CARIBBEAN

CARIBBEAN POWER

CARIBBEAN POWER

COLIN RICKARDS

LONDON: DENNIS DOBSON

First published in Great Britain in 1963 by
Dobson Books Ltd., 80 Kensington Church Street, London W.8.
Printed in Great Britain by Clarke, Doble and Brendon Ltd.,
Cattedown, Plymouth

CONTENTS

7

Their pictures appear between pages 188 and 189

AUTHOR'S PREFACE

The islands in and the countries which surround the Caribbean Sea are rapidly becoming vitally important in the defence of the Western Hemisphere.

Strategically, the area is vital because it lies between highly-developed North America and under-developed South America, and because it is the gateway to the Panama Canal. And it is always in the news.

To the north the Caribbean Sea is bounded by the Greater Antilles: Jamaica, Cuba, Haiti, the Dominican Republic and Puerto Rico. The eastern extremity of the sea washes the Lesser Antilles, a string of golden islands extending from the United States Virgin Islands to Trinidad. To the south lies half a continent—South America—and the coastlines of Venezuela and Colombia. To the west is Central America and the shores of Panama, Costa Rica, Nicaragua, Honduras, Guatemala and British Honduras.

"This is neither Latin America nor Spanish America. This is Caribbean America," wrote the distinguished Colombian political commentator Germán Arciniegas in his book *The State of Latin America*. "It is a patchwork of colonies, semi-colonies, protectorates, republics, pseudo-republics, democracies and anti-democracies."

But when he spoke of Caribbean America Señor Arciniegas meant only the islands and Central America. He did not include the two South American countries with Caribbean seaboards as I have done.

In Caribbean America live some 50 million people—roughly the same population as Great Britain. Their leaders and régimes are as varied as the territories themselves. There are democratic governments and there are dictatorships. And in between these two there are semi-democracies, colonial legislatures and potentially totalitarian governments.

In this book I have tried to present the leaders of Caribbean America as they are—not always as the outside world sees them—and to show what they are doing in their countries.

9

In writing of these political leaders I have included two whose countries are geographically just out of the Caribbean but which are so inextricably linked with it that they are fairly considered West Indian. These are British Guiana, lying next door to Venezuela and as West Indian in its outlook as any of the Caribbean Islands; and Barbados, out in the Atlantic, a hundred miles east of the Lesser Antilles, but part of the British West Indies and destined to be the seat of the proposed Eastern Caribbean Federation.

Conversely, all the Central American countries have Caribbean coastlines except the smallest—El Salvador—and I have left this out, despite the fact that it is linked geographically and culturally with its neighbours. Neither have I written of two tiny British colonies, the Cayman Islands and the British Virgin Islands.

I have not written of the Dutch territories in Caribbean America, nor of the French. Surinam, once Dutch Guiana, is an independent state under the Dutch Crown. The Dutch islands in the Lesser Antilles and off the South American mainland have their own forms of government within the Netherlands kingdom. The French territories—Martinique, Guadeloupe and French Guiana—are Departments of Metropolitan France and as such send their Deputies to the Parliament of the mother country.

I have concentrated on the mainland territories of Central and South America—plus British Guiana—the independent islands in the Caribbean Sea and the British colonial possessions which are working towards independence.

For these are the countries to watch in Caribbean America.

I travelled more than 25,000 miles gathering information for this book and in all the countries I visited I was given every assistance and shown every friendliness by many people. In most of them I was able to see the politicians. However, in some territories— either dictatorships or countries where authoritarian government is a real possibility—new-made friends talked only on the understanding that I did not call their names in any acknowledgement I might make in this book. Because of this I have decided to leave out acknowledgement completely. Friends who supplied information will recognize what they told me in the relevant chapters, and nobody is going to be pilloried for talking, because those who might persecute cannot know who talked.

So the only thanks I publicly acknowledge are to Mrs. Meena

Stentiford who laboured to read such parts of the original draft as I had written by hand and turned it into carefully-typed manuscript.

To the many nameless informants and friends, my sincere thanks for their assistance.

COLIN RICKARDS

Polperro, Cornwall,
May, 1963

INTRODUCTION

The Caribbean Sea lies like a slightly off-shaped coffee bean between North and South America. Its boundaries are two groups of islands—the Greater and Lesser Antilles—and the mainlands of Central and South America. Around its edges live a vastly complex population drawn from every corner of the globe. A tiny handful are indigenous to the region, though even they came from Asia as migrants centuries ago. The vast majority are immigrants of the more recent past. They came as conquerors, as indentured labourers, as slaves. They came seeking gold and silver, seeking freedom from religious and political persecution, or simply seeking better opportunities in the New World.

They brought with them their own cultures—European, African and Asian; and their own religions—Christianity, Hinduism, Mohammedanism, and the pagan religions of Africa. They brought their own foodstuffs and grew them in new surroundings; and where necessary they brought foods from other tropical regions and planted them. They brought their own styles of buildings; and their own patterns of life.

Around the enchanted sea they settled in small numbers and grew until today they number more than 50 million. The indigenous Arawaks are extinct. The flesh-eating Caribs—from whom the sea gets its name—are now a mere handful. In the five hundred years that they have been there the newcomers have taken over.

In the Caribbean Sea are the islands, some independent, some still the colonies of European powers, and some the offshore adjuncts of the mainland territories of Central and South America. Around the sea are the mainland countries, all of them former colonies of Spain.

Jamaica, once Spanish and then for 307 years a British colony, became independent in 1962; Cuba, once Spanish, once British, sometimes occupied by America, is independent but fast becoming a satellite of Russia; Haiti, once Spanish, once French, became the second oldest—and only Negro—republic in the New World and is today under a dictatorship; the same island is shared by the Dominican Republic, which has been in turn Spanish, Haitian,

13

independent, occupied by the Americans and which—in 1961—
threw off a thirty-year dictatorship; Puerto Rico, Spanish then
briefly independent, was seized by the United States in the Spanish
American War of 1898 and is now closely linked to America as
"a freely associated state". These are the Greater Antilles.

The United States Virgin Islands are an American colony in all
but name; the neighbouring British Virgin Islands definitely are
one. The beautiful string of islands, extending southwards to South
America are a mixed bag. Some of them belong to European
countries, some are independent and some soon will become
independent. Antigua, St. Kitts-Nevis-Anguilla, and Montserrat
are the most northerly British islands. All of them plan membership of the new Federation of The West Indies, the off-shoot of the
defunct Federation which lasted less than four years. Their
neighbours are the Dutch islands of Saba, St. Eustatius and Sint
Maarten, the last-named shared by France and shown as St. Martin
on their maps. Other French islands in the area are St. Barthélemy,
the tiny Islands of the Saints and Marie Galante. These are
dependencies of Guadeloupe, like Martinique a Department of
Metropolitan France. The British islands of Dominica, St. Lucia
and St. Vincent plan to be part of the new Federation. Grenada
was going to be a part but may now join Trinidad and Tobago
which became independent in 1962. Barbados, a hundred miles
east of the island chain, will be the seat of the new Federation.
These are the Lesser Antilles.

Off the coast of the mainland of South America are islands
belonging to Colombia and Venezuela. Off the same coast are the
Dutch oil colonies of Aruba, Bonaire and Curaçao. Off Central
America are islands which belong to British Honduras—they are
called Cayes; and islands which belong to the republic of Honduras, some of which have been leased to the United States. There
is also the British colony of the Cayman Islands, some 160 miles
north-east of Jamaica.

The Caribbean has been called the "sea of troubles". And
certainly her political history has been as full of revolutions,
uprisings and bloodshed, as her turbulent period when the great
wooden-walled ships of Europe fought for loot, land, supremacy
and power.

The political history of the British colonies has been compara-
tively quiet. Strikes and imprisonments, but seldom bloodshed,

have been the pattern for the emerging nations. In the other islands it has been far more violent. Cuba, the Dominican Republic and Haiti have seen bloodshed and insurrections in the name of political freedom for the past 150 years. Only Puerto Rico has been reasonably peaceful, gaining autonomy by negotiation with Spain, only to lose it two weeks later to conquering Americans, and then gaining semi-autonomy from the United States, once more by negotiation. Even so, a fanatically independence-minded minority have shed some blood.

On the mainland of Central America things have been far from peaceful. Revolts, dictatorships, border wars and *coups d'etat* have been the order of the day in most of them. And the same is true for the South American territories.

But often even the revolts have been tinged with a hint of humour. The Austrian general who said: "The situation is constantly desperate—but never serious", might well have been speaking of the politics in the republics, most of whom exchanged Spanish rule for home-grown dictators.

The United States has done much to promote stability in Caribbean America. Recently the Alliance for Progress has taken the place of indiscriminate hand-outs, and this is all to the good. The fear of half a continent to the south under possible Communist domination has finally brought America to her senses.

But the United States also has a great deal to answer for— both in the past and the present.

American business interests have been championed to the detriment of the common people in a number of the Caribbean American republics. Armed intervention and the landing of Marines have featured in the affairs of Nicaragua, Honduras, Haiti and the Dominican Republic. Puerto Rico and Cuba were seized by the United States. The Panama Canal would never have become the bone of U.S.-Panamanian contention that it is, had not President Theodore Roosevelt, with his "walk softly and carry a big stick" policy, fomented a revolution and then virtually blackmailed the breakaway Republic of Panama into giving him the Canal Zone "in perpetuity".

The intervention of American Marines in Nicaragua made it possible for Anastasio Somoza to step into the position of Chief of Police and Commander of the National Guard and then into the role of dictator when the Americans left. His sons still hold the country in a dictatorship. The same is virtually true of the Dominican Republic, where Rafael Trujillo's star of ascendancy followed the same pattern as that of Somoza. Dictators in Colombia and Venezuela have had United States backing much to the dissatisfaction of the general populace.

Rather than disrupt American business interests the State Department has too often been pleased to recognize dictators, to pander to them, and sometimes to shower them with honours, medals and glories.

Commented American Senator William Benton in his book *The Voice of Latin America*: "These medallic symbols ... offset hundreds of millions of dollars in U.S. good deeds."

Today there are only three of the old-style dictatorships left in the New World. And two of them are in Caribbean America: Haiti and Nicaragua. The other is in South America: Paraguay. The United States shamelessly supports and panders to both the Somoza dictatorship in Nicaragua and the Duvalier régime in Haiti.

But the United States record in recent years has been largely offset by their actions in Puerto Rico, now a thriving economy. And by the Alliance for Progress scheme. Both these factors have helped to redeem the unfavourable picture of Uncle Sam that has grown up in the area. Stable leadership in the region, coupled with self-help and American aid, will eventually bring the countries of Caribbean America into a position where they represent a dominant and important collective voice in the councils of the world and in the cause of world peace.

PART ONE
THE ISLANDS

"The pivot of America lies in the Antilles. If enslaved, they would be nothing but a pontoon between an imperialist republic and a jealous, superior world resentful of its power, a mere outpost of the Rome of America. But if free, and worthy of being so by the existence of a just and effective freedom, they would be a guarantee of the stability of the continent."

JOSÉ MARTÍ

CHAPTER ONE

JAMAICA

Sir Alexander Bustamante

When Sir Alexander Bustamante became Prime Minister of Jamaica at the age of 78 he joined the ranks of the world's oldest Heads of State. Topping him for age was Germany's Konrad Adenauer, 85. Just behind were Israel's David Ben Gurion, 76, and France's de Gaulle, 72.

The election, in April, 1962, which brought Sir Alexander to power was the culmination of a distinguished and flamboyant political career: a career which gave him the opportunity to lead his country into independence after 307 years of British rule.

In a political arena where social pressures have brought about radical changes and older politicians have given way to younger men, Sir Alexander has shown a resilience and zest for life which is little short of remarkable.

This larger-than-life master showman, with his mop of unruly white hair and hawk nose, can still show the youngsters a thing or two. Visit him in his home and he is quite likely to drop to the floor and do an impressive series of press-ups.

"I can still wrestle with a man half my age," he says in his slightly off-key, high-pitched voice. "Fit as a fiddle, that's me. They can't find a thing wrong with my heart."

And behind the impishness and showmanship, the flair for publicity, the white bow tie that was for so long his trademark, is a keen, sharp and alert brain.

And Lady Bustamante, hovering discreetly in the background, smiles a proud smile and glasses are filled with more champagne— Sir Alexander's favourite tipple.

"I drink a magnum of champagne a day, except when I have a

cold, then I drink rum," Sir Alexander says. "Champagne stimulates me and keeps my strength up." (A qualified dietician, he eats mainly beef and vegetables and drinks vast quantities of carrot juice).

Lady Bustamante has known her husband for a long time. As Miss Gladys Longbridge, she went to work as his secretary in 1935 when he was a prosperous moneylender in Jamaica's capital, Kingston, and stuck with him through thick and thin, fortune and depression, from then on. And in September, 1962, Miss Gladys Longbridge, secretary to the Prime Minister, became Lady Bustamante, wife of the Prime Minister.

"I owe all my success to her," says Sir Alexander, and his voice drops to a sentimental softness. "She made me. Whether I go to a common rum shop or the best place, she goes with me."

And then, remembering hard times and prison bars, he laughs: "And when I'm in jail she carries on until I get out."

Lady Bustamante—Lady B she is called—has been more than a secretary to the big, bluff, jovial man who was for so long her boss and is now her husband. She has been confidante, counsellor and guardian angel. She never gets in a temper, deals with his tantrums with a calm smile—and then gets on with the business in hand.

"When he blows up, I keep quiet," she says simply.

And that is only part of the secret of the success of this remarkable woman.

Jamaica has been well-blessed politically in having Sir Alexander and his cousin Norman Manley alternately in control of the island since 1944 when the people first went out to vote under universal adult suffrage. They have been spared the uncomfortable business of political parties changing heads with monotonous frequency.

But the two men are poles apart—not only politically but personally.

Bustamante is colourful, dynamic and forceful. Often untidy in his dress—if he can escape the ministrations of the ever-vigilant Lady B—colloquial in his speech, and with a common touch that politicians thousands of miles from Jamaica can envy. He is the embodiment of Jamaica.

Manley is hard-thinking, serious—and, to some extent, ruthless. He is nearly always a symphony in pearl-grey suiting, a red rose in his buttonhole, contriving to keep knife-edge creases in his trousers on the hottest of days. But he falls far short of Bustamante both in personal magnetism and in his contacts with the people.

Revered and adored by his fervent supporters, Bustamante has spent nearly as much of his life away from his native Jamaica as he has in the midst of its multi-racial boiling pot.

He was born William Alexander Clarke on 24th February, 1884, in Blenheim, in the western end of the island. His father was an Irish immigrant farmer; his mother a Jamaican girl. Young William Alexander inherited his father's fair complexion—he is light-skinned with hardly a visible trace of his Negro ancestry. He also developed to a fine degree his father's Irish blarney.

There are many stories of his early life. Almost every Jamaican has a different version. And Bustamante, who moves in an aura of melodrama and fantasy, has never gone to the trouble to tell his side of the story or to correct mis-statements.

"One day I'll write my autobiography and then the world will know it," he likes to say.

When he was 14 he left home to work on a relative's farm. That was in 1898. Five years later he went to Cuba. And that, so the stories go, was when he first began to call himself Bustamante.

"My mother had thirteen children," he told me once. "We were so poor that different people adopted us. I was adopted by Lieutenant-Colonel Bustamante, a Spaniard, and studied in Spain."

In his early twenties Bustamante was in North Africa serving as a trooper in the Spanish Cavalry. In the camps of the Spaniards opposing Abdel Krim in the Riff Wars he became a crack shot with a pistol. Later in his life he carried two holstered .38 calibre revolvers and several times produced them with lightning speed when in a tight corner.

"I never shot anyone in Jamaica," he told me with a grin. "Never had to. But I've shot men in North Africa. Don't ask me about dates—I can never remember them."

Later he returned to the New World to work as timekeeper for a tramway in Panama. He was a policeman in Cuba. Then it was North America. He lived in Canada for a short time. In Chicago he was a hospital orderly. In New York he was a waiter before he qualified as a dietician, in 1926, and set himself up in business. Three years later he began dabbling in the New York stock market. Like many people he made money. Unlike a lot of them he held on to it.

"My formula for making a fortune was hard work, saving at great personal sacrifice, and taking a chance," he says. "The years of the Wall Street crash were my golden years. I had saved several thousand dollars during the three years I had been in New York working as a dietician at $350 a month. I was born poor and I meant to escape from poverty.

"When stock prices slumped I bought heavily in General Motors, International Hotels, United Fruit Company and Chryslers. Prices went up. I made money, sold out and left for Jamaica."

He arrived back in Jamaica in 1934 financially "well fixed", as he likes to put it. How "well fixed" he does not say, but once, when heckled at a meeting in London, he admitted that his personal fortune is something in the region of £75,000.

"In Jamaica I lent money, bought houses and land, but I have not made money in Jamaica," he says. "My fortune is probably smaller these days than it was when I first went into politics." As Jamaica's Prime Minister his salary is £2,500 a year.

But the prosperous Bustamante who returned to Jamaica was shattered to see the appalling conditions the people were living in. The country's peasant farmers especially were in an almost desperate plight. Jobs—when there were any—were too often only seasonal. The white and light-skinned Jamaicans lived in comparative prosperity. The majority, the black peasantry, were starving in petrol-can shanty-towns on the outskirts of Kingston or scratching a bare living on smallholdings.

Despite emigration to Panama, Central America, Cuba, the United States and later to Britain, there are more than 1,600,000 people packed into the 4,411 square miles of island which lies a scant ninety miles from Cuba.

Lion-maned Bustamante began to get interested in union activities. He lent his support to the Jamaica Workers' and Tradesmen's Union who were working to get the rock-bottom wages raised enough to let people enjoy a reasonable standard of living instead of barely existing.

Conditions throughout the West Indies were in an economically depressed state. There had been strikes and minor rioting in Trinidad in 1934. Tiny St. Kitts had seen bloodshed on sugar estates the following year and British Guiana, Barbados and St.

Vincent were living on the edge of economic crisis and possible violence.

In 1937 Bustamante sent a telegram to the King urging better conditions and wages for the Jamaican people. And, as conditions worsened rather than bettered, trouble simmered just beneath the surface. January, 1938, ushered in big things which began with minor strikes and clashes and built up to the firing of Tate and Lyle's sugar estate at Frome on 2nd May.

And it is from this date that Bustamante's political career can really be said to have begun.

In a bungling attempt to arrest one man the police killed four with gunfire. Suddenly Jamaica was electrified with wild rumours. In his Kingston loan office Bustamante knew that his hour had come.

He ran out into the street in his shirt sleeves, climbed onto the base of Queen Victoria's statue in North Parade and yelled to a crowd which quickly assembled.

"I want the Governor to know that Alexander Bustamante is prepared to fight and that he has 100,000 people behind him," he shouted.

This was something that people could understand. Bustamante found himself the accepted leader of the working people. "Busta" or "The Chief" they called him. And they sang "We Will Follow Bustamante Till We Die".

He launched a campaign against the Governor, Sir Edward Denham, and the upper-crust Jamaicans, who, he charged, thought of themselves, "as a black royal family of the island".

On 23rd May, Bustamante was addressing a meeting when the police swooped. In a pitched battle he was arrested along with scores of his audience. Hauled down to the police headquarters, he was tossed into a cell charged with "sedition and excitement". When he was refused bail—though he offered to go as high as £10,000—he went on hunger strike.

Two days later his brilliant barrister cousin Norman Washington Manley came to his rescue and managed to get him released.

"I am an agitator," he told his first public meeting after his release. "I do not deny it. I am fighting to make conditions better for posterity. I'm above those who are opposing us. They want to live well forever. But I am ready to die today if I can help you."

Wherever there was a strike, a demonstration, a public meeting,

Bustamante was there. He spoke from the nearest vantage point: a rickety donkey cart, a motor car, a gnarled stump—even from the branches of a tree.

"I don't believe in mob rule," he always told his audiences. "I believe in peaceful persuasion. I believe in agitating to the core and then soothing, so gently soothing. I will settle these strikes if the owners will be fair.

"I don't want bloodshed. I want peace."

And, "agitating to the core", he sent cables to Whitehall requesting a Royal Commission. More cables to the King. He wrote letters to Opposition leader Clement (now Lord) Attlee and to Lord Olivier, who, as Sir Sidney Olivier, had been Governor of Jamaica.

Sir Edward Denham postponed his three months' leave to face up to the problems and released funds to be spent on roadbuilding and housing schemes. Two days after his leave should have started he died of overwork. Bustamante kept on holding meetings. Sir Arthur Richards (now Lord Milverton) hastened to Jamaica to become Governor.

When Bustamante told his audience "I am one of you" he was speaking the truth. For his early life had been as hard as theirs. His fiery oratory held them. Once, during a dock strike, he stood on a soap box from 9 a.m. until dusk haranguing the crowd.

"Don't give in," he told them. "Fight. Don't let them frighten you. If you are strong they will pay you."

Days later, when there was looting and arson, Bustamante was one of 700 people arrested. Eight men were killed and 171 wounded before the police got the position under control.

When he was released Bustamante formed his own union. He called it—much against the wishes of the Governor—the Bustamante Industrial Trades Union. He became President for life and built his all-embracing union into a powerful force. His secretary, then Miss Longbridge, now Lady Bustamante, became Treasurer.

Labour and Independent M.P., W. J. Brown, himself a union organizer, wrote of Bustamante's union: "His powers make me green with envy. He has the right to appoint key men; the general secretary and treasurer are appointed by him; he has no time for Communists and must be the only trade union leader in the world who is not troubled by them."

In August, 1938, a Royal Commission under Lord Moyne arrived in the Caribbean with instructions to "investigate social and economic conditions in all the West Indian territories, and make recommendations". Bustamante spoke to trade union chief Sir Walter Citrine and brought home the Jamaican situation with characteristic forcefulness.

The following month Norman Manley formed the People's National Party and began to campaign for a new constitution. His carefully-planned campaign appealed to the thinking man, for Manley speaks to the head. This distinguished barrister who won the Military Medal in the First World War, was a Rhodes Scholar at Oxford, and rapidly became a King's Counsel, has always appealed to the intellectual.

He appeals to the head; Bustamante appeals to the heart.

Sir Grantley Adams, at the time Prime Minister of the Federation of The West Indies, summed up the cousins for me most succinctly. He said: "Manley is a statesman who will never be a politician. Bustamante is a politician who will never be a statesman."

The Royal Commission made their report after fifteen months and as a direct result of their recommendations the Colonial Development and Welfare Act was passed through the British Parliament. Britain was at war with Germany by then but made good her promises by pumping money into the West Indies.

In September, 1940, Sir Arthur Richards decided that Bustamante was a security risk and put him behind bars. Manley held the people together—incidentally wooing some of Bustamante's trade unionists into the P N P—and when Bustamante came out in February, 1942, he still had his power.

But a number of Communists and fellow travellers had climbed on to Manley's party machine while Bustamante was in jail and the Chief, with his passionate hatred for Communists, broke away from his cousin and brought about the birth of the Jamaica Labour Party on 8th July, 1943, as the political wing of the Bustamante Industrial Trades Union. Manley formed the Trades Union Council affiliated to the P N P.

The words People's and Labour are almost obligatory in British West Indian political parties—Labour the more so if the party concerned tends to be Right-wing which was the case of the Jamaica Labour Party.

In 1944, after much campaigning and lobbying by both Bustamante and Manley, Jamaica was granted a new constitution, the only British colonial territory to get one during the war years. And with it came universal adult suffrage. A bi-cameral legislature was introduced with the Legislative Assembly being made up of officials and nominated members and the House of Representatives of elected members.

In December, 1944, the island went to the polls and returned Bustamante with twenty-two out of the thirty-two seats. Manley's P N P got only five. He became Minister of Communications and top man in the Government.

The Chief was packing two holstered .38 calibre pistols now. "I carried them for protection," he explains. "I never knew when some fanatic might want to bump me off." They also made for good showmanship.

In the middle of 1946 Bustamante and his Minister of Social Services, Frank Pixley, found themselves on a manslaughter charge arising out of the death of a man during a clash between P N P and J L P supporters at the Kingston Mental Hospital in March. Hauled into court, Bustamante told his story simply. He had gone to the mental hospital in an effort to end the strike, he said.

The Judge, Sir Hector Hearne, tore the Crown's case to pieces, challenged witnesses and found them to be P N P supporters, and virtually instructed the jury to find Bustamante and Pixley not guilty. It took them less than twenty-five minutes to do so.

The Chief was carried from the courtroom to triumphant singing of "We Will Follow Bustamante Till We Die". He led them in "God Save the King" and "Rule Britannia", made a short speech and went back to his office to get on with more pressing problems.

Unemployment was still acute and Servicemen returning from Europe made the situation even worse. Jobs were created, immediately filled and still the people clamoured for work. On 12th May, 1947, Bustamante's office was beseiged by banner-waving crowds who sang "Busta, where art thou hiding from the Lord?" until he came out.

But as soon as he made for his car the crowd surged forward threateningly. In their faces was all the pent-up frustration of men willing to work but unable to get jobs.

Anything could have happened.

Completely in character the Chief, with an incredibly swift

movement, snatched his guns from their holsters and menaced the crowd.

"Keep back," he cautioned them. And then, to clear the way to his car, he fired a shot into the ground. Momentarily uncertain, the crowd wavered. And in that moment the Chief leapt into his car and drove away.

The same year a conference at Jamaica's Montego Bay gave birth to the idea of federating the British West Indian islands, a scheme which both Bustamante and Manley favoured.

Later Bustamante travelled to London to seek a loan with the PNP demand for independence ringing in his ears. He met the Royal Family and became an even more ardent royalist.

"You cannot beg and demand independence at the same time," he said on arrival. He got his money, went back to Jamaica and began campaigning for the 1949 election.

Once again he was swept back into power—but with a reduced majority— JLP seventeen seats, PNP thirteen seats. He had already lost some ground when the PNP captured fifty-two seats in local government elections to the JLP's fifty-three. Independents held another eighty-six.

In 1951 there was more union strife. On one occasion the Chief fired a shot into the air when his car was stoned by sugar workers. On another occasion police with fixed bayonets charged Bustamante's union headquarters and arrested 100 men who had kept them at bay with a storm of stones and bottles for two hours. The same year Manley cleaned the Communists out of his party and started the National Workers' Union.

By the time the 1955 elections came around it seemed that Bustamante was losing his grip. There were 106 candidates for the thirty-two House of Representative seats including Independents, candidates from the newly-formed Farmers' Party, the National Labour Party and the Communist-dominated People's Freedom Movement.

Norman Manley won eighteen seats to Bustamante's fourteen seats, and for the first time Jamaica had a PNP Government.

The Chief was knighted the same year.

The following year the West Indies Federation was launched and Manley became the Founder-President of the West Indies Federal Labour Party. He did not run for Federal office and neither did Trinidad's Premier Dr. Eric Williams with whose party the WIFLP was linked. Barbados's Premier Sir Grantley Adams did run and became Federal Prime Minister.

But Bustamante had joined forces with Eric Williams's Opposition to form the Democratic Labour Party of The West Indies and his party's candidates won seventeen of the twenty-two seats Jamaica was allotted in the Federal House of Representatives.

The Jamaican election of 1959 returned Manley for another term, this time under a new constitution giving full internal self-government. Manley held twenty-nine seats and Bustamante sixteen seats in the forty-five-seat House.

By the middle of 1960 Bustamante had become convinced that Federation was bad for Jamaicans. He was variously accused of being insular in his outlook and of trying to stir up feeling and get back into the limelight himself.

But he continued and in June, 1960, resigned as leader of the Democratic Labour Party.

"We are determined to rule ourselves and not be ruled by Trinidadians, Barbadians, St. Kittitians—or whatever they may be," he said.

He began a vigorous anti-Federation campaign whipping up fervour wherever he spoke. His platform was simple. Jamaica would have to support a great many of the small islands in an independent Federation. She had enough problems at home to use up all her money and a great deal more besides. Why carry others when charity begins at home?

In May, 1961, Premiers and Chief Ministers from the ten units of the Federation gathered in London to fix a Federal constitution and a date for independence. At the end of their conference they returned home with the matter settled. Independence would come on 31st May, 1962.

There was just one snag. Manley had promised Bustamante a referendum to see whether or not the Jamaican electorate wanted Federation. There was no reason for Manley to have offered a referendum. No provision in the Federal Constitution allowed for the secession of a territory and Manley was in power so could have taken Jamaica in.

But Manley has an arrogant streak and saw, in offering a referendum, a chance to break Bustamante for good. He was supremely confident and assured the then Colonial Secretary, Iain Macleod, that the result was a foregone conclusion.

But he had reckoned without the Chief. While Manley toured Jamaica speaking in every constituency many of his Ministers did not even move out of Kingston. Some of them did not make one speech during the referendum campaign.

Manley went for the economic advantages of a Federation. He used his normal tactic—appealing to the head.

The Chief went to the country with a very simple formula.

"You got three goats?" he demanded in the rural constituencies where his greatest strength is. "You get Federation, you got only two goats—Federationists send the other one to Trinidad."

In the face of this challenging platform from the Chief and his party who went all-out to win the campaign, it was little use Manley talking about Customs Union and West Indian identity.

When it came to polling day—in September, 1961—the Chief netted 251,935 votes (53.8 per cent); Manley got 216,400 votes (46.2 per cent). Jamaica was out of the Federation. A constitutional conference in London followed five months later and Jamaica was given independence on 6th August, 1962.

But before independence there had to be an election to give the people a chance to decide who they wanted to go into a new status under.

Manley's position was acutely embarrassing. For years he had been telling Jamaicans that they should be federated. Now he had to go to them and say that Jamaica should be on her own. He faced the crisis with a "great I am" campaign, banging the drum of the personality cult, cutting short hecklers with arrogant outbursts and putting himself forward as "The Man With The Plan". (Bustamante referred to him as "The Clot With The Plot".)

The Chief simply went to the country districts, climbed on to platforms and asked "Who has been your friend all along?" His party members tackled the danger of Communism and the nearness of Cuba.

On 10th April, 1962, Bustamante's Jamaica Labour Party was back in power with twenty-six seats to Manley's nineteen. The Chief tallied 283,351 votes (49.73 per cent) and Manley got 278,704 (48.91 per cent). The other fraction went to a newly formed racialist party.

He immediately declared his stand: "My Government is anti-Communist, and anything that is against the Church we are

B

against. We are too small to be neutral. I should like to sign a treaty with the U.S. for help in case of foreign invasion."

Before him the vibrant old man of Caribbean politics has a tremendous job. The "safety valve" of immigration to Britain has been screwed down a little tighter by the Commonwealth Immigrants Act; illiteracy is still a pressing problem; there are not enough schools, hospitals or roads; and the biggest problem of all is unemployment.

Bustamante is backed by good administrators and able men, outstanding among them Minister of Finance Donald Sangster and Minister of Trade and Industry Robert Lightbourne. In many ways these two men and their Chief symbolize the fighting spirit of the Jamaica Labour Party. The Chief is the figurehead, the lodestone of the party; Sangster is the brain—financially speaking; and Lightbourne—one of the best public speakers in the island —is the voice.

Jamaicans like to say "push Busta in front when something new crops up—and then bring Manley in later to organize it."

And this could well happen. For the margin of majority in the votes is very close between the two parties. And a large body of the voters of Jamaica fluctuate in their loyalties. If Manley uses the breathing space of Bustamante's term of office to give his party a much-needed shot in the arm, he could well have it sufficiently rejuvenated to give the Chief a very close run at the next election. Certainly much will depend on the success of the Jamaica Labour Party in this all-important first government after independence.

"People either love me or hate me," says the Chief. "But they can't ignore me."

And he is right at that.

For Bustamante and Jamaica go together. He is like one of the great natural hazards of the Caribbean: earthquake, fire and hurricane. And people adore or abhor him.

But he is there just the same.

CHAPTER TWO

CUBA

Dr. Fidel Castro

Fidel Castro is probably not a Communist. He is a revolutionary, an intellectual, a rabid nationalist, a genuine Socialist reformer and a dreamer. He is flamboyant, ruthless, brave, noisy and naïve. He is all these things and a great many more.

But it is unlikely that he is the die-hard, West-hating Red that he is most often tagged.

Cuba's firebrand Prime Minister knows that he is many things to many people. He knows that he is the liberator of his country; he knows that he has done more for the peasants in four years than his predecessors did in four centuries; he knows that he is idolized, loved, respected and copied. He also knows that people call him a dictator and say that he has sold out to Russia, trading Cuba's former dependency on the United States for complete domination by the Soviet *bloc*. He knows that he is hated, feared, derided and plotted against.

But to Fidel Castro—liberator or dictator—it is enough that he is accepted, by the great mass of Cubans, as the twentieth century successor to National Hero José Martí.

For more than a third of his life he has been a rebel, a fighter for one thing alone: Liberty. He has been jailed for it, hunted for it, and persecuted for it. He has fought for it, bled for it, killed for it.

And ironically, at the very moment that he had it in his hands, it has been spirited away from him by a group of masters far more internationally dangerous than the ones he overthrew in Liberty's name.

Cuba covers 44,178 square miles, is easily the largest of the

Greater Antilles and stretches for 700 miles across the top of the
Caribbean Sea. To the north, only ninety miles away, is Key
West, Florida and the United States. The same distance to the
south is Jamaica. Haiti is only forty-nine miles to the east across
the Windward Passage. Mexico lies little more than 100 miles to
the west. More than 6¼ million people live in the island. Some
44 per cent are of mixed descent; 30 per cent are European—
mostly from Spain; 24 per cent are of Negro origin—some the
descendants of slaves taken to the island, and some Negroes from
the British West Indian islands, mainly Jamaica, who went to
work on the sugar plantations; 2 per cent are Chinese.

For centuries Cuba was a Spanish colony. And for more than
a hundred years America watched the island, supremely conscious
of its importance. "We must have Cuba," said Thomas Jefferson.
And in due course America had it. In 1868 a wealthy planter
named Carlos Manuel de Céspedes collected some kindred spirits
in an attempt to drive out the Spanish. Maximo (The Fox) Gómez
and Antonio (The Lion) Maceo rallied to the flag in a ten-year
"Freedom or Death" war which cost the lives of a quarter of a
million Cubans. Then the Spaniards offered terms. On a promise
of reforms for peace the rebels hung up their guns. The
Spanish kept up to their bargain for a while, and then the old
régime returned. Eventually the idealistic young poet José Martí
recruited The Fox and The Lion in another attempt to oust the
Spanish. They landed in Oriente Province in 1895—as Fidel Castro
was to do some sixty years later—and before the end of the
year Martí had been killed in battle to become the National Hero
of Cuba.

The fight for freedom was still going on three years later when
the American battleship *Maine* blew up—or was blown up—in
Havana harbour and the United States declared war on Spain. The
war gained her Cuba and Puerto Rico in the Caribbean and various
other Spanish territories scattered across the face of the globe. It
opened the way for American influence, and the possibility of
actual armed intervention in Cuban affairs which was to last until
1934. And it built up, to a great extent, the average Cuban's anti-
American feeling which has been traded upon by a long line of
local politicians.

In exchanging Spanish rule for American occupation and then
independence, Cuba ushered in a new era of home-grown oppres-

sors. The first President, Tomás Estrada Palma (1902-06), was honest and died penniless; his successor retired in immense wealth; the third President made a personal fortune of £12 million; the fourth stole from the peasants through his taxation; the fifth was Gerardo "The Butcher" Machado (1925-33), an incredibly violent and corrupt man who was overthrown largely through the efforts of American diplomats. After the rioting, bloodshed and mayhem a little part-Negro, part-Chinese Army sergeant-stenographer of obscure origins seized power and restored order to the island. His name was Fulgencio Batista y Zaldívar.

At first Batista—he was from Oriente Province—was content to be the power behind the scenes. He deposed the temporary President, put in a five-man Directory which lasted for five days, and then named Dr. Ramón Grau San Martín as President. But America refused to recognize the new régime. Batista fired the President and in doing so he made himself a lasting enemy. Then followed in succession Dr. Carlos Hevia—he served for one day only, 15th January, 1934—Colonel Carlos Mendieta, José Barnet, Dr. Miguel Mariano Gómez and Francisco Laredo Brú. In his role as President-maker-and-breaker Batista gave Cuba a total of seven Presidents in as many years, and went on record as saying: "I can never be President of the country".

But by October, 1940, he had changed his mind. He stood for election and became President for the constitutional term of four years. At that period in his career he was a remarkable figure in Caribbean American politics. For he had brought off a seizure of power, but had not forced a dictatorship which so many other military men had done under similar circumstances in neighbouring countries.

Batista's Acción Popular party, contested the 1944 election— the first completely honest one in the island's history—and lost. The winner was ex-President Ramón Grau San Martín running on a Partido Revolucionario Cubano ticket. Four years later the same party won again and Grau San Martín gave way to Carlos Prío Socarrás who was to make himself a personal fortune of several millions before being ousted from power.

Fidel Castro's father, Angel Castro, went to Cuba from the Galicia region of Spain, an area which has a long tradition of emigration to Cuba and South America. By hard work, sweat and toil he built up a sugar plantation worth £250,000 at Mayarí, some fifty miles from Santiago de Cuba, in Oriente Province, at the eastern tip of the island. He married a Cuban girl from a wealthy land-owning family and they had seven children, four boys and three girls. Fidel Castro Ruz was born on 13th August, 1926.

A devout Roman Catholic, he attended the Jesuit Belén College and then went to Havana University to study law in 1945. A tall, gangling young man with black hypnotic eyes weakened by astigmatism, student Castro debated well, studied law and became interested in the sinister machinations of Generalissimo Rafael Trujillo in the near-by Dominican Republic.

He became so interested in fact, that in 1947 the bespectacled Castro joined eleven hundred Dominican Republic exiles and anti-Trujillo Cubans and set sail for the dictator's island with the intention of overthrowing him. But the attack was a failure. Intercepted by gunboats, their ships shot out of the water, the rebels admitted defeat. Castro swam two miles to the nearest shore emerging from the sea a very wet and disillusioned revolutionary.

He went back to Cuba and the university, immersed himself in his studies, surfaced for long enough to marry Mirta Díaz Balart in 1948, and then went back to work. When he left the University in 1950 to go into partnership with two friends in establishing a law firm, he had two legal degrees, one of them his doctorate. His wife presented him with a son—Fidelito—the same year.

But politics and the struggle for power interested him. So did the abysmal conditions of the great majority of the Cuban people, the exploitation of the country by top Cubans and American business interests, and the illiteracy and poverty of the vast majority of the population. He became an active worker for the Ortodoxo party—a breakaway group which opposed the corruption of the Partido Revolucionario Cubano. In due course he became the Chairman of the Ortodoxo Party in Havana Province.

Elections were due on 1st June, 1952, to choose a President to succeed Carlos Prío Socarrás. The Partido Revolucionario Cubano, commonly called Auténtico, put up Carlos Hevia—he of the one-day Presidency; the Ortodoxo Party named Dr. Roberto Agramonte; and Batista's Acción Popular party, nominated Batista.

Fidel Castro campaigned vigorously for Dr. Agramonte and the general reckoning gave him the edge on his opponents as the election day grew near. Castro's favourite line to the electorate was the iniquity which gave Cuba—on paper—the second highest *per capita* income in Caribbean America—oil-rich Venezuela's was higher—but kept the majority of the people at virtual starvation level while a few at the top enjoyed immense wealth.

But Agramonte's hopes of the Presidency were dashed by Fulgencio Batista. On 10th March, 1952, he suddenly seized power, ousted President Carlos Prío Socarrás who fled into exile, dissolved Congress and declared himself Chief of State. By this act he destroyed his reputation as a patriot—for he had restored order out of chaos in 1933 and ruled with a moderately wise hand both from behind the scenes and as President—and established himself as a military opportunist and dictator of the traditional Caribbean American stamp.

And by the same move Batista set in motion a chain of events which were to finish him.

For Fidel Castro, the freshly-qualified lawyer, became Fidel Castro the fanatical rebel. He organized his friends into a 200-strong fighting force, trained them in the mountains at weekends, under the guise of student climbing parties, and armed them for an attack on the Government. His brother Raúl became his trusted lieutenant and when they thought that their troops were ready the Castros took them into the field. Their arms hidden in rice sacks, the rebels headed for Santiago de Cuba, capital of Oriente Province. The target was heavily-defended Moncada Barracks. They attacked at dawn on 26th July, 1953, hoping to carry the barracks by surprise and seize the arms and ammunition they needed for a full-scale revolt against Batista.

"I felt very strange," says Castro. "I am a Roman Catholic and had never thought of killing people."

But the ascetic young lawyer had become a revolutionary and had no thoughts of turning back.

Moncada Barracks held out and the automatic weapons of the highly-trained Batista troops were no match for the shotguns and small calibre rifles of Castro's men. The battle soon turned against them, and, with his men dying all around him, he surrendered on the promise of amnesty. Instead the rebels were jailed as insurgents. Castro had surrendered with 113 men and two women. Only fifty of them were to come before the courts. The rest died in Batista's jails.

After seventy-six days in solitary confinement, Castro himself came before a Special Tribunal at Santiago de Cuba to face a treason charge. The trial was a farce, the verdict a foregone conclusion. And Castro, after conducting his own defence, made his three-hour summing-up a memorable piece of oratory, which has gone down in Cuban history as a legal masterpiece and a shattering indictment of Batista's régime.

He began by quoting from the Bible, Martin Luther, Milton, John Knox and a round dozen philosophers, and then, hitting his stride, spoke of the Cuban peasants—"the 900,000 farmers and workers, miserably exploited, with perennial work their only future and the grave their only rest".

Pointing a long, accusing finger at the judges, he said: "We were born in a free country, and we would rather see this island sink to the bottom of the ocean than consent to be anybody's slave. I know that for me imprisonment will be harder than it ever was for anyone, but I do not fear it as I do not fear the fury of the miserable tyrant who killed my brothers.

"Condemn me," he cried. "It does not matter. History will absolve me."

Unimpressed, the judges handed down a fifteen-year sentence. Raúl Castro received thirteen years. They were sent to the Isle of Pines and Fidel Castro's first seven months were spent in solitary confinement, denied even books to read. It was 16th October, 1953.

Meanwhile Batista was preparing the way for "elections" to add a democratic touch to his seizure of power. They were held in November, 1954, but his old enemy Dr. Ramón Grau San Martín, who had planned to contest the Presidency, withdrew before polling day claiming that the voting would be rigged. Batista therefore claimed to have won and declared himself "Constitutional President". Castro's wife divorced him in 1955 and the same year—in May—Batista granted an amnesty to Fidel and Raúl Castro and they were released from the Isle of Pines.

It was the worst mistake that Batista ever made.

The brothers left for the United States. Weeks later they were in Mexico with a band of Cuban exiles they had picked up on the way. Castro rented several adjoining farms and began training his men for the next move against Batista. The Mexican Government, aware that military training was being done on their soil, ignored it for the moment and gave Castro the breathing space he needed to get his plans moving.

He called his rebels "The 26th July Movement" in memory of the brave men who had died at his side in the abortive Moncada Barracks attack. He needed money for arms and soon got it from one of the many men who had no reason to love Fulgencio Batista: ousted President Carlos Prío Socarrás. In American-style combat gear the men trained, the black and red armbands marked MR 26-7 showing up against the jungle-green. The rebel flag was black and red.

As Castro's fame spread, fighting men joined him from all over Caribbean America. Cuban exiles from Venezuela flocked to the rebel banner along with English soldiers of fortune, American filibusters and barefoot Mexican peons.

For a long time the Mexican authorities turned a blind eye to the activities of "The 26th July Movement". And then they let it be known that they must put a stop to the soldiering.

Castro had just bought a 62-foot yacht called the *Granma* with money given him by ex-President Prío Socarrás. It was a leaky old tub which badly needed overhauling, but the imminent advance of the Mexican authorities made this impossible and the rebels had to advance their plans. On 25th November, 1956, the *Granma* upped anchor and sailed from Tuxpán with eighty-two heavily-armed men on board. Among them were two men who more than any others would be responsible for Cuba's swing to the left: Raúl Castro and an Argentinian surgeon named Ernesto "Ché" Guevara.

The assault on Cuba had begun.

Said Fidel Castro: "If Batista loses, he will lose for good. If I lose I will just start all over again."

And what an assault it was. A few hours out the hardy rebels were nearly all seasick. On the third day out one of the *Granma*'s diesel engines broke down and the radio died. They had sailed south through the Yucatan Straits and on past Grand Cayman Island when the bilge pump stopped. On the seventh day a man fell overboard and Castro ordered a rescue operation. After several hours the swimming rebel was picked up and the *Granma* creaked and wallowed on her way.

On 2nd December, a Cuban Government gunboat surprised the rebels off the coast of Oriente Province and the *Granma* made a run for the shore. They beached in thick mud, lost all the heavy equipment, and made a mad dash for the hills just as a squadron of Batista's B-26 patrol bombers droned across the island. Three days later they were surrounded by General Díaz Tamayo's crack First Regiment and most of Castro's army were killed on the spot. Eighteen, captured wounded, were tortured to death. But Fidel Castro escaped into the bush with eleven other survivors.

The voyage of liberation had ended in complete failure.

The rebels hid in the bush for nineteen days living on berries and fruit as they worked their way up into the Sierra Maestra range. But not for a minute did Castro's burning faith desert him. The first recruit for the new rebel army was an ex-butcher, the second was a Negro cane-cutter. More followed. From nothing, as he had done before, Fidel Castro began rebuilding his revolutionary army. They did not shave for days on end and when at last they could do so, Castro declined.

"I shall not shave my beard until I give Cuba a good, honest and corruption-free Government," he said.

On 16th January, 1957, the rebels attacked an Army post at La Plata, killed five soldiers, wounded fourteen and fled with a dozen Thompson machine-guns. By the end of the month they had smashed three more outposts and in May they stormed the Uvero garrison. Now hundreds of recruits were joining Castro in his stronghold in the Sierra Maestra.

His name had become a symbol of freedom from the tyranny of Batista. His oath not to shave gave him a glamour and when his men copied the idea they became "los barbudos"—"the bearded ones".

By mid-1957 Castro's rebels were well armed and equipped and their stand against Batista's troops had inspired other rebel organizations to take to the hills all over Cuba. One band, quite unconnected with "The 26th July Movement", was active in the hills around Santa Clara, capital of Las Villas Province, in the centre of the island.

The notorious Military Intelligence Service—s I M—became more frightened and violent as the rebel forces grew. The Cuban Communist Party—which had worked with Batista during his behind-the-scenes reign and his first Presidency—was still working closely with him. They were especially powerful in the Ministry of Labour. But as the revolution gathered force the leaders—anxious to be on the winning side—began to think again. For the time being, however, they remained on the fence.

But even though the organization was growing, the odds were always against the rebels. Their rifles were never far from hand and their temporary hideouts—they seldom slept in the same place two nights running—were never unguarded. The men learned to be as merciless as Batista's troops and the much-feared s I M. Their attacks on lone outposts and stronger military garrisons were ruthlessly and brutally efficient. And as their successes mounted so did their fighting efficiency and techniques.

"We took Hemingway's *For Whom The Bell Tolls* up to the hills with us," says Castro. "It told us about modern civil war. Other books don't teach us that."

And what they did not adapt from Hemingway came from the methods of the French wartime Maquis and the tactical brilliance of Tito's Jugoslavian fighters.

In the few moments of relaxation that the rebels allowed themselves, Castro would light one of the 3s. 6d. Montecristo cigars which are his only luxury, and settle down to read a highbrow book, his green fatigue cap tilted back on his head. Occasionally he played marbles with his men. They held prayers daily—Castro wears a religious medallion—and had a priest among them. Swearing was forbidden, drinking kept down to a bare minimum. Castro himself hardly ever touches strong liquor. And in the mountains he became a Yogi.

Money came pouring in to the rebels. Cuban exiles sent funds through secret channels; a non-redeemable bond-issue in Venezuela raised £50,000; American sympathizers sent £10,000 a month at the height of the fund-raising campaign; local sugar kings dipped into their pockets and donated money. The band grew ever-larger and better equipped. Soon the mere handful who had dared the might of Batista's 40,000-strong army had blossomed into several thousands in the hills, and a spy system which stretched across the length and breadth of the island.

Almost every night there was a raid somewhere. Swiftly, silently the rebels struck. They moved in darkness, passing like shadows along the high ridges, descending into the valleys to fire a police post or blow a bridge, and when the dawn light began to creep across the Sierra Maestra range they returned carrying their wounded.

But though he fought with guns, Castro never underestimated the power of publicity. Foreign correspondents from American and British newspapers who were ingenious enough to find a rebel contact man and then hardy enough to follow him into the mountains, were received with great cordiality by Castro. In February, 1958, he kidnapped world champion racing driver Juan Fangio on the eve of the Cuban Grand Prix. On other occasions he spirited away American tourists, later releasing them unharmed but full of tales of their dangerous adventure.

In April, 1958, Castro tried to topple Batista through a general strike. But it was a costly failure. The sadistic SIM excelled themselves in the violence with which they put down the attempt, and their orgy of killing and torture-chamber tactics convinced Castro that further strikes would be similarly dealt with. An estimated 20,000 Cubans were killed and countless other thousands branded and maimed by the SIM during the last few months of Batista's rule.

A few Cuban Communists went into the mountains during 1958 to join either Castro or other rebel leaders. Others stayed on with the Government and played a busy part in Batista-ism right up to the last minute.

By August, 1958, Cuba was beginning to contract on Batista. Castro had cut all road links between Havana and Santiago de Cuba, the island's two largest cities. Travel between them was impossible. The following month another rebel group assisted in cutting Havana off from the central Las Villas Province. Castro's lieutenant "Ché" Guevara was sent with a column of "26th July" rebels to help lay siege to Santa Clara, capital of Las Villas Province. In November, another rebel group, made up of Auténtico partisans, laid siege to Pinar del Río in the island's west end and Castro's own men surrounded Santiago de Cuba.

The revolt was drawing to a close. Castro contacted General Cantillo, a top man in Batista's Army who was close to the dictator, and made a deal for him to arrest Batista when the régime fell.

The final stroke in the revolt came when Santa Clara gave in to the besiegers in the last days of December, 1958. Batista saw the red light and secretly made arrangements to leave. On 1st January, 1959, the dictator, his family and a few men close to him, flew out of Havana and sought refuge in Trujillo's Dominican Republic. General Cantillo saw Batista off at the airport instead of arresting him.

During the first few days of January Fidel Castro made a

triumphal journey across Cuba from Oriente Province, entered Havana riding on an armoured car, and was hailed as the great liberator. Months earlier he had named lawyer Manuel Urrutia as Provisional President and Dr. Miró Cardona as Prime Minister. Colonel Barquin replaced the untrustworthy General Cantillo as Chief of Staff.

"For myself," said Castro, "I ask nothing more than to be given the rank of major."

Almost at once the executions began. The key men in Batista's Government, Army and police were rounded up, tried at drumhead courts martial and summarily executed in the dried-up moat of La Cabaña fortress across from Havana harbour. Officers of SIM were arrested and shot. World opinion, which had been with Castro for most of the rebellion, now began to change.

But Castro was adamant: "They are criminals," he said. "Everybody knows that. We have given them a fair trial. We have given orders to shoot every last one of these murderers, and if we have to oppose world opinion to carry out justice, we will do it."

And in the midst of the riotous joy of the new régime a disturbing gap began to appear. Castro gave every credit to members of "The 26th July Movement", but steadfastly refused to recognize that other rebel groups had played an important part in the fight against dictatorship. He turned the "Movement" into the National Army and Raúl Castro became the Commander-in-Chief.

Only six weeks after Batista fell, Prime Minister Cardona resigned from office saying that the post should go to revolutionary hero Fidel Castro. And the man who only wanted to "be given the rank of major", the owner of the world's most famous beard, became the Prime Minister of Cuba on 16th February, 1959. Ex-Prime Minister Cardona was appointed Ambassador to Washington. He went to the United States, resigned from his post and is now in exile in Miami as the head of the Cuban Revolutionary Council.

Prime Minister Castro promised elections within eighteen months or two years.

"The parties must have time to reorganize," he explained. "If we held elections tomorrow, we would win. People tire easily. In eighteen months the people may be very tired of us."

It soon became apparent that Castro saw himself as the heir of National Hero José Martí. It was Martí on the bus tickets, in the shop windows and on the vast posters that began to appear on the streets of Havana. When it was not Martí, it was Fidel. And the symbol of the revolutionary Government seemed to be death. It jingled in the pockets of the people. "Patria o Muerte"—"My Country Or Death"—was stamped on the coins, glared down from the neon signs all over the city, and became the national slogan.

Fidel Castro hates formality, in fact he has made a virtue of informality. He is seen around Havana at all times of the day and night. He works a fourteen-hour day which often begins about noon and ends in the kitchen of the former Havana Hilton Hotel —now the Habana Libre—for a scratch meal in the small hours of the morning. Work is done during the day, the Castro image spread during the evening. A rounding-off of his working day is often the casual meeting of Castro and other nocturnal intellectuals in a down-town bar in the very early hours. He appears at sporting functions—usually to hit out at the first throw in a baseball game—in beret or campaign hat, the image of the man of the people. He hates desks and—much to the exasperation of his office staff—is seldom behind one when needed to sign papers. The drudgery of administrative work he leaves to others. He is never on time for functions, arrives at big parties with a casually-crumpled look and an engaging smile. He speaks fairly fluent English, apparently better than he understands it. His chauffeur and bodyguards wait around the bullet-proof car for him to come out. He will stop to sign autographs at the first sight of a collector with pencil in hand.

Castro made immediate overtures to the United States which were cordially received. He went to Washington in April, 1959, lived in a Harlem hotel and took time off to lay a wreath before the seated figure of Abraham Lincoln which dominates the Lincoln Memorial.

But then, as American opinion changed towards him over the mass executions, he embarked on a violently anti-American campaign which had some appeal in Cuba because of the tradition of hostility to the larger neighbour. He attacked the existence of the United States military base at Guantánamo, and began a mass nationalization scheme throughout the island. A total of 382 companies were nationalized. By far the greater number of them were American-owned. United States investors and companies held 40 per cent of the sugar mills as well as land, banks and businesses, giving them virtual control of one quarter of the island's economy. All banks—except the Bank of Nova Scotia and the Royal Bank of Canada—also fell to nationalization.

In July, 1959, Osvaldo Dorticós Torrado became President of Cuba. Castro's cabinet by this time included two survivors of the *Granma*. One was the Argentinian surgeon Ernesto "Ché" Guevara who was Minister for Industry. The other was Faustino Pérez, the Minister for the Recovery of Stolen Government Property.

Castro has never been slow to try to extend his influence to other Caribbean American and Latin American countries, and one of his first targets was a noisy campaign against the Dominican Republic. "Trujillo is next," he boasted. And both Cuba and Venezuela were instrumental in supplying arms and men aimed at toppling the dictator. They failed, and in November, 1959, Trujillo sentenced in their absence Fidel and Raúl Castro of Cuba and President Rómulo Betancourt of Venezuela to thirty years at hard labour for "crimes against State security".

Castro had promised elections "within eighteen months or two years" but by the end of 1960 things had changed. From this ideal, the internal political situation degenerated into the spectacle of vast crowds listening to Castro speaking in a public place. Euphemistically it was called "the sovereign organ of the National Will of the Cuban Nation", and to raise a hand at the end of a policy speech was "to vote". Soon anyone who spoke of elections was branded "counter-revolutionary" and Castro went on record as saying that elections were "unnecessary" as he knew what the people wanted.

This was a first step towards totalitarianism.

The American Government became increasingly critical of the new régime and Castro continued to build up his nationalistic following with tirades against the northern neighbour. As American goods were drawn into the trade blockade he had an even bigger stick with which to beat them. But he kept his dislike for the Government, not the people, of the United States.

"I am a friend of the Americans," he said. "I don't hate the American people. They can't get the truth. Their radio and newspapers are controlled by big business. All give a false story."

The inept, American-inspired—but not fully backed-up—Bay of Pigs invasion of April, 1961, gave him an ideal and lasting peg upon which to hang more and more "anti-imperialist" propaganda. And he used it to full advantage—especially when it was revealed that the American Central Intelligence Agency had spent some £160,000 on training the 1,500 Cuban exiles engaged in the abortive landing.

In July the same year Raúl Castro was injured in a bomb explosion in Santiago de Cuba which is one of the least pro-Castro areas in the island.

Right from the beginning Castro's dream has been to better the lot of the Cuban peasants, and one of his first moves was to break down the illiteracy. In 1961 he made a full-scale attack on it after building more schools in two years than his predecessors had built in two centuries. His classrooms ready, he called for volunteers to teach the illiterates of all ages. Almost every adult who could spell out words took on the job of teaching at least one less fortunately endowed. Secondary school children participated in the plan and often taught their own parents. True they were teaching people from Marxist books, but they were teaching just the same.

For this Castro received the Lenin Peace Prize.

Castro's anti-American tirades on television and in public grew in volume and all Cuba was nurtured on his hatred for the United States Government. When he makes his long, but captivatingly hypnotic speeches, Castro's hands are never still. When he is not spreading them afar, banging home a point, or clenching his big fist in defiance, his long tapering fingers are at work making continuous and unnecessary adjustments to the microphones. His deep voice, and the way he has of rolling his Rs, have a fascination all their own.

And as the anti-American feeling grew, the cult of Fidel grew with it. Vast posters of a smiling, gun-toting Castro in crumpled fatigue gear beamed down in every conceivable corner of Cuba. Castro says he is against the "personality cult". But in every way he encourages its growth. And in it lies his strength. For while people may criticize the Government for promises broken, they personally idolize the Prime Minister.

Publicly he tells reporters: "This is the century of the masses—the need produces the leader. It wasn't Churchill who won the war, but the soldiers and the workers. Here it is not Fidel—it is the people who matter."

But Castro knows that if he ever loses his magnetic appeal for the average Cuban it will be the end of him. The Communists cannot rule without him—but they would like to. If he loses his popularity he will lose everything, probably even his life.

And while Fidel Castro propagated the Castro image and immersed himself in his plans for the peasants, the two men who are really the power in Cuba were hard at work: Raúl Castro and "Ché" Guevara. Both dedicated Communists, they set in motion the machinery for a big Soviet *bloc* move-in. The anti-American stand taken by Fidel, the increasing shortages of food, spare parts for the U.S.-made equipment in the island, and the contracting outlets for the island's traditional products, made their job of swinging the island to the Left a great deal easier.

Cuba has done well out of the revolution in many ways. In other ways she has done incredibly badly.

On the credit side is the long list of reforms which Castro promised when he came to power and which he has tried faithfully to fulfil. All back taxes have been collected; the colour bar—never as odious as in parts of the United States, but there nevertheless—has been effectively ended; workers' rents have been cut by half and so have the prices of electricity and transport; and untold millions of dollars have been seized from the safe deposit boxes where they had been stored by corrupt Batista officials.

Castro's particular dream was to see the peasants decently housed, fed and clothed. And his Agrarian Reform Bill of April, 1959, went a long way towards seeing this dream become a reality. The 500,000 sugar workers, who had previously had to tighten their belts for more than half the year because they could work for only five months on the estates, are now guaranteed a round-the-year wage. The Instituo Nacional de Reforma Agraria —INRA—runs the co-operatives and the marketing divisions through which all produce is channelled. The vast holdings of American sugar and fruit companies have been nationalized and Castro has promised the workers their own land.

In one of his mammoth four-hour television broadcasts he spoke volubly of the foreign land holdings.

"More than half our best cultivatable land is in foreign hands. In Oriente Province the lands in possession of the United Fruit

Company, taken with those held by the West India Company, extend unbroken across our country from coast to coast. Two hundred thousand Cuban peasant families are without land, whereas 300,000 caballerías of our best land is in the hands of foreign interests." (A caballería is approximately 33 acres).

The squalid hovels in which many peasant families spent their lives have been largely replaced by row upon row of neat prefabricated concrete bungalows with four rooms, electric light at the flick of a switch and fresh water at the turn of a tap. They are not pretty, but they are utilitarian, and gone are the three-mile walks to the nearest spring or stand-pipe. Newly-literate hands have scrawled "Gracias Fidel" on countless doorways.

Equally spectacular is the revolution's debit side. The peasants have not got the land that was promised to them yet—and they probably will never get it. Just under half of Cuba's land is still in the hands of private individuals who market their produce through the none-too-efficient I N R A marketing boards. Religion still plays a large part in Cuban life although its influence is on the decline. Roman Catholic churches are less full as the belief grows— particularly among the young people—that "there is no need for religion in a Socialist State". And Castro himself was excommunicated by the Pope in January, 1962, for "impeding and imprisoning" Roman Catholic bishops. A noisy anti-church campaign by youngsters has overtones of José Martí—for the National Hero himself was anti-cleric.

The civil service—already too large under Batista—has swollen to three times its pre-revolutionary size. The £70 million held in foreign reserves at the time of Castro's ascendancy has all gone. And the sugar crop—the island's mainstay—has been mortgaged to the Soviet *bloc* until 1965. The inefficiency of I N R A, and the inexperience of the volunteer cane cutters, caused a tremendous wastage in the 1961 crop and Castro had to tell the Soviet Governments that there would be less than the three million tons they had expected. Tourism, once the biggest earner after sugar, is virtually non-existent.

Thousands of Cubans have left the island and still more would like to go. They are leaving at the rate of 300 a day. More than 29,000 left last year alone and about 350,000 have left since the revolution. Others would go if there were more flights out and fewer forms to fill in.

It takes about 120 days to leave the island and the paperwork to be completed means residence in Havana for access to the many offices which must be visited. The Government thinks that it is better to let the dissatisfied leave. But it makes it far from easy. All money, property and furniture must be turned over to the State—the furniture, it is said, is sold to Soviet *bloc* countries. A man may take out three suits; a woman five dresses and a change of underwear. All personal belongings must be left behind. No one may take out even a wristwatch or the little gold cross on a chain that Cubans are so fond of. The outgoing cash allowance is only 8s. per person.

After continuous exposure to every kind of humiliation the departing Cubans complete the requirements and make their way to the José Martí Airport—another of Castro's attempts to create a national feeling and link himself with the National Hero. On the way out are huge papiermâché peace doves, hammers and sickles painted on buildings, and vast posters of Castro, Lenin and other Communist heroes all along the road. And if it is not their pictures it is their quotes: quotes from Castro, from Lenin and from Mao Tse-tung.

And the last thing that the departing Cubans—branded by their own people as "traitors to the cause of Socialist solidarity"—see is a poster proclaiming that they are just leaving "Cuba—Territorio Libre de América", "The First Socialist State in America".

As Cuba's future became clear, Castro came more and more under critical overseas comment, especially over his antipathy towards the idea of elections.

"I am a dictator in the Roman sense," he admitted with disarming candour. "But I am not yet a tyrant. The day I am forced to kill, I will kill 40,000 people once and for all. It is not my fault if the revolution I lead and the methods I have used are similar to those of Communism."

When he came to power in 1959 Castro prophesied that 450 people would die in front of his firing squads. He also said that they would be Batista followers and criminals. But soon those who had "betrayed" Cuba were joined by those who opposed Castro. By mid-1962 there had been 680 admitted executions and probably at least an equal number of unadmitted ones.

Says Castro: "The firing wall works in the Socialist revolution."

Batista's sadistic, brutal and corrupt Military Intelligence Service—s I M—has been replaced by a less sadistic, less brutal and less corrupt secret police organization patterned on the Communist style and called G.2. But if they are more socially desirable than s I M, they are certainly as efficient and some 35,000 "enemies of the revolution" are in jail to prove it.

Batista's Army of 40,000 has been purged and re-organized frequently and it is now re-grouped under Commander-in-Chief Raúl Castro as a standing army of 100,000 men. In addition, there are some 300,000 part-time troops—thousands of them teenagers and young women—who have received basic military training in guerilla fighting and the handling of the Czechoslovakian and Russian automatic weapons which have been shipped to the island in bulk.

The American trade blockade brought two things to Cuba: an increasing shortage of food, and a dearth in U.S. consumer goods and spare parts. But it welded the people into an even more solidly anti-American front than before.

When rationing came into force in March, 1962, the people had to tighten their belts. But they did so in the belief that shortages were caused by outside influences—which was partly true—and not by the bungling inexperience of their Government.

In 1953—the last pre-revolutionary statistics available—Cubans ate an average of 146 lb. of their staple rice and beans per person, per year. Now they have been cut by more than half. The ration per person, per month is 6 lb. rice; 1½ lb. beans; 1 lb. lard; 2 oz. butter; 3½ lb. potatoes; and 5 eggs. Meat is a rarity and so is fish, although the sea around teems with every kind.

But as the Cuban housewife queues for her food, her plastic-covered ration book clutched tightly in her hand, posters tell her that she is doing it for the future prosperity of Cuba and that it is necessary because of the "imperialist aggressors".

And even with the rationing and shortages, the average Cuban gets enough to eat and the standard of living is higher than it is in some Communist countries in Europe.

As the face of Cuba was changed, so were Castro's own views. In December, 1961, he made a speech in which he described himself as a "Marxist-Leninist". And in this somewhat autobiographical piece of oratory he went on to answer some of the "then and now" questions which the revolution-to-Communism line of his political career had raised.

"Am I a convinced revolutionary? Yes, I am a convinced revolutionary," he said. "For the benefit of those who have asked me whether my opinions at the time of the attack on the Moncada Barracks were the same as today, I can answer that they were *very similar* to my opinions today. This is the truth. . . .

"Do I believe in Marxism? I believe absolutely in Marxism. Did I believe in it on January 1? I did believe in it on January 1. Did I believe in it on July 26? I did believe in it on July 26. Did I interpret it then as I interpret it today? Between the way I interpreted it then and the way I interpret it now there is a big difference. Was I prejudiced? Yes, I was prejudiced on July 26. Was I a thorough-going revolutionary on July 26? No, I could not call myself a thorough-going revolutionary. Was I a thorough-going revolutionary on January 1? No, only to a certain extent. Am I a thorough-going revolutionary today? That would mean that I was satisfied with what I know and I am not satisfied—far from it. Have I any doubts about Marxism and do I think that certain interpretations are wrong and should be revised? I have no doubts whatever."

Castro has never had much time for the Cuban Communist Party—P S P—and frequently accused them—with justification—of working with Batista. Few of them went into the hills to fight the dictator and Castro has never been slow to remind them of this.

His disappearance from public life during the last two weeks of February, 1962—itself an unprecedented event—sparked off a crop of rumours that he had been toppled by the P S P and was hiding in the Mexican embassy; that he was dead; and that he had been kidnapped and sent to Moscow.

But the resilient, bearded leader came bouncing back two weeks later to announce his rationing programme and to launch a blistering attack on the P S P. Before his tirade, and the traditional Communist-style purge which followed it, had run their course, Aníbal Escalante, a top Cuban Communist, had been accused of infiltrating P S P members into cushy jobs in the over-staffed Administration, and had been sent into exile.

Castro's family life also underwent changes in 1962. In February his son Fidelito was kidnapped from his mother in Rome, and flown back to his father by way of Moscow. And in October Castro married Isabel Coto from Santiago de Cuba, proving that not everyone in the island's second largest city dislikes him.

Then came the crisis of October when the world was poised
on the brink of nuclear war. The diplomacy of major participants
Kennedy and Khrushchev saved the situation, but Cubans exulted
in the crisis which changed their island from a Caribbean American pawn into a nation of world importance and seemingly
nuclear standing.

The Cuban revolution has been a strangely mixed up entity.
While the average man-in-the-Cuban-Street has benefited, he has
also lost. Hunger—despite rationing—has virtually been wiped
out; so has illiteracy. And with them have gone much personal
freedom. But if the Cuban peasant has suffered, his old bosses, the
Cuban middle class, have lost more and suffered more. For the
first time the peasant is not being ignored, on the contrary, he is
considered important. And for most of the peasants this makes up
for a lot of other things.

When he came to power Castro had little to build on. There
was no non-political civil service; no police force he could trust;
no National Army which he could consider even vaguely loyal.
He had to start from scratch. And if he started his rule like
Machado and Batista, this was only to be expected from a band
of non-politicians with a "do it yourself" Government.

In an unintentionally prophetic moment, early in the revolution's
success, Castro remarked: "We are not politicians. We made our
revolution to get the politicians out. This is a social revolution."

But he made two big mistakes: he refused to turn "The 26th
July Movement" into a political party—thus giving the green
light to Communists and defeating the original radical intention of
the revolution; and he allowed his personal plans and dreams for
the betterment of the peasants to blind him to the dangerous men
at his side. For while Castro bypassed the drudgery of administrative routine and put his own plans into operation, brother Raúl
and friend "Ché" Guevara, the die-hard Communists in his inner
circle, changed the face and political colour of Cuba.

One of the favourite "counter-revolutionary" jokes told in
Cuba is indicative of the belief of the great mass of Cubans that
Castro himself is not steeped in Communist doctrine, and is a
Radical rather than a Red. The joke—invariably told by strongly
pro-Castro Cubans—is one of several so-called "counter-revolutionary" jokes which are never told by genuine "counter-revolu-
tionaries". It goes like this:

The "counter-revolution" has been successful and all Communists are sentenced to be buried in mud up to the extent of their Communism. Fidel Castro, up to his thighs, sees brother Raúl only up to his ankles.

Fidel: "Why are *you* only up to your ankles?"

Raúl: "Shhh! I'm standing on 'Ché's' head."

Now the Cuban situation is as it will probably be for a long, long time. The Cuban Communists cannot rule Cuba without Moscow. And Moscow cannot rule without Castro.

He is everything that they dislike: too independent; too much of a personality; too much the beatnik; too emotional. But they cannot do without him. For the people eat out of the palm of his hand.

A fighter, a genuine social reformer, a naïve politician, and an intellectual dreamer, Fidel Castro will go down in history in two versions. The history books of the Soviet *bloc* will show him as an inspired visionary who fought for his country for the good of the people. In the annals of the West he will go down as a mere pawn in Moscow's game for the highest Western Hemisphere stakes.

But to thousands of his own countrymen—both in Cuba and in exile beyond its shores—neither of these versions will be correct.

For they will remember him as a liberator whose romantic idealism and political folly made him the betrayer of a great revolution.

CHAPTER THREE

HAITI

Dr. François Duvalier

The three ancient French field-guns simmered in the sun in Port-au-Prince's main square, the Champ de Mars. Gun crews, their eyes squinting in the shimmering glare, peered across the square at the Dessalines Barracks where the rebel general was dug in.

It was 25th May, 1957, mid-way through a year of political turmoil that had given Haiti, the second oldest—and only Negro —republic in the New World, a total of five governments in as many months.

Colonel Armand, the artillery commander, had sent a note to rebel General Cantave to vacate his stronghold or be blown to pieces. The General had replied with a burst of gunfire.

The Colonel gave the order to fire and Haiti's most tragi-comic battle began.

One field-gun exploded at the first shot and killed its crew. The other two, with consistent and impressive inaccuracy, sent shell after shell whistling over the roof of the barracks to drop into the harbour on the other side. Several narrowly missed a Dutch ship which was just docking.

Then the Air Force launched their attack. An ancient transport plane, the only aircraft capable of carrying a bomb, staggered into the air with an 18-year-old blockbuster and droned low across the glistening, domed Presidential Palace towards the barracks.

When the pilot thought that he was roughly over it the bomb was kicked out through the open door and hurtled down into the Champ de Mars. It failed to explode and, bouncing, knocked over a civilian and broke his leg.

Meanwhile the Haitian Navy's only gunboat chugged up and down the harbour vainly trying to make its single gun fire.

Finally General Cantave ordered his men out in a charge. And the artillerymen, who had forgotten to bring along small arms for their own protection, were massacred in a bloody orgy of killing beneath the bougainvillaea and poinsettias in the square.

Colonel Armand managed to reach the airport and take the first plane out for the United States. General Cantave's *coup* came to nothing. And Daniel Fignolé, who had appeared and seized power during the battle, was arrested, imprisoned and exiled within weeks.

That year there were seven different governments. Even for Haiti, scene of 130 revolutions in 158 years of independence, it was a record.

American Marines occupied Haiti, the western third of the island that Columbus called Hispaniola, between 1915 and 1934. They were in the eastern neighbour, the Dominican Republic, at the same time. And ever since they left American money has kept the one crop—coffee—economy going.

The mountainous, densely wooded country covers 10,748 square miles and barely supports its 3,700,000 population. Ninety-five per cent of them are of almost pure Negro stock. Some 5 per cent are mulatto. Education is compulsory, but this is seldom enforced for there are not enough schools. As a result the population is 90 per cent illiterate and the budget allocation of 13 per cent for education does little to combat this. Only 2 per cent of it goes on education in the country with the result that 92 per cent of the rural children never have a day's schooling. French is the official language but less than 5 per cent of the population speak it. Creole is the universal tongue.

Ever since Jean Jacques Dessalines, the great liberator, finally wrested Haiti from the French in 1803, the country has been in turmoil. In this land of Dessalines, Toussaint l'Ouverture, Pétion and Henri Christophe only two things have mattered—power and colour.

When a black President has been in power the mulattos have been stripped of rank, property and often freedom. When the mulattos have held the reins of Government the blacks have suffered. It was Dessalines himself who, ripping the white from the French Tricolour, gave Haiti her flag and a rigid caste system which makes mulattos claim white ancestors and Negroes deride them. Even today mulattos will proudly point out that they have, say, ninety parts Negro to 229 parts white blood, and will consider themselves better than fellow mulattos with a higher percentage of Negro ancestry. Generally, unless a Negro can claim lineal descent from one of the famous liberators, the black people are the workers, the mulattos the professionals, the merchants and the *élite*.

Four years before the Americans left Haiti a strong and sincere man—a mulatto—became President. He was Sténio Joseph Vincent and he stayed at his country's head until 1941. Élie Lescot—also a mulatto—who succeeded him held power until 1946 when he was deposed for allegedly fascist tendencies and exiled to Canada. Dumarsais Estimé, the next President, who was a Negro, tried to change the constitution to allow himself to be re-elected and was succeeded after a *coup* in 1950 by General Paul "Iron Pants" Magloire, a remarkable man who attempted in six years to improve the conditions of his impoverished people.

He encouraged tourism and built it up until it was a great revenue earner—second only to coffee. He built workers' housing, diversified and improved the agriculture, opened up bauxite mines, and established social services. He borrowed money where he could — £10½ million from the Export-Import Bank for a hydro-electric scheme, £1 million from the World Bank for roads. His stable government encouraged the United States to give money in larger amounts than ever before.

Even so, the people live in poverty. Fishermen can seldom afford to replace their gear lost at sea. If they are lucky they earn about 1s. 9d. a day. Sugar factory workers get about 5s. a day. Workers in towns get between 5s. 6d. and 10s. a day. The country's average wage is £35 a year.

But, for all his improvements, Magloire was not to last. A general strike in December, 1956, finally lost him the Presidency and plunged Haiti into a ferment which lasted for nine months. Other strikes forced two Presidents and an Executive Council composed of all Presidential candidates from office in a few months.

Then came the battle of 25th May, 1957, and the bloody killings on the Champ de Mars. Daniel Fignolé, who had seized power while the military fought, was himself deposed at gunpoint a few weeks later and sent into exile. A 48-year-old Army officer named Antonio Kebreau established a three-man military junta with himself at the head. The country was declared to be in a state of seige, fifty people died in the rioting that followed, and General Kebreau prepared for honest elections.

"There must be calm in the streets and in the hearts of the people," he said.

Kebreau went to work to bring about elections which would be the first under universal adult suffrage. There were difficulties. The million-and-a-half voters were 90 per cent illiterate. The greatest illiteracy was in the inaccessible mountain regions and not in Port-au-Prince's mere 200,000 population. And then there was the age-old colour problem between the two most likely Presidential candidates.

Louis Dejoie, wealthy, of good family, merchant and importer, was a mulatto. He could count on the mulatto votes and a certain percentage of the more prosperous Negro votes. François Duvalier, fairly wealthy, of humble beginnings, a country doctor, hardly known in Port-au-Prince, was a Negro of immense influence in rural areas.

The clash of their personalities and policies was immediate. Dejoie branded Duvalier "a treacherous, corrupt nobody" who was steeped in voodoo practices. Duvalier retaliated, canvassing his crowds on a colour basis. Mulattos had held the reins of government far too often in the past, he told them.

But just who was this sad-faced, soft-spoken, bespectacled black "nobody" who would soon become the President of his country; this man who would change gradually from a humane politician offering freedom from fear, corruption, arbitrary government and bloodshed, into one of the harshest dictators that Haiti has ever known in her long association with harsh dictators?

François Duvalier was born in the country in 1907 and grew up with the peasants who scratched a bare existence from the erosion-prone soil, as generations of peasants had done before them. He lived with them and was in fact one of them for all his formative years. He knew their good times and their bad; he understood their problems and their weaknesses; he knew their despair and took part in their voodoo rites in the secret compounds of the *houngans*—priests.

When the nights are fragrant with tropical blossoms and the

throb of drums lifts across the hills and valleys, the sound is nothing less than the heartbeat of Africa.

After a spell at the Lycée Alexandre Pétion and the Faculty of Medicine in Port-au-Prince, a lucky chance sent Duvalier to America and he qualified as a doctor. When he returned to Port-au-Prince he became a physician at the St. Francis-Xavier Hospital and began to move in influential Negro circles—but he never forgot his friends in the country. A resurgence in national pride was under way among Negro intellectuals, and Duvalier, passionately interested in the country's ethnology and anthropology took a lively interest. While the mulattos, for the most part, derided folk lore and peasant cultures and remained headily aloof from their champions, Duvalier gathered about him a small clique of men like himself.

In 1927 he, and intellectuals Lorimer Denis and Carl Brouard, founded a society combining African ideas and culture with socialist economic principles. Subsequently Duvalier became head of the Bureau of Ethnology. He studied voodoo very seriously and wrote learned papers for internationally-known ethnological journals.

But first and foremost he was a doctor. And it was as a doctor that he went into the country to fight disease and take modern medical techniques to the most remote villages and settlements in the interior. Once he worked for an American-sponsored anti-yaws campaign. Later, he was Director of the Gressier Rural Clinic. At other times he was just a country practitioner.

And, when it came to politics, Duvalier was on the scene. He offered himself for the Presidency with complete confidence in 1957 and went to Port-au-Prince to do battle with Louis Dejoie for the highest post in the country.

In his favour he had his knowledge of the country people and of how they thought. His platform was freedom from tyranny, more food for their children, more work and better homes. And his skin, like theirs, was black. He banked on the country districts. Dejoie banked on the towns, and on Port-au-Prince in particular.

But when, in September, 1957, under the rigorous scrutiny of the military junta of General Kebreau, the votes came in it was the country doctor who had won with a total of 679,884 votes, giving him complete command of the Senate and thirty-two of the thirty-seven seats in the Assembly.

Vainly Dejoie alleged fraud. He claimed that Duvalier had tallied 18,000 votes in a district that had a population of only 7,000. He resurrected the story that Duvalier was steeped in voodoo and had used the *houngans* to frighten the people into voting for him.

Mobs of angry Duvalier supporters broke up Dejoie's house. Police machine-gunned his close supporters after a series of bomb incidents that rocked the capital, and sent the defeated candidate into hiding with a price of £5,000 on his head. He escaped to Mexico. Many of his supporters were not so lucky and were thrown into the National Penitentiary.

Duvalier took power at a crucial point in his country's history. A poor coffee crop had depleted the exchequer; the nine months of troubles had frightened away all but the hardiest of tourists and with them the £3 million they annually brought to Haiti; gross public debts stood at £22 million—more than twice the recent annual budgets.

On a widely publicized slogan of "Unity and Peace" Dr. François Duvalier, £8,000-a-year President of Haiti, went to work.

The country operates on an annual budget of about £8½ million and a privately administered fund—most of the money coming from the United States—of about the same size. But about 62 per cent of both is spent on the Army. The Government is the country's biggest employer. In direct aid the United States annually gives some £4½ million, thus virtually underwriting about half the national budget.

From his Presidential desk in the great white national palace in the centre of Port-au-Prince, Duvalier issued a never-ending stream of missives, orders and memos. Many of his decisions were unpopular, not only with the people but with his own party. But such is his personality that he was able to pass them through Government regardless. He felt that he alone understood his country's needs and problems, and that he alone must face up to them. The Presidency of a place like Haiti is a lonely job, fraught with the possibility of assassination. Because his guards are strong it might be hard to get him with a gun. It would also be hard to do it with poison. For Duvalier has two full-time "food tasters".

One of his first acts was to establish—in the face of fierce opposition—a permanent civil service. This had been recommended by the United Nations in 1951 but had never been implemented. Previously, when a Government fell everyone fell with it, from the President to the road sweeper.

Another early object for Presidential scrutiny was the 5,000-man Army. The military had always been the prime target for any would-be usurper. So Duvalier packed the top places with men he knew were loyal to him—and he has reshuffled them often. No Chief of Staff has lasted more than a year. And in case these loyal officers ever changed their minds he established a 2,000-strong Palace Guard of hand-picked troops. Six hundred of them sleep in the basement of the palace making him what must be the best-guarded President in the world. As a third precaution, he enrolled some 5,000 general roustabouts, strong-arm men, former riot police and voodoo worshippers as a form of island-wide secret police and spy system. They became known as the Ton Ton Macoute—roughly translated Creole for Bogeymen. Nothing of significance happens in any part of Haiti without Duvalier knowing about it through his spies within a matter of hours.

He launched a great publicity campaign to project his personality to the people in an attempt to win over those of the public who were not convinced that he was the man to lead Haiti. And when this failed he launched another personality-cult campaign aimed at keeping the peasants loyal to him. Initially it was done through pro-Duvalier newspapers—others had been closed during a Press censorship campaign and their editors incarcerated in the National Penitentiary.

Papers carried the banner: "The Haitian who does not love President François Duvalier is a dangerous enemy to his fatherland." Another of his widely-spread lines, aimed at the simple people who believed in voodoo, was: "The President can see into the minds and hearts of his people. He knows all."

And when the written word failed to reach the illiterates it was the Ton Ton Macoute who received orders to spread it about the country that President Duvalier had come to stay—and that it was just as well for Haiti that he had.

Mystical and clairvoyant powers were attributed to him. This, coupled with the fact that he knew of every movement in the island hours after it happened, made it easier for the Ton Ton Macoute to spread the message that "The President knows all". To a simple people who still believe in Damballah, the African

Snake-god, Duvalier's apparently all-seeing and all-knowing figure was to be feared and revered. He must, they felt, indeed be a powerful *houngan* himself.

The Roman Catholic Church, despite voodoo—which is a combination of African and Catholic religions anyway—held strong sway, particularly in the rural areas. And when Duvalier discovered that the priests were trying to combat his publicity machine with logic he had to move fast. Roman Catholic bishops were deported from the island. This act brought the fury of the Roman Church down on the President's head, and finally got him excommunicated by order of the Pope. But otherwise it did little or nothing to alter his hold on the people.

Still seeking money for his country Duvalier began a new line of approach. Fidel Castro had come to power in Cuba, a scant forty-nine miles from Haiti across the Windward Passage. And when he saw how worried the Americans were becoming over the growing Communist threat, Duvalier began subtly to suggest that unless more dollars reached Haiti there might be what he described as "a Castro-style" revolt in the country.

In fact it is unlikely that Communism could get a really strong hold in Haiti. For Duvalier's administrative machinery would deal with it too fast. It would be the biggest threat to his continued well-being in the country and would be stamped out as ruthlessly and efficiently as have minor risings and abortive plots on his life.

But now Duvalier, who had risen to power as a great bringer of freedom and democracy to his people, had degenerated into a violent and corrupt dictator whose position was well secured by his own careful planning.

He passed through Parliament a bill reducing the Senate and Assembly to a one chamber legislature. Announcing this, he also declared that there would be fresh elections for the new legislature. Fifty-eight seats were to be contested and fifty-eight hand-picked Duvalier supporters prepared themselves to "contest" them. A fifty-ninth candidate withdrew his name on the eve of the polls for what he called "urgent and personal reasons". Cynics said he wanted to stay alive.

On 30th April, 1961, Haitians went out to vote. It was a foregone conclusion. Few of them even remarked on the fact that at the top of each ballot paper was printed in neat, small letters "President François Duvalier". But five days after the election they were stunned by an announcement from the palace that President Duvalier had been "unanimously re-elected" for a further six year term of office. At that time he still had two and a half years of his previous term to run.

On 22nd May, he was re-inaugurated in the new single chamber legislature. Army trucks transported thousands of peasants from outlying districts into the capital to attend celebrations—and then left them to find their own way back home. Despite his still recent excommunication by Rome a High Mass was said at a "Thanksgiving Service" in the cathedral.

Said Duvalier: "My brother Haitians. With Me, you must procreate, give birth to the new Haiti, and make her live all the great dreams of which she has so long been frustrated."

The same month General Rafael Trujillo, the immensely rich, completely ruthless and staggeringly corrupt dictator of Haiti's neighbour, the Dominican Republic, was machine-gunned to death. Duvalier momentarily panicked and then sent troops dashing for the border. Ostensibly they were to prevent refugees crossing into Haiti. In fact their mission was to prevent any slight feelings of unrest that the news of Trujillo's assassination might have raised in the Haitians. It was not until September that any actual plot could be discovered and then it was efficiently cleared up. A former Army officer and his two sons, allegedly planning to assassinate Duvalier, were arrested and the affair blew over.

Soon after the re-inauguration celebrations the sinister Ton Ton Macoute began a new phase. The President, always seeking money for his country—an estimated £2 million a year finds its way into private pockets—announced the formation of a National Renovation Movement and put the Ton Ton Macoute in charge of raising the cash.

Foreign businessmen soon had unwelcome callers who informed them that they were expected to "contribute" to the Movement. Figures varying between £10 and £300 a month were named. Most paid. The threat of damage to business property, staff and themselves was enough inducement.

But Cromwell James, a coloured British subject from the Eastern Caribbean spice island of Grenada, was one man who stood out in the face of this blatant "shakedown" racket. Stubbornly he refused to pay up. The Ton Ton Macoute decided that an example must be made. Framed on a robbery charge,

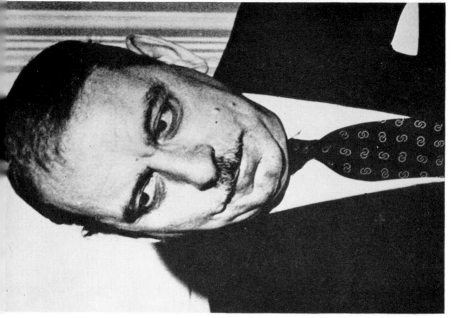

LUIS MUÑOZ MARÍN
Governor of Puerto Rico

Alex McCulloch

SIR ALEXANDER BUSTAMANTE
Prime Minister of Jamaica

DR. FIDEL CASTRO
Prime Minister of Cuba

PROFESSOR JUAN BOSCH
President of the Dominican Republic

DR. FRANÇOIS DUVALIER
President of Haiti

Camera Press

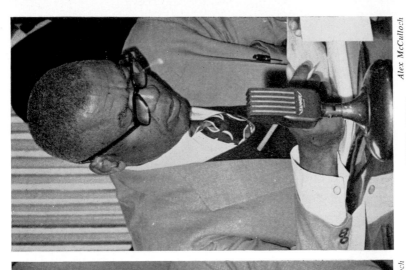

VERE BIRD
Chief Minister of Antigua

WILLIAM BRAMBLE
Chief Minister of Montserrat

THE LEEWARD ISLANDS

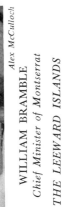

C. A. P. SOUTHWELL,
*Chief Minister of St. Kitts,
Nevis and Anguilla*

ERROL BARROW
Premier of Barbados

EDWARD LE BLANC
Chief Minister of Dominica

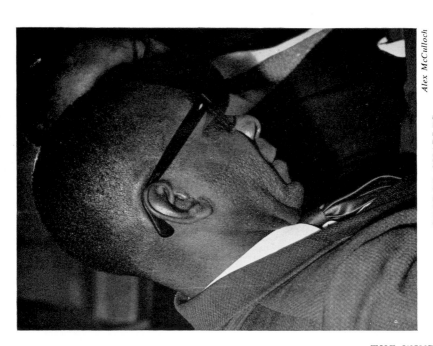

GEORGE CHARLES
Chief Minister of St. Lucia

HERBERT BLAIZE
Chief Minister of Grenada

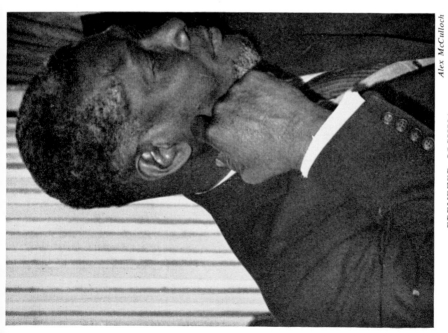

Alex McCulloch

EBENEZER JOSHUA
Chief Minister of St. Vincent

Alex McCulloch

DR. ERIC WILLIAMS
Prime Minister of Trinidad and Tobago

James was hauled down to the National Penitentiary and spent five days undergoing almost continuous beatings and torture before the British Ambassador, Mr. G. T. Corley Smith, was able to get him released. Two days later he died from his injuries.

Mr. Corley Smith visited the other embassies and as a result a concerted plan of action was agreed upon. Forthwith Mr. Corley Smith, as spokesman for the Ambassadors of Canada, Italy, the United States and France, called upon the Minister of the Interior. He protested on behalf of the British Government over the death of Mr. James, and on behalf of his diplomatic colleagues over the activities of the Ton Ton Macoute. In March, 1962, he was ordered out of the country and Anglo-Haitian diplomatic relations were broken off.

On 22nd May, 1962—a year to the day of his re-inauguration ceremony—Duvalier declared that a national holiday would henceforth be observed to mark a Day of National Sovereignty.

This small incident put the United States in an acutely embarrassing position. Between Duvalier's rise to power in September, 1957, and mid-1962, they had put some £10,700,000 into Haiti in addition to their normal annual grants and gifts. What had started as a duly elected Presidency had degenerated into a harsh and corrupt dictatorship with all the usual trappings. Now they were being asked to celebrate as a Day of National Sovereignty the anniversary of a completely dishonest election.

Looking for a way out, a State Department official dreamed up the idea of calling the Ambassador and his deputy back to Washington for a "high level conference" which would last just long enough to ensure that both men were out of Haiti for the celebrations.

In fact Haiti will be a problem child for America for some time to come. They despaired of the régime in September, 1962, and cut off some aid, risking Duvalier turning to the East for help. But it has made the already desperate plight of the Haitian peasants much worse. Corruption, graft and extortion have ruined the economy. It may, with time, bring about the fall of Duvalier. But the Americans are loath to risk another Cuba. Glittering Miami is only 500 miles away. In the Dominican Republic democracy is about to begin again with strong American backing.

Currently Duvalier has taken over all financial and economic responsibilities and has issued 5 per cent bonds called "certificates

c

of economic liberation". Everyone must buy them in relation to
their earnings. He slashed the budget to £9 million and assured
Haitians that the "certificates of economic liberation" will be
sufficient to make up for the loss of the dollars.

"We shall prove it as many times as may be necessary," he said
confidently.

Duvalier will be ousted eventually. It is unlikely that he will
stand down constitutionally. Whichever way things go the United
States is watching closely and supporting him in a small way
financially, but with misgivings. They have supported dictatorships before—Trujillo had a benevolent friendship with
America—and are in fact doing so now—with the Somozas in
Nicaragua.

They are in an embarrassing position and wide open for criticism. But the way they see it they have little choice in the matter.

Haiti's tragic story is one of too much too soon, a story that the
leaders of many of the newly-independent African and soon-to-
be-independent Caribbean territories might well study and learn
from.

Duvalier is there. So is Government by decree. The United
States are on the sidelines. And that will probably be the position
for some time. Years ago the schoolchildren used to sing a little
song called *Merci, Papa Vincent*. And when President Vincent
retired they sang *Merci, Papa Lescot*.

They will probably never, willingly, sing *Merci, Papa Doc*.

CHAPTER FOUR

DOMINICAN REPUBLIC

Professor Juan Bosch

When Rafael Leónidas Trujillo, the Caribbean's toughest, smoothest and most dictatorial of dictators, was assassinated on the night of 30th May, 1961, the country which he had ruled with an iron hand for thirty-one years was thrown into a panic.

The peasant's son who became President of his country and the tyrant of the Dominican Republic, was shot down with machine-guns as he drove out along George Washington Avenue in the capital, Ciudad Trujillo, on his way to visit his 94-year-old mother. The man who had bossed, run, bullied, cajoled, frightened, awed, coerced and sat upon his fellow Dominicans for thirty-one years; who had five elaborate houses, yachts, bullet-proof cars and a personal fortune of £280 million; who had boasted: "The man who takes a shot at me had better be a good shot"; that man was dead.

On the spot where he was killed his family erected a monument to his memory. And on the monument was a plaque to inform all those who cared to look that El Benefactor had been "sacrificed on the tragic night of 30th May, 1961".

But six months later, after his sorrowing family had smuggled the dead dictator's body to France and interred it in a £16,000 plot in a Paris cemetery, the monument was pulled down. And in its place, on the first anniversary of Trujillo's death, another monument was erected. This time it was to the memory of "the heroic liberating act"; to the memory of the men who had died on that night so that the country they loved might be free of tyranny, corruption, oppression and fear; to the assassins.

Now the days of Trujillo are only a memory. The Council of

State who organized the first free elections in thirty-eight years have seen a man of an entirely different calibre get into the Presidential chair: a man from the "democratic left" who had been in exile for twenty-five years and who had returned to lead his country towards a new place in the Caribbean.

Professor Juan Bosch, scholar, novelist and exile, had left everything behind him when he slipped out of the Dominican Republic in 1937 to seek a new life and living away from the evil hand of Rafael Trujillo. He had been hunted out of Cuba twenty-two years later, and then, when Trujillo fell, he returned from his chosen home of exile in Costa Rica to take part in the Presidential elections.

Covering 19,327 square miles at the eastern two-thirds of the island which Columbus called Hispaniola, the Dominican Republic shares a common 193-mile border with Haiti to the west and is separated from Puerto Rico to the east by a narrow strip of sea. It is the home of just over 3,000,000 people of mixed Spanish and Negro descent, a people who have been in a permanent state of revolt or suppression for almost the entire history of their country.

It was in 1697 that the island was first cut in two. The western portion was France's richest colony in the New World. The eastern portion was Spanish, wealthy, seat of the oldest university in the oldest city in the Western Hemisphere, and the burial place of Columbus. But after a Spanish rule of only ninety-eight years the island became all French again. After the slave revolt which set up Haiti as an independent country the whole island was under the rule of the black Kings, Emperors and Presidents until the people of what is now the Dominican Republic rebelled in 1809 and offered themselves to Spain once more. The offer was taken up, but in 1821 they thought that they had had enough of colonial rule. The whole of Central and South America had shaken off the shackles of the Spanish Empire and the Dominicans thought to do so too. They proclaimed their independence and tried to join Simón Bolivar's Greater Colombian Federation.

The following year the Haitians crossed the border and took the country back. Another revolt twenty-two years later was successful and the Dominicans again declared independence. But neither peace nor political stability were to come to the strife-torn republic. At the outbreak of the American Civil War in 1861 they asked Spain to accept them as a colony once more. Spain did so. But only for four years. For when the American Civil War ended the Dominicans again proclaimed independence, and Spain, now thoroughly tired of the fickle Dominicans, withdrew for the last time. In 1869 a Dominican request to be incorporated as a part of the United States reached the American Senate but failed to be ratified by only one vote.

By the turn of the century the economy was in ruins; great debts were piling up and the ships of the European Powers of the time were threatening to blockade the bankrupt republic to claim their money. The United States, at this imperialistic point in their history, used this as an excuse to land marines and take control of the country to prevent, they said, any violation of the Monroe Doctrine by a European Power. They invaded in 1905, took over the customs—and so were able to ensure that their debt at least was paid—and finally took complete control of the country in all matters in 1916.

Their occupation of the Dominican Republic was in fact a dictatorship. Few Dominicans would co-operate with them and they were fighting a rebel guerilla war in the mountains for several years. Their rule was a harsh and bloody one, even by the bloody and repressive standards accepted in the country.

And during this period a young Dominican offered his services to the National Guard, setting in motion a chain of events which would lead him to the highest and most lucrative position in the land: the Presidency.

His name was Rafael Leónidas Trujillo Molina, a name unknown then, but one which would be heard with fear, distaste and disgust for more than forty violent years.

The son of a peasant—although he later went to elaborate lengths to conceal this fact—Rafael Trujillo was born in San Cristóbal on 24th October, 1891, the third of a family of eleven. In 1918 he became a telephone operator in the country's ancient and historic capital Santo Domingo, the city whose name he would later change to Ciudad Trujillo. Three years later he was fighting with the American-controlled National Guard in the wars against patriots in the mountains. A particularly penetrating description of the young Trujillo was given by his American commander who, mentioning him in dispatches, called him "calm, even tempered, forceful, active and painstaking".

He graduated from the Haina Military Academy, became an officer in the regular Army, and was a major when the United States began a withdrawal from the republic in 1924. The administration was handed over to the Dominicans as the Americans pulled out, leaving only a handful of marines as the armed force until the country could get on its feet again. Horacio Vázquez, elected in an honest, U.S.-scrutinized poll, was President and he rapidly made Trujillo a lieutenant-colonel and gave him special power over the police. In 1927 he was again promoted, this time to brigadier-general, and made Chief of Staff. Mussolini sent him a decoration and soon afterwards he was ready to make his bid for power.

The weak and vacillating Vázquez was generally unpopular and Trujillo had been awaiting an opportunity to oust him. But in 1930 the job was done for him. For a small-scale revolt blossomed into a serious overthrow bid when Chief of Staff Trujillo refused to order his troops and police out of their barracks to quell the rebels. When it was too late for Vázquez' government to be saved, Trujillo marched out his troops, suppressed the rebels and put Estrella Ureña into power as Provisional President. From behind the scenes Trujillo wielded his power while the machinery was set up for an election. He had complete control of the police and Army and when the promised polls were held he made certain that he was the winner. On 16th August, 1930, he assumed the Presidency of the Dominican Republic.

He never looked back. His Partido Dominicano was the only party allowed to function. He was its President from 1930 until 1952. Other parties were driven underground and gradually suppressed or died out as their organizers were captured or fled the country. He appointed members of Congress, judges, councillors, policemen and other public officials, requiring them to deliver to him their formal resignations, signed but undated, before taking office. In one four year term of Congress—during which there were no elections, even Trujillo-style—there was a 200 per cent turnover of members as Trujillo made and broke his politicians as he felt like it.

On 3rd September, 1930, the worst hurricane in the history of the Dominican Republic ripped in from the Caribbean and left Santo Domingo in a shattered, chaotic mess. Here was a challenge for Trujillo and he rose to it with stupendous drive and initiative.

The old Spanish city, lying in a mangled, battered state, was cleaned up and rebuilt as a plushy modern capital. The country districts, which normally would have taken years to get back on their feet after the beating they had taken, were rehabilitated with surprising speed.

For this great work Trujillo wanted just one thing. And on 11th January, 1936, he got it when Acting Vice-President Jacinto "Mozo" Peynado approved a change of name for the capital. The oldest city in the New World, founded in 1496, after 440 years under one name, overnight became Ciudad Trujillo, in honour of the man who rebuilt it from rubble and dust.

He bestowed names, titles and decorations upon himself. In 1936, for rebuilding the capital, he ordered the dons of the university to put him forward for the Nobel Peace Prize. When he did not get it he consoled himself with his own honours. He called himself Generalissimo of the Armed Forces . . . Restorer of Financial Independence . . . Founder and Supreme Chief of the Partido Dominicano . . . Saviour of the Country . . . Captain of God . . . and First Journalist of the Republic (he owned two newspapers). But the name he preferred was Benefactor of the Fatherland.

The megalomania of this brash and showy *hombre* knew no bounds. Soon all over the country busts, statues and monuments of him were going up. In a prominent position in every store were photographs of him. No home was complete without its draped picture of him, sometimes dazzlingly bemedalled with a dark sash and a sardonic smile, sometimes in a natty American-style suit with a snap-brim hat. He had a mania for clothes and maintained complete wardrobes—even to full-dress military uniforms—at each of his five residences.

Neon signs all over Ciudad Trujillo illuminated the tropic nights as at five-second intervals they blinked out "God and Trujillo". "In this house Trujillo is Chief" warned the notices in public buildings. His newspapers, *La Nación* and *El Caribe*, daily proclaimed his glories. And anxious civil servants scanned their front pages to see whether or not they still had jobs. For when El Benefactor was displeased with a man he merely added the date to the signed resignation deposited with him and announced that man's resignation in a special column of his newspapers.

On 16th August, 1934, Trujillo began his second term as President after being "unanimously" elected. His organization was booming. More than 160 relatives had found cushy jobs in the Government service. His own fortune was estimated at £1 million. He owned five elaborate houses, yachts, thousands of acres of land and almost any woman he liked to name in the entire country. And all the time he was expanding.

His secret police organization was the most ruthlessly efficient in the Caribbean. They packed the National Penitentiary with Trujillo's enemies. Men began to drop from sight and were never heard of again. They were not accused; they were not tried; they just vanished.

In 1937 Trujillo ordered the most atrocious crime—of the many atrocious crimes—of his career. For years Haitian peasants had drifted across the ill-defined border between the two countries to scratch a bare living from the erosion-prone soil. But Trujillo put a stop to that. He ordered them killed. And by the time his Army and police had finished their work at least 12,000 Haitians had been chopped down with machetes or bullets. When the news of the mass killings leaked out Trujillo put on a good face, said that he had had nothing to do with the affair, and paid out some compensation to the Haitian Government whose President had the bad taste to name a main thoroughfare in Port-au-Prince after the murderous despot.

After eight years in office he had had enough of the Presidency, for the moment at least, and on 8th March, 1938, he put Jacinto "Mozo" Peynado into the chair. He retained the National Guard and the police for himself and they were the real power in the land. Peynado knew it, and even if he had had any ideas about being the big boss they would have been impossible to execute.

Trujillo visited Europe in 1939 and the United States the following year. Always strongly pro-American, he was fêted officially and unofficially wherever he went. He returned home in time to deal with a group of plotting Army officers who were working towards a revolution. They just disappeared. A shake-up of the Partido Dominicano followed and from it emerged an inner party of close adherants called the Partido Trujillista.

El Benefactor married three times and had four legitimate children. His pampered, film-star-chasing playboy son Rámfis, the apple of his father's eye, was made a colonel at £150-a-month when he was three years old; "Protector of the Poor Children" at the age of 6; brigadier-general at 9; and ambassador at 20. When he went to the United States for military training at Fort Leavenworth—he subsequently spent most of his time in Hollywood—proud father handed him £400,000 to be going on with and sent an additional £30,000 a month pocket money. The American Government noted with concern that it was approximately the same amount as they annually gave to the Dominican Republic in foreign aid.

Trujillo looked after his family, close relatives, not so close ones and ones who possibly were not relatives at all. One brother owned the radio and television station; another ran the vice business; still others were in high Government positions or owned factories, plantations and property. Between them the Trujillo family owned 35 per cent of all the cultivatable land in the Dominican Republic. There were seventeen sugar mills in the country—and the Trujillos owned thirteen of them.

Foreign firms doing business in the country paid import taxes and excise taxes and in addition a "special tax" which went to El Benefactor. One American firm doing some sewerage contracting were instructed to add £600,000 to their estimate and Trujillo got half of it. He wrote a school primer which was required reading, and sold thousands of copies of it to the education ministry at a fat profit. He dominated salt, tobacco and beer enterprises. His personal fortune rose to £280 million—in cash alone.

After his spell as Commander-in-Chief of the National Guard, Trujillo decided that it was time for another round in the Presidential chair and was "unanimously" elected again on 16th August, 1942. There was a new constitution this time raising the term of office from four to five years and he began his fourth Presidency on 16th August, 1947.

Other parties were outlawed in the Dominican Republic, but they sprang up and flourished wherever Dominican exiles gathered. The oldest was the Partido Revolucionario Dominicano headed by exiled novelist and literary figure Juan Bosch. It had been founded in 1939 in Havana and had branches in New York City, Mexico City and Caracas. The Vanguardia Revolucionaria Dominicana, established in 1956, had branches in Puerto Rico and New York City. Other exile parties included the Frente Unido and the Partido Populista. All were impotent while El

Benefactor was alive. In the republic itself there was a price of
£350 on the head of any man suspected of being disloyal to the
régime and Trujillo's secret police had devious ways of extracting
information which were brutally efficient.

A Spaniard in Trujillo's service wrote a book about El Benefactor in which he likened him to Bolivar, the Great Liberator. He
wrote: "Like that great Don Simón of Venezuela, this great Don
Rafael of Santo Domingo cannot be confined with the narrow
limits of his nation."

And Trujillo could not be. His evil hands reached out to deal
coldly and effectively with anyone he feared, hated or distrusted.
Mauricio Báez, a trade unionist, disappeared from his Havana exile
in 1950. . . . The same year the Haitian Government protested to
the Organization of American States that Trujillo's diplomats in
Port-au-Prince were supplying arms and guns to rebels in the
hills. . . . Sergio Bencosme was murdered in New York City. . . .
In 1952, Andres Requena, editor of an anti-Trujillo newspaper,
was murdered gangster-style in New York City. . . . "Pippi"
Hernández was killed in Havana in 1954. . . . Tancredo Martínez
was luckier and survived an assassination attempt in Mexico City
in 1957.

Dr. Jesús de Galindez, a Spaniard who had lived for some
years in the Dominican Republic, prepared a dossier of facts about
Trujillo which he was due to present at Columbia University in
the United States. He had been lecturing there while gathering
his material. But in March, 1956, only a few days before he would
have made his facts public, Dr. Galindez was snatched from the
streets of New York City, bundled into a car and driven to a
landing field where a charter plane was waiting with its engine
ticking over. He was flown to the Dominican Republic and
killed. Rumours trickled out that his body had been fed into the
furnaces of the navy's flagship. Then Gerald Murphy, the
American pilot-for-hire who had flown the captive out of the
United States, was murdered so that he could not talk and the
story was put around that he had been killed in a brawl by a
Dominican pilot.

Trujillo was not above taking on the Presidents of other
Caribbean American countries. In 1957, El Benefactor sent two
gunmen to San José, capital of Costa Rica, to kill President José
"Pepe" Figueres who had criticized the Trujillo régime. They

were picked up before they could get into action. . . . In July, 1957, Carlos Castillo Armas, President of Guatemala, another of Trujillo's enemies, was shot down supposedly by his own guard. But later the Guatemalan Government uncovered proof that Trujillo had been behind the assassination. . . . In 1960, as President Rómulo Betancourt of Venezuela—another critic of Trujillo— was driving to an Army parade a bomb was exploded by remote control near his car. Three people died but the President escaped. Evidence tied Trujillo in with the murder bid and the Organization of American States announced an economic blockade of the Dominican Republic.

An unsuccessful invasion from Cuba in 1947—it included an unknown young Cuban lawyer named Fidel Castro—was one of the first serious attempts to overthrow Trujillo. Later there were other minor and equally abortive invasions. But by June, 1959, when Fidel Castro, after deposing dictator Batista, had been in power in Cuba for six months and had been shouting "Trujillo is next" for three of them, there was a better planned invasion bid. Captain Enrique Jiménez Moya, leading a battalion of sixty-three airborne troops and a sea invasion force of 150, engaged Trujillo's troops at the town of Costanza and captured it for a short time before being dislodged and defeated by half of the dictator's 23,000-strong Army, 4,500 police and several of his nineteen-ship navy.

Trujillo, frightened that the revolt had been as successful as it was, sentenced Fidel Castro to death in his absence for "crimes against the State", added the same sentence for Venezuela's Rómulo Betancourt, whom he accused of giving arms and men for the invasion, and set about building up a Dominican "Foreign Legion". Up in a lonely fort in the mountains scores of soldiers of fortune from half the nations of Europe, mercenaries from Latin America, men from Franco's "Blue Division", former German S.S. troopers and Italian Fascists flocked to the high-paying Trujillo banner after entering the country as "agricultural immigrants".

Boasted Trujillo: "If anyone wants to see their beards and brains fly like butterflies, let them approach the shores of the Dominican Republic."

The name of Trujillo and his long-suffering country became notorious across the Western Hemisphere as the haven for

deposed dictators, sadistic military men and political undesir-
ables. Trujillo was the perfect host. To his home-from-home
for the unprincipled, the ambitious and the crooked came Juan
Peron, deposed dictator of Argentina; General Gustavo Rojas
Pinilla, deposed dictator of Colombia; Colonel Marcos Pérez
Jiménez, deposed dictator of Venezuela; and Colonel Fulgencio
Batista, deposed dictator of Cuba.

But all good—and most bad—things must end. And for
Generalissimo Rafael Leónidas Trujillo the night of 30th May,
1961, was his last.

As he drove out along George Washington Avenue in Ciudad
Trujillo seven men were waiting for him at a crossroads a mile
out of town. His bullet-proof limousine screeched to a stop as
machine-gun carrying assassins drove another car across its path.
Trujillo's chauffeur, machine-gun in hand, leapt out and opened
fire. The Generalissimo grabbed another machine-gun and joined
in. But the odds were seven to two. The chauffeur went down
first and seconds later El Benefactor's body fell across the dead
driver. The assassins picked him up, bundled the body into the
boot of a car and drove off, later abandoning the vehicle and
making good their escape, for a while at least.

The country was thrown into a state of armed rebellion and
military panic. Six of the assassins were hunted down and killed.
The men, led by Brigadier-General Juan Tomás Días, a retired
officer, included Antonio Imbert, the brothers Antonio and Rafael
Delamaza, Huascar Tejeda Reina, Pedro Lirio Cedeño and Amado
Garcia Guerrero. Only Antonio Imbert escaped the unleashed
fury of Trujillo's family and Army officers. He hid in a friend's
shuttered room for six months, wore a .45 calibre automatic at all
times and kept an American M-1 rifle at hand. Even when the
immediate danger from Trujillo's henchmen had passed he continued to wear the pistol and he still does so today.

For a while the huge neon lights which blinked down "God and
Trujillo" from every corner stayed blinking. Great wreathes with
black bows and mourning cards arrived at Trujillo's official
residence the Rhadames Estancia. Newspapers vied with each
other to produce the most flattering and extravagant obituaries.
Said one: "Trujillo was good and just". And they went on to
add that only two good and just men had been born in the last
two thousand years and that the other one was Jesus Christ.

Immediately after the assassination of his father, Rámfis Trujillo, the favoured son, tried to do what Luis and Tachito Somoza succeeded in doing in Nicaragua after their dictator father was assassinated: establish a hereditary dictatorship. But his attempt failed miserably. In order to placate the United States and so, he hoped, strengthen his own hand, Rámfis packed off the most politically disreputable of his relatives on extended holidays. El Benefactor had ceased to be President in 1952 and had passed the office to his brother Héctor. He had served the statutory five years, been re-elected in 1957, for a further term, and then deposed by El Benefactor in 1960 after the economic blockade enforced by the Organization of American States. This had been a political move aimed at bringing a better outward face to the Dominican Republic—and a face which was not fronted by a Trujillo. Dr. Joaquín Balaguer had been made President on 3rd August, 1960. Now Rámfis hastily packed Uncle Héctor off on a trip to Bermuda. Uncle José Arismendi was given a Caribbean cruise on the navy's flagship.

Rámfis promised to turn £40 million-worth of family sugar estates and lands over to the Government and went on record as saying: "To some this may sound socialistic, but a recent Papal encyclical approves of state ownership of property for the good of the people. If I were a politician, I would be a Leftist."

President Balaguer, as anxious as Rámfis to keep the Trujillo family in business, and himself at the same time, did a quick purge of the most obvious of the family, promising them that the retirement was only temporary. Out went Lieutenant-General José Garcia Trujillo, Minister of Armed Forces, and Dr. Luis Ruiz Trujillo, Minister for the Presidency. But Balaguer had been for too long the friend of Trujillo and after the initial feeling of insecurity, the people of the Dominican Republic began to clamour for a new deal. The "God and Trujillo" signs blinked for the last time and went out. Framed portraits of the dictator, for so long almost obligatory furnishings for shops and homes, were burned in piles in the streets. Rámfis saw the red light and packed his bags. What family cash and valuables he could not get out of the country stayed behind and he fled to Europe taking his father's body with him for burial in Paris. By Christmas, 1961, the country was ripe for a change.

It came on New Year's Day when Dr. Balaguer resigned following popular demonstrations. Into his place stepped a seven-man Council of State. Dr. Rafael Bonnelly, a mild, scholarly man who calls himself "a liberal in the truly democratic sense", was its Vice-President. Bonnelly, convinced in 1939 that there was a beneficial side to El Benefactor after all, had entered politics. He had become a Deputy in the National Assembly, later a Senator and finally Minister of the Interior and Police. He resigned to go back to his old job, teaching law at the university, only to be tempted back into politics by Trujillo who made him Minister of Labour and National Economy for a short time in 1946. Later he was ambassador in Spain and then Venezuela and was there when the Peron régime fell in Argentina. Peron reached Caracas, was granted political asylum by Bonnelly and finally arrived in the Dominican Republic. From Venezuela Bonnelly returned home to become rector of the university.

But in January, 1960, he was among several thousand people arrested for suspected complicity in an attempt on El Benefactor's life. His youngest son, Rafael Francisco Bonnelly, was among 1,500 people jailed and Bonnelly senior was put under house arrest at the home of his brother-in-law and remained there reading sociology and politics from the beginning of 1960 until June, 1961.

The seven-man Council of State included a truckline operator, two heart specialists, a businessman, a Roman Catholic priest (two archbishops have been President of the Dominican Republic), and Antonio Imbert, the only survivor of the assassins.

They seized £11 million of Trujillo assets, retired 1,300 violently pro-Trujillo officers, drew several embryo political parties together to form the anti-Communist National Civic Union, and invited exiles to return home.

The United States rushed a speedy £10 million to the country and Governor Luis Muñoz Marín of Puerto Rico sent in technicians and financial experts to help untangle the Governmental and financial mess the dead dictator's régime had left. Another £13 million of Trujillo monies was seized to establish a Puerto Rican-managed Industrial Development Corporation.

But on 17th January, 1962, General Rodriguez Echavarria, who had been made Chief of Staff after Trujillo's death, suddenly deposed Bonnelly and set himself in power at the head of a seven-man military-civil junta. Echavarria rushed Bonnelly to the San

Isidro Air Base and held him prisoner. The *coup* was not announced but several junior officers began to suspect that all was not as it should be. Forty-eight hours after the Council had been deposed, Echavarria and some junior officers visited Bonnelly and one of the officers asked the deposed leader if he was being held prisoner. As Bonnelly nodded several other officers pulled out their pistols and pointed them at Echavarria's stomach. His junta was in turn deposed and Bonnelly re-established with his Council of State. This time he was made President of it.

He began working towards the first free elections for thirty-eight years. Exiles were encouraged to return and did so in great numbers. The United States, which had pandered so shamelessly to Trujillo, now heaved a sigh of relief and began to pour money into the country in an attempt to atone for the past and ensure that democracy and not dictatorship—either Right or Left wing brands—would replace El Benefactor. Under the auspices of the Alliance for Progress plan they put £8 million into the republic. Special sugar prices were arranged—more than 60 per cent of the country's exports are in sugar—and a special grant of £5 million compensation was paid for the discontinuation of the sugar quota during the last days of the Trujillo régime.

Then Bonnelly changed the name of the capital from Ciudad Trujillo back to Santo Domingo, its name for 440 pre-Trujillo years.

The illiteracy rate was well over 50 per cent of the population so money was found to build schools; an estimated 89 per cent of the population had less than primary education while only 0.4 per cent had completed secondary education; special adult literacy and other educational classes were set up. Some 500,000 people out of a population of just over 3,000,000 were unemployed so jobs were created by the Government. An unexpected outright grant of £10 million from the United States helped in this and in rehousing slum dwellers; a self-help housing scheme, similar to that pioneered by Muñoz Marín in Puerto Rico, was started and quickly caught the public imagination; a Los Angeles policeman was loaned to instruct the Dominican police force in riot control; a U.S. marine colonel was flown down to reorganize the purged Armed Forces; special advisers from the United States and Puerto Rico arrived to oversee many of the new schemes.

Bonnelly made a valiant attempt to pay off the public debt and managed to do so at a rate of £150,000 a month from local revenues. He pushed through a progressive income tax law. And he balanced the budget. A special advisory group from the Organization of American States arrived to give further technical assistance.

And all the time Bonnelly was working for the elections. In the rush to organize political parties after a lapse of thirty-two years dozens of tiny pressure groups sprang up, dissolved, amalgamated, split again and died. Only the hardiest survived. But there were twenty-eight of them even after the two Communist-dominated parties—the Popular Socialists and the Dominican Popular Movement—had been outlawed. Bonnelly announced that he would hold elections on 20th December, 1962. The country's estimated 70,000 Communists announced that they would boycott any elections—and darkly hinted that they would put a stop to any taking place or else rig the polls by working through some unbanned party.

With admirable judgement Bonnelly persuaded the Council of State that none of its members should run for election or take any part in the political campaigning. He let his National Civic Union get on with its electioneering without him. Their candidate, 67-year-old Dr. Viriato Fiallo, set about trying to win the election.

Said Bonnelly: "We have only one task: to prepare our country for elections and a democratic Government. My Government is committed to this historic transference of power, but its success will much depend on the parties and the candidates contesting the election. My Government will take no part in the election but will do everything it can to see that the election is held."

Professor Juan Bosch, the eminent literary figure who had left the republic in 1937 and started the Partido Revolucionario Dominicano in exile in Havana, returned from his exile in Costa Rica to establish his party and contest the election. Stubby, silver-haired Bosch, home again after twenty-five years in exile, described himself as a member of the "democratic left" and announced his intention, if he got in, to help the little man. His campaigning was soon felt in the rural areas in particular.

Juan Bosch was born in La Vega on 30th June, 1909, and early in his career as a journalist established himself as one of the leading literary figures of the Dominican Republic. He was a founder of a literary and artistic group which met at the home of a well-known poet who lived the life of a semi-recluse. He only went out at night and the group called itself *La Cueva*—The Cave—because of their association with him. Bosch wrote four books before leaving the Dominican Republic. The first novel was *La Mañosa* and he followed it with *Camino Real, Indios* and *Volumen de Cuentos*—Volume of Tales. He left the country soon after Trujillo's massacre of the Haitian peasants in 1937 and established himself in Havana. There he married a Cuban girl whose parents had come from Spain. Bosch's own family were Catalan. He wrote a biography of Simón Bolivar which is now a textbook used in schools throughout Bolivar's own country, Venezuela. When the Batista régime fell to Castro, Bosch took his wife and went to live in Costa Rica. His in-laws lost everything in Castro's campaign to break the wealthy.

"I don't say that I knew that Castro was a Communist," Bosch says of his leaving Cuba. "But I felt that he was not a democrat and I was afraid of what might happen."

Bosch campaigned vigorously in the rural districts with his left-of-centre policy. Dr. Viriato Fiallo, considered right-of-centre, tended to concentrate on the towns, conceding that Bosch would win the country districts.

There were six Presidential candidates for the election and each one had a ballot form of a different colour. This had been agreed upon to assist the illiterate voters although it was generally believed that there would be a very small turn-out for the actual polling. Each form was perforated, as not only a President was to be chosen but also a complete new Chamber of Deputies and Senate. The Government printed 19,000,000 ballot papers, expecting that a large number of them would be ruined immediately as enthusiastic but inexperienced voters ran amok. There were 3,500 polling stations and for weeks before the election the radio stations gave out continuous instruction on how to fill in a ballot paper and on the importance of elections. For two generations of electors had never been to the polls and badly needed advice and coaching.

"We were a party without funds and without a voice—a newspaper, that is. I talked on the radio every day for fourteen months. I kept my remarks on a level which a 14-year-old could understand—especially on politics," soft-spoken Bosch told me.

"I never asked anyone to vote for us, but they did. I knew they would. The radio became a school of democracy and that was what the people wanted to hear about."

It was obvious after a short time that either Juan Bosch's Partido Revolucionario Dominicano or Dr. Viriato Fiallo's National Civic Union was going to win. The danger lay in the support that the other four candidates would get from the extremists. There was also the danger of fraud and corrupt practices in both the voting and the counting.

But it did not worry Bosch.

"Fraud will not rob me of victory," he said confidently. "They might steal 15,000 or even 30,000 votes—but never 100,000. I shall win."

Dr. Fiallo's party had more appeal to the middle classes and the businessmen. He spoke volubly about the Alliance for Progress plan and his confidence that it would raise the standard of living for the whole country and not just a few.

"The new impulse of the money under the plan is as great for us as the Marshall Plan was for Europe after the war," he said. "And because we are such a small country, the force of the programme is that much stronger."

Bosch, whose campaign slogan was "Dignity Against Money", went all out for the peasants' vote, promising to break up the great Trujillo estates—and any others the Government might take over on compulsory purchase orders with compensation attached—and distribute sixteen-acre plots to 70,000 landless peasants. He also promised the workers to try to raise the minimum monthly wage to £30.

A week before the elections he nearly withdrew from the polls altogether after a minor Roman Catholic priest had said publicly that some of Bosch's writings and speeches smacked of Communism. Bosch, a violent anti-Communist who has travelled widely in Latin America preaching "democratic left" ideals on the lines of Puerto Rico's Muñoz Marín, Venezuela's Rómulo Betancourt and Costa Rica's José Figueres, felt this smear deeply. He confronted the priest on television, pronounced his ideals again and damned Communist ideologies, got the cleric to withdraw his comments and apologize, and made some very useful votes in the process.

On polling day, 20th December, 1962, trouble was expected and steel-helmeted riot police stood by as the people went out to vote. The papers for the National Civic Union—candidate Dr. Viriato Fiallo—were white; for the Partido Revolucionario Dominicano —candidate Professor Juan Bosch—they were blue; the third largest party, the Social Christian Revolutionary Party—candidate Alfonso Moreno Martínez—had green papers. The other parties contesting were the Dominican Revolutionary Vanguard —candidate Horacio Ornes; the Social Democrat Alliance— candidate Juan Isidro Jiménez Grullon; and the Democratic Nationalist Revolutionary Party—candidate Virgilio Maindardi. All but one of the candidates had been in exile during the Trujillo régime. There would have been a seventh candidate but Dr. Bonnelly's Council of State refused to allow Dr. Joaquín Balaguer, Trujillo's puppet President who had been deposed in January, 1962, to return to the Dominican Republic from the United States whence he had flown.

Despite the low poll expected and the violence anticipated, more than one million Dominicans went out in a quiet and orderly manner to vote Juan Bosch and his Partido Revolucionario Dominicano into power with a two to one majority over Dr. Viriato Fiallo and the National Civic Union. When the counting came in Bosch had gained 628,495 votes for himself out of the 1,050,867 cast. This was 312,618 more than Dr. Fiallo received. The party also gained control of the legislature.

Bosch hastened to the United States to talk to President Kennedy and to Teodoro Moscoso, the Puerto Rican head of the Alliance for Progress, and lay down firm foundations for rebuilding the Dominican Republic. While he was away the police and Army clashed with a strange religious sect in the mountains, and in a brief but bloody battle killed twenty-five of them, wounded fifty and captured 673.

Juan Bosch was proclaimed President of the Dominican Republic under a new constitution on 27th February, 1963. Before him is an immense task and he has many problems to face. He must make good his election promises regarding land distribution and minimum wages; continue breaking down the illiteracy; clear the slums and re-house the poor; and rebuild the shaky economy. Much of the initial ground work was done by Dr. Bonnelly and the Council of State, but Bosch must use their efforts as a foundation and build upon them.

He must also ensure that the flow of American capital—the Almighty Dollar—continues to be received with good will, and does not attract the smear of tainted money which it has in other parts of Caribbean America and the vast continent south of the Amazon where the Alliance for Progress is often jeeringly referred to as "Kennedy's Castro Plan". The United States will give him all the help they can for they have learned the hard way that it is very difficult to give away money and thereby earn gratitude. They are becoming experienced in matters of this kind —and, in the Dominican Republic, they are anxious to erase the unfavourable picture of themselves that their support of Trujillo built up over the years in the minds of the people.

Political organization will be allowed in the Dominican Republic and the new constitution allows for complete freedom—as long as a party is not opposed to democracy.

Bosch feels that the danger from extremists—either Fascist or Communist—has been largely averted.

"After Trujillo fell people thought that there was only extremism. We could have had trouble, but did not. Now we have built up a faith in democracy and many of the extremists are re-examining their own feelings and coming round to our side now that they see we are trying to make democracy work," he told me.

Bosch is not a man who talks glibly or for the sake of hearing his own voice. Everything he says is carefully weighed up and balanced in his agile mind before it is spoken.

For the future he sees hope—but does not blind himself to possible danger. The one thing Bosch needs most is time; time to work, to shape, to think; time in fact, to build a democracy.

"The danger to democracy will come if we cannot do what we must do," he says. "The transition from dictatorship to democracy is not an easy one."

CHAPTER FIVE

PUERTO RICO

Luis Muñoz Marín

Two weeks after Spain's stablest, richest and most conservative possession in the New World set up its own legislature after achieving autonomy under the Spanish Crown, hundreds of American troops landed on the island and took it after seventeen days of fighting and bloodshed.

General Nelson A. Miles, fresh from the Western Plains and full of honours as an Indian fighter, promised Puerto Ricans that America would "bestow upon you the blessings and immunities of our liberal Government". Rough Rider Colonel Theodore Roosevelt—later President of the United States—breathed a sigh of relief. Months before he had told Congressional friends worried about the Spanish-American War: "Prevent any talk of peace until we get Puerto Rico". The United States immediately made General Miles's words a mockery, enforced a Government which denied Puerto Ricans the right of U.S. citizenship, and made every local law subject to summary Congressional repeal.

And in a house a few hundred yards from La Fortaleza, the palace of the former Spanish Governor, a five-month-old baby gurgled in his cot while his statesman-politician father, Luis Muñoz Rivera, tried to help the American conquerors restore some sort of order from the chaos of war.

The baby was Luis Muñoz Marín, (say it Moonyos Marine), born on 18th February, 1898, and destined to shape his country's political and economic future and to become one of the most respected politicians in Caribbean America.

The island was an embarrassment to the United States almost from the beginning. From being Spain's richest possession in the

Caribbean, it rapidly became a slum of the worst kind. New changes were on the move in the United States and new leaders, unwilling to admit that they had, in an imperialistic moment, seized the island by force of arms, were troubled about just what to do with it. Legally, a U.S. Supreme Court judge had ruled in 1901, it was "a possession" and "an organized but unincorporated territory of the United States"—which meant a dependency— one step lower than Alaska which had been bought from Russia and was an "incorporated" territory.

The island, covering 3,435 square miles—half the size of Wales —lies sandwiched between the Dominican Republic to the west and the U.S. Virgin Islands (bought from Denmark in 1917) to the east. Miami is eleven hundred miles to the north; the Panama Canal is twelve hundred miles to the west; Trinidad, the smallest member of the Commonwealth, lies 657 miles to the south-east.

Sugar was king and remained so for many years after the Americans came to the island. For the first nineteen years of their rule Puerto Rico was virtually a backwater, hardly moving forward, sometimes moving back, always a millstone round its wealthy patron's neck, gradually building up vast problems for itself and its master. Puerto Ricans lived in a kind of political limbo from 1898 until 1917 when the Organic Act granted them United States citizenship.

The American, Washington-appointed Governor was the power in the land. He held sway in the legislature and carried the almost limitless power of any chief executive in an occupied territory. The islanders had no power in the United States and very little in their own country.

Luis Muñoz Rivera, who had been largely responsible for the enlightened autonomous constitution that Spain had granted just before the Americans took the island, did his best to work with the new masters. The island was granted a Resident Commissioner in Washington in 1910 with a seat—but no vote—in the House of Representatives. Luis Muñoz Rivera became the Commissioner and took his family to Washington.

His son Luis Muñoz Marín (under Spanish tradition the mother's surname is tacked on behind the father's) after two years at school in the United States, showed a rare brilliance and was enrolled at Georgetown University at the age of 14. Several years later, much to the despair of his father, he quit and went to live in New

York's bohemian Greenwich Village, eking out a slender living as a poet, becoming a chain-smoker and mixing with the famous and aspiring figures of the literary world. He also became a socialist and a passionate nationalist, demanding that Puerto Rico be freed from colonial rule and declared independent.

He was 28 years old in 1926, a physically and mentally powerful young man, contemptuous of formality, careless in his dress, passionate in his nationalism and fantastically hard-working. That year he returned home to do battle with the oppressors.

He became a member of the island's Liberal Party, a gentlemanly, ultra-conservative group which advocated statehood, mixed socially with the wealthy Americans, accepted large sums of money for party funds from the United States sugar interests, and was their voice in the legislature. Muñoz soon lost some of his socialism, but not his nationalism or his highly critical opinion of the sugar kings.

He rose high in the party, got into the legislature in the 1932 election and became a senator. But he carried on his crusade for independence, his party's official line to the contrary. From the floor of the House he made impassioned pleas for freedom, attacked the sugar kings and earned their unanimous and undying hatred, railed against the United States, and built for himself a key position in' both politics and the hearts of the people.

He branded the United States an "opulent kleptomaniac" and charged that they "filched life-giving pennies from the pockets of a pauper".

"Puerto Rico," he said, "is a factory worked by peons, fought over by lawyers, bossed by absent industrialists and clerked by politicians."

He was re-elected in 1936 and by the following year the sugar kings could take no more. They told the Liberal high-ups that Muñoz had to go, enforcing their demand by refusing to contribute one cent more to party funds until he was pushed out.

The Liberals expelled him and have regretted it ever since.

By July, 1938, he had founded the Popular Democratic Party and was beginning to tour the country, building the framework for the national campaign which would sweep him to victory in the elections two years later.

The Nationalist Party, ardent Yankee-haters, watched with interest. They too demanded independence. Muñoz appeared as if he might be a powerful ally. The main difference between the parties was that his campaign was peaceful, theirs violent. In 1930, Pedro Albizu Campos had become their leader. A Harvard-educated lawyer of mixed Spanish and Negro descent, he had mustered into a Negro regiment during the First World War, become an excellent officer and returned to Puerto Rico an avowed nationalist. In the 1932 election his black-shirted followers got 10,000— 2 per cent—of the votes, and in 1936, the year before Muñoz was expelled by the Liberals, Albizu had launched a campaign of violence which started with the assassination of San Juan's police chief, E. F. Riggs. Arrested, he underwent two sensational trials and was sent to Atlanta Penitentiary for ten years for "conspiracy to overthrow the Government of Puerto Rico by armed force". Able and equally independence-dedicated supporters carried on his work with the party.

Luis Muñoz Marín wanted independence, but he wanted it constitutionally—not by force of arms. Elections were less than two years off and he soon had his party organization whipped into shape. He made heavy demands on the time and loyalty of the men closest to him, and even heavier ones on himself. A round-the-clock worker, he planned a campaign with the skill of a military leader, dreamed up improbable ideas, discarded them for even more improbable ones, and came up with a brilliant tactical plan to beat the Government.

He travelled from one end of the island to the other, making contacts, setting up little groups as party campaigners wherever he could, making speeches, offering much, promising little. For he is a man who likes to state the possibilities, but never makes promises that he may not be able to fulfil. He spoke from ox-carts in dusty squares, the backs of open cars, donkey-carts. To his growing number of followers he was "Don Luis" or "*El Vate*"— "The Bard".

His newly-launched newspaper, *El Batey*, boomed. He sold the advertising himself, raised enough to put out a four-page party voice and soon built its circulation from nil to 100,000. As the elections drew closer he put his party machine into top gear and drove himself even harder. Proudly he says that he made 100,000 speeches in fifty days. Impossible? Not for Muñoz. He used his dwindling party funds to have gramophone records of a political speech made at a cost of 3s. 6d. a record. These he sent into 200 villages with instructions to his party agents that they were to be played ten times a day from the gramophones and public address systems he had had fixed up in ox-carts which moved slowly down the streets with his voice booming out.

Traditionally, workers had sold their votes for $2 each at election time. Muñoz countered this, but not with money.

"Two dollars will buy a lot of food for your family," he said. "But do you want the two dollars—or do you want justice? You can't have both. Lend me your vote. Don't sell it to others."

His campaign slogan became "Bread, Land and Liberty".

There were four schools of thought on Puerto Rico's future: José Celso Barbosa demanded statehood; Luis Muñoz Marín was for autonomy; José de Diego demanded complete independence; and Eugenio Maria de Hostos of the Patriotic League dreamed of an Antillian Confederation.

While the Liberals campaigned for statehood and the Nationalists for independence, Muñoz went his own way. He put aside his own demands for independence and spoke instead of more food, more work, better houses, electricity, sewerage, and social services.

"I refused to make use of the independence issue in the campaign because it would have divided the people on an abstract issue which the election could not possibly settle," he explains.

And to prove that he was not just talking when he spoke of reforms, he personally drafted twenty-two Bills to set before the House of Representatives if he won. Each Bill, the work of days and even weeks, was complete down to the last detail, full stops, commas and all.

The election was held in November, 1940, and when the votes were counted Luis Muñoz Marín and the Popular Democratic Party had won 38 per cent of them, giving him ten seats in the Senate and exactly half of the thirty-six seats in the House of Representatives. The other half were won by Liberals, Socialists and Republicans who, to make an opposition to Muñoz, would need to form a coalition. As they were poles apart this seemed unlikely. But Muñoz was taking no chances. He wooed away three of the opposition members, gaining complete control, and became President of the Senate.

Immediately he put his plans into action. He called his campaign *"Fomento"*—"a stirring up"—and the first to feel the change of

Government were his long-time enemies who had plotted his political destruction, the sugar kings.

An old law forbade any one company, individual, or corporation to own more than 500 acres of land. But the sugar estates were vast and for years the law had been openly defied, often with the connivance of the Government, always with their tacit silence. In 1930 it was estimated that 367 landowners had violated the law and controlled a third of the agricultural land. The other 58,004 landowners made out as best they could with the remaining two-thirds. Muñoz enforced the law, redistributed the land and turned to a new series of projects.

But the energetic genius was pushing himself too hard. Illness confined him to his bed for weeks and the doctors thought he would die. Even the optimistic Muñoz thought so. He named his mother, Doña Amalia Muñoz, as his political heir and lay back to see what would happen. But he recovered, and during the long period of convalescence fumed and fussed at his doctors, schemed and planned for his return to active political life.

At last he could contain himself no longer. Defying the doctors he went back to work, presenting himself dramatically in the House of Representatives in an overcoat, scarf and cap and accompanied by an attendant to make sure that he got his medicine at the correct times.

The agricultural economy that Puerto Rico had existed on for so long was barely able to keep the population alive. Muñoz knew that the only thing to raise the country's standard of living was industrialization. He began a series of moves which were to raise the country from poverty to something like prosperity. And which, under his guidance, would raise the political status from that of a neglected child to that of a favoured nephew.

American economists had described Puerto Rico's problems as "insoluble". Muñoz set out to prove them wrong. But he had a vast job ahead of him. Half of the island's 70,000 children of school age got no education because there were not enough schools or teachers. The average wage of the peasant was £27 a year, 1s. 6d. a day. Infant mortality was the highest in the world, four times that of the United States. The population in 1940 was 1,800,000 making Puerto Rico the second most densely populated place in the world—Java was worse off and Barbados only a little behind Puerto Rico.

Muñoz' answer to the situation was characteristic: "We must live like angels and produce like the devil," he said.

The appointment of a new Governor who was interested in his job was an asset to Muñoz during his term of office. For Professor Rexford Guy Tugwell changed the traditional stick-in-the-mud reputation of the Washington-appointed Governor. He worked hard, giving the Government what aid he could.

Muñoz built schools, started a self-help housing scheme, installed electricity where it had never been before, constructed new office blocks, roads and sewers. San Juan, the capital, stands on an island between a lagoon and a bay. Vast sprawling slums on stilts surrounded it. Muñoz tore them down as soon as new houses could be built for the poor. In 1942 he launched the highly successful "Operation Bootstrap"—designed to pull Puerto Rico up by its own efforts and bootstraps. Generous industrial tax holidays aimed at attracting investors brought businessmen down from the United States to investigate. Soon new factories went up making fountain pens, baby shoes, wall tiles and clothing.

The island enjoyed tariff concessions from the United States, and a considerable degree of autonomy. Local but not Federal taxes were levied—this because the Resident Commissioner in Washington had the right to sit, speak and introduce Bills into Congress but not to vote, the United States observing their unwritten code of "no taxation without representation".

"Puerto Rico has no natural resources except land, people and hope," Muñoz told would-be investors.

This was not quite so. For the lovely beaches awaiting development were a natural resource. Muñoz was quick to see tourism as a substantial source of income and tried to interest American investors to sink some money into it. When he was only partially successful his Government built a £2½ million hotel and then invited Conrad Hilton to add it to his chain and run it on a profit-sharing basis. Today tourists spend some £10 million a year in Puerto Rico—about £4 for every man, woman and child in the island.

He set up factories to manufacture cement, glass, paper, ceramics, and shoes and then turned four of them over to Luis Ferré, a leading industrialist and Muñoz' political foe.

"We think Ferré has better sense about industry than about politics," he explained.

Muñoz won again at the 1944 elections—his party got 64 per cent of the votes—and about this time he finally gave up his ideas of independence for Puerto Rico. Experience had shown him that the island's vast problems needed enormous sums of money and that by retaining links with the United States it might be forthcoming. The tariff concessions, local and not Federal taxes, Federal welfare services, unlimited immigration to the United States, and technical and financial aid from America were vitally necessary and played an important part in his plans for the future. Many of these benefits would be lost with either independence or statehood.

"The proponents of nationalism prefer the despotic government of their own to the democratic rule of those removed from them," he said.

Worried by the rapidly increasing population—some 50,000 a year—Muñoz set up Government-sponsored birth control clinics. A Roman Catholic, he is also a free thinker who believes that a man has the right to determine his own personal creed and act accordingly. The Catholic Church immediately launched an attack on him but he did not care. The clinics were there if people wanted to use them.

"If we don't hold down our population the island will sink into the sea through sheer weight of numbers," he says.

"There is an old saying here that a man must do three things in his life: plant trees, write books and have sons. I wish they would plant more trees and write more books."

In 1947 President Truman granted Puerto Rico the right to select their own, local, Governor. Muñoz was the obvious choice. Elections were held on 2nd November, 1948, and his slogan "*Jalda Arriba*"—"Up and On"—gave him victory with 63 per cent of the votes.

Puerto Rico went up and on.

New roadways were built; highways crossed and recrossed the island; great concrete, glass and metal buildings changed the sky-line of San Juan; more and more industries came, lured by the tax concessions.

The Nationalists busied themselves with renewed violence in support of their independence claim and launched attacks on Governor Muñoz and President Truman. On 30th October, 1950, five gunmen attacked La Fortaleza, the Governor's palace. Four were killed, Muñoz escaped. An armed band of forty were captured in the hills. Pedro Albizu Campos, as leader, was jailed again. Two days later—1st November—two would-be assassins tried to shoot their way into President Truman's temporary home at Blair House on Washington's Pennsylvania Avenue. Griselio Torresola was killed outright. Oscar Collazo, although badly wounded, survived to make an impassioned plea for independence at his trial, was sentenced to death and then reprieved. He is still in prison in the United States. An attempt to blow up the Puerto Rican office in New York also failed.

Muñoz himself is unique among politicians. For he thinks that he is paid enough. When the Senate proposed to raise the Governor's salary from £3,500-a-year to £7,000-a-year, Muñoz gave notice that he would veto the Bill. The Senate was adamant. So was Muñoz. Eventually both won. The Governor's salary was raised. Muñoz stays at £3,500. The next Governor will get the raise. Muñoz travels economy class when he flies to the United States. He has eleven years still to run on the mortgage on his private house near San Juan. Statistics published just before the 1956 election showed he had private assets of only just over £200 to his name.

In 1950 he drafted a constitution which would give Puerto Rico a unique political status. The United States Congress approved it the same year. Puerto Ricans ratified it by referendum. The legislature was increased to give twenty-seven seats in the Senate and fifty-one in the House of Representatives. The island was styled "The Commonwealth of Puerto Rico", and linked to the United States as "a freely associated State" with its own flag, taxes and internal laws—freed at last from repeal by the U.S. Congress.

The election which brought in the new constitution, and with it a new era for Puerto Rico, was held on 25th July, 1952. Muñoz' Popular Democratic Party netted 65 per cent of the votes cast. His nearest rivals, the pro-statehood Liberals, got 19 per cent.

"In its negotiations with Puerto Rico the United States has been so forgetful of its bigness that it has fully disclosed its greatness," he says.

But the overwhelming win in 1952 worried Muñoz. He felt that his Popular Democratic Party was, if anything, too popular. To make certain that they could never get into a position where they had all the seats, he made constitutional provisions that guarantee Opposition parties one third of the seats in both the Senate and the House of Representatives.

"A healthy democracy needs a strong opposition," he says.

In 1954 the disgruntled nationalists made another attempt to draw attention to their claim. They opened fire from the Visitors' Gallery on members of the House of Representatives in Washington. The four Puerto Rican gunmen wounded five members, causing one of them to sink to the floor at the first burst of gunfire with the time-honoured cry of "They got me!", in the mistaken belief that he had been fatally punctured.

Two years later Muñoz won another election. The same year he won the coveted Freedom House Award—previous winners had been Sir Winston Churchill and President Eisenhower. In 1960 his party got 59 per cent of the votes.

Muñoz rises early, goes to bed late. His normal working day lasts about sixteen hours. A heavily-built, slightly-stooping, grey-haired figure, he is revered throughout the island. He has bushy eyebrows, a toothbrush moustache, and a fierce temper. It takes a lot to bring him to the boil, but when he does the result is violent, vivid and frequently profane. He gave up chain-smoking in 1947 after nearly twenty years. Despite his work he still finds time to write some poetry—he likes being referred to as the "poet leader" —and to spend as much of his time as possible with his attractive wife Inez and daughters Viviana and Victoria.

Hard-working himself, he makes heavy demands on his staff, keeps three secretaries busy, and does many things himself which could well be delegated to subordinates. When his colleagues criticize him for wasting time on trivial details, he laughs. "What can you expect from a poet?" he demands.

He will interrupt a conference of prime importance to watch a sunset, often lards his conversation with quotations, and blandly tells his supporters: "Distrust all politicians—even me".

After a hard day at the office he will return to La Fortaleza, settle down at his desk and continue working until mealtime. Two birds have the freedom of the house and garden and roost on the chandelier above the Governor's desk. Meals are interrupted by telephone calls, casual visitors and sometimes conferences.

Muñoz numbers among his friends such men as José Figueres, ex-President of Costa Rica, and Rómulo Betancourt, now President of Venezuela but once an exile who spent several years in Puerto Rico. The magnificent 400-year-old Governor's palace, La Fortaleza, a former Spanish fort, looks out over San Juan Bay. Since the Muñoz family moved in it has become something of a home-from-home for democratic Latin American leaders exiled by dictators, visiting men of letters—especially poets—and journalists writing of Puerto Rico's amazing progress.

The Governor also has an official country home at the top of a 2,600-foot mountain with a twenty-five mile view of the sparkling Caribbean. But his favourite home is his own modest cottage on a plot of land near San Juan.

"This is where I'm going to retire to and write poetry," he says with a smile. And he adds: "The sooner the better."

The Nationalists still want independence. But they now see that revolution and violence is not the answer. Their demands are verbal. When President Eisenhower visited the island in 1960 he was greeted by banner-waving demonstrators bearing slogans like: "Yankee Go Home", "Independence or Death", "We Want Freedom" and "Viva Castro".

Muñoz maintains that Puerto Rico has had its revolution: a peaceful, industrial one.

He says: "Part of our revolution was to put hope into people, give them the feeling that they could achieve a better way of life through hard work. They have that feeling now and they have the feeling that something of importance is happening here."

Industries have flooded into the island. Most have survived and boomed. A few have gone under the way businesses occasionally do. Labour troubles are rare. Muñoz backs labour and is a fierce fighter for their rights. But he will oppose them if he believes that they are wrong. Once he went on the radio and condemned a threatened bus strike. It collapsed. His industrial development policy has brought a degree of prosperity to the island. He has set a target of 2,500 new factories by 1975. The 650th one was opened in mid-1958, the 800th one in 1961, they are going up at the rate of 100 a year. His aim is a living standard by 1975 equal to that of the United States now.

Some time during 1963 Puerto Ricans will vote in a plebiscite to determine their future status: Independence, Statehood or a stronger Commonwealth link. Muñoz, of course, is for bigger and better Commonwealth ties with the United States.

"Puerto Rico can never be rich. Our people must learn to strive for a decent way of life, an education for their children and a comfortable old age—and not to be unhappy because they don't have everything their neighbours have," he says.

A lot has been done in his twenty-three years as leader of the Government. In 1940 the *per capita* income was around £40 a year. Today it is about £220. In the same period the island's agricultural income has risen from £25 million to £80 million.

But a lot remains to be done. The population has grown despite the large-scale immigration to the United States and the considerable success of the Government's birth-control campaign. In 1940 it was 1,800,000: today it is 2,300,000. Unemployment stands at 13 per cent of the working population. There are still slums in many parts of the island and tar-paper shacks cling to the hillsides around San Juan.

Recently a visitor, looking at the progress, asked Muñoz: "Where do you go from here?"

Snapped the "poet leader": "Man, we're not even here yet."

CHAPTER SIX

THE LEEWARD ISLANDS

ANTIGUA

Vere Bird

A lean and grizzled former Captain in the Salvation Army is the Chief Minister of Antigua, largest of the Leeward Islands. In his 54 years he has seen many changes come to the island. Many of them have been as a direct result of his efforts.

Antigua was one unit of the defunct Federation of the West Indies and will be one unit of the proposed new Federation. The island covers 108 square miles and is the home of nearly 60,000 people of mainly African descent. The capital is St. John's which has a population of 12,000. The dependencies of Barbuda—sixty-two square miles, population 1,000—and Redonda—half a square mile of uninhabited rock—bring Antigua's size as a single unit up to 171 square miles and make it the third largest British territory in the Eastern Caribbean. Barbados and St. Kitts are larger. Antigua lies twenty-seven miles north-east of Montserrat, forty miles east of Nevis and about the same distance north of Guadeloupe.

Columbus discovered the island in 1493 and named it after a church in Seville. Britain and France fought for it on and off until it finally became British in 1667. In the past Antigua, Barbuda and Montserrat were administered as a single government and neighbouring St. Kitts, Nevis, Anguilla and the British Virgin Islands as a single colony. But after fifty-five years under this grouping the Federation of the Leeward Islands came into being in 1871 and five Presidencies were established: Antigua, St. Kitts-Nevis-Anguilla, Montserrat, the British Virgin Islands and Dominica. In 1940 Dominica was given a new geographical status and became part of the Windward Islands.

There were labour troubles through the West Indies in the

1930s, and between 1937 and 1938, in an effort to appease the
people by giving them a larger say in the islands' affairs, elected
members were added to the Legislative Councils. Eventually
radical constitutional advances came into force in 1950.

Vere Cornwall Bird was born in Antigua in 1909. He left school
to join the Salvation Army and rose to the rank of Captain, a 6 feet
3 inches, brown-skinned human dynamo. His close contacts with
the people of the island gradually interested him in trade unionism
—and later politics—and he became President of the Antigua
Trades and Labour Union in September, 1951, after being a
leading light in it for some time.

The constitutional changes of 1950 were to be put into force
after an election in December, 1951. Vere Bird decided to go into
politics and contest the eight Legislative Assembly seats which
were to be chosen by a much larger electorate than ever before—
suffrage was limited to those who were literate. He formed the
Antigua Labour Party, put up his candidates and won. The older
and more conservative of the island's politicians were mostly
members of the upper class who strongly resented the changes
which would give the people more of a say. In reprisal they
boycotted the four seats they had at first planned to contest and
Bird's Antigua Labour Party romped home with wins in all eight
constituencies. Bird himself won one of the four seats which
would not have been contested anyway, that of St. John's Rural
West. In January, 1952, he was appointed to the Executive Council, the island's main policy-making body.

Right from the start Bird made it quite obvious that he was a
man to watch. He pressed hard for the betterment of the peasant
population and was delighted when the Government passed plans
to acquire lands for peasant resettlement. Another of his pet
themes was that Antigua could not live on an agricultural economy
alone. He encouraged industries when he could find people interested in investing in the island. And he saw the great potential in
tourism. Now it is a large industry in the island and the American
visitors spend thousands of badly-needed dollars there every year.

His peasant re-settlement scheme was a success and the island's
sugar industry has seen great changes. Before the Second World
War peasant growers supplied less than 20 per cent of the sugar
cane to the mills, and only about 25 per cent of the cotton for the
sea island cotton industry. By far the greater share was produced

by the large land-holders, the remnants of the landed "plantocracy" of the last century. Today the peasants produce 50 per cent of the sugar—it is an expensive crop to produce and is cheaper if grown on large plantations—and some 80 per cent of the cotton.

Bird was re-elected President of the Antigua Trades and Labour Union in October, 1952, and as his policies began to bear fruit he became the most important politician in the island. Since he came into politics little more than a decade ago, the growth of the living standard of the people has been little short of spectacular. In 1951 Antigua's national *per capita* income was almost the lowest in the Eastern Caribbean averaging about £25. In 1959 it was about £72. It is still astonishingly low. But Bird has brought about a remarkable series of changes which have provided a much wider distribution of the wealth in the agricultural section of the community.

In May, 1955, he was appointed a Commissioner of the Caribbean Commission (now the Caribbean Organization). In January, 1956, he was in trouble for remarks he was alleged to have made at a union meeting, and was charged with contempt of court. He was freed on 13th March.

The same year additional constitutional changes brought into force a ministerial system of Government. Bird was returned to the Legislative Council—again unopposed and again with all eight seats going to the Antigua Labour Party—on 26th October, 1956, and became the Minister for Trade and Production.

A strong believer in the federating of the West Indies he soon became a key voice in the decisions taken at the various meetings which preceded the coming into being of the Federation of the West Indies in 1958. During its four-year life Bird was an important figure in the Federation and will work hard to ensure that the new Eastern Caribbean Federation does not fail as dismally as its predecessor. It is also probable that he will be a strong contender for the office of Prime Minister of the new Federation. If Barbados' Premier Errol Barrow declines to stand for election, Bird will probably get the post.

His Government bought land for an industrial estate and soon established a modern cotton ginnery for the superior quality sea island cotton which Antigua produces. An edible oil refining plant was installed and industries for the manufacture of cigarettes, cornmeal and garments were established.

The older politicians who made up the conservative elements of Antigua's political scene not only resented the bold and hard-working newcomer, but branded him a dictator, pointing out that there was no opposition. Bird countered this by reminding them that he had won all the seats fairly. Because he is a man of humble origins, Bird had come in for a great deal of class discrimination which may account for his somewhat dour appearance.

The Leeward and Windward Islands received new constitutions on 1st January, 1960, and Antigua's Legislative Council was enlarged to give 10 elected seats. In the election which followed Bird was again victorious and his party captured every seat. This time he became Chief Minister and Minister of Planning.

Antigua works on an annual budget of £2½ million practically all of which is taken up with Government services, administration and imports. Exports total a little over £1 million.

Whether they see Bird as a dictator or a saviour, Antiguans cannot deny that he has done much for his island and given a chance will do even more.

* * *

MONTSERRAT

William Bramble

Tiny Montserrat is the smallest, most southerly, and the poorest of the three units which make up the Leeward Islands. It is also one of the prettiest of the British West Indian islands.

The pear-shaped island, covering a mere thirty-two square miles and supporting some 14,000 people of predominantly African descent, lies twenty-seven miles south-west of Antigua, twenty-three miles south-east of Nevis and is the nearest of the Leeward Islands to the French island of Guadeloupe, some forty miles to the south-west.

Top man in this pretty, impoverished island—the main export is the high quality sea island cotton—is William Henry Bramble, a squat, very dark Negro politician whose self-effacing attitude hides

an engaging and charming personality. His quiet and steady outlook has earned him the respect of more vociferous Eastern Caribbean politicians and he is one of the least shakable in his area.

He has come up the hard way and the pathway to Chief
Minister of his island has been a long, tortuous and often hungry
one. Born on 8th October, 1901, Bramble was educated at St.
Mary's College, Montserrat, worked on the plantations for some
years and then became a dealer in sea island cotton. Later he
became a skilled carpenter and was an undertaker for a short time
before entering politics.

Montserrat is unique in the Caribbean in that it is more Irish in
its outlook than West Indian. This dates back to the Cromwellian
period when a large number of Irish rebels were deported to the
island—it then being about as far as he could send anyone and
still keep them in the Empire. Today traces of them are still to
be found in abundance. Other islands have their towns and their
families with French or Spanish names. But in Montserrat there
are Negroes with Irish brogues and names like Kelly, O'Flaherty,
Riley and O'Brien, and towns called Kerry, Cork and Kinsale.

There is no skilled labour in the island and immigration to
Britain has drawn off more than a third of the working population. The average wage-earner makes a mere £46 a year and no
other island in the British Caribbean is as dependent on the grant-
in-aid handouts of the United Kingdom Treasury. This money
made up some 44 per cent of the 1958 budget and without this
annual dole out the island would almost certainly starve.

The island's capital is Plymouth, a small, picturesque town of
2,500 people. Chance Peak with its semi-active volcano towers
above the island at a height of 3,002 feet. The people live mainly
by market gardening and working small plots of ground which
raise the basic foodstuffs.

Like the other Leeward Islands, Montserrat has been through
many political federations and is now lining up to take part in
another. The only difference is that this one is self-chosen while
all the others except the last have been arbitrarily decreed by the
British Government.

After years of shuffling back and forth from French to British
rule the island finally became British in 1784 and has remained so
ever since. The munificence with which English kings handed out
grants of islands to faithful courtiers involved Montserrat—it was

discovered in 1493, by Christopher Columbus—when the Earl of Carlisle was granted letters patent to all the Caribbean islands in 1627. Just under two hundred years later—in 1816—Montserrat, Antigua and Barbuda were given a form of government which separated them from the other islands which now make up the Leeward Islands. In 1871 the Federation of the Leeward Islands came into being uniting in five Presidencies, Antigua, St. Kitts-Nevis-Anguilla, Montserrat, the British Virgin Islands and Dominica. In 1940 Dominica ceased to be one of the Leeward Islands and became one of the Windwards. And in 1956 the Leeward Islands Federation itself was dissolved.

The economic suffering which had caused rioting in Trinidad, Barbados, St. Kitts and Jamaica during the late 1930s brought a gradual increase in elected responsibility. Universal adult suffrage was introduced with the constitutional reforms in the Leeward Islands effected between 1950 and 1954.

William Bramble by that time was President of the Montserrat Trades and Labour Union, a leading light in the Montserrat Labour Party and the representative on the Legislative Council of five elected seats for the constituency designated as Windward District. He was elected in February, 1952, and returned for a second term in March, 1955.

The island had high hopes of economic benefit from membership of the West Indies Federation of which it became the smallest of the ten units. And Bramble, with two terms in the Montserrat Legislative Council behind him, turned his back on the island's own politics to contest the Federal elections of March, 1958. He won a seat and right from the start let it be known that despite Montserrat's small size he, as its representative, did not intend to see the island pushed around in the arena of Federal politics.

But some twenty months later, with constitutional reforms for Montserrat in the immediate offing, he resigned from the Federal Parliament and returned home to contest a by-election in the Southern Electoral District, winning the seat on 18th December, 1959.

A new constitution came into force on New Year's Day, 1960 and William Bramble became Chief Minister and Minister of Trade and Production. His dual portfolio has meant untiring, but —through no fault of his own—not very successful efforts to bring a new prosperity to the island.

Tourism is in its infancy as a money-earning industry. The sea island cotton is still a mainstay of the economy, and Montserrat has no skilled labour, natural resources or geographical affinity with big markets to offer outside investors. Jamaica, much closer to the United States, managed to persuade Americans to put up clothing factories and baseball-making plants in the island. Montserrat can offer little for any foreign investor at the moment.

And Bramble has been far more concerned in trying to diversify the island's agricultural economy and feed his people than in trying to bring in grandiose schemes.

Bramble, despite the unhappy end of the first West Indies Federation, is still federation-minded and has expressed an interest in taking the island into the proposed federation which will be based on Barbados.

In time Montserrat may prosper. Right now she is trying to balance her budget.

*   *   *

ST. KITTS-NEVIS-ANGUILLA

C.A.P. Southwell

Three islands make up this one unit of the Leeward Islands group. They share a Government; were one unit of the defunct Federation; will be one unit of the new one. And their Chief Minister comes from none of them.

For big, ponderous C. A. P. Southwell is from neighbouring Dominica.

Anguilla is the most northerly of the Leeward Islands—the Virgin Island group excluded—and is separated from her partners of St. Kitts and Nevis by some sixty miles of island-spattered sea. Between Anguilla and her sisters lie French St. Barthélemy, Dutch Saba and St. Eustatius, and St. Martin which is both French and Dutch. Pear-shaped St. Kitts lies forty-five miles west of Antigua and two miles north of circular Nevis. Montserrat is thirty-five miles to the south-east. And away to the north-west of Anguilla is the little uninhabited rock Sombrero, so named because it looks like a Mexican hat.

As a single unit St. Kitts, Nevis and Anguilla cover 153 square miles. Little Sombrero increases the area by two square miles. St. Kitts itself covers sixty-eight square miles; Nevis covers fifty square miles; and Anguilla covers thirty-five square miles. The total population is about 60,000 people of mainly African descent and some 15,000 of them live in the capital, Basseterre.

To St. Kitts—then called St. Christopher's—fell the distinction of being the first West Indian island to be colonized by the British. That was in 1623 when Sir Thomas Warner arrived with a party of colonists and settled on the island which Columbus had discovered 130 years earlier. French settlers came too. But soon they were evicted by the Spaniards. Eventually the Spanish withdrew and the island was shuttled back and forth by the French and British in wars and treaties until it finally became British in 1783.

The main industries of the three islands complement each other, but still fail to provide enough work for all the population. In St. Kitts sugar is king; in Nevis they produce fine-quality sea island cotton; in Anguilla cattle are raised and salt is produced. But it is sugar that amounts to some 90 per cent of the islands' exports.

St. Kitts suffered from the same chronic conditions of poverty and unemployment as the other West Indian islands in the 1930s. And in 1935 there were labour riots and sugar estates were burned. Soon afterwards trade unions were formed.

And in that period a man came forward to lead his people and earn a sure and dear place in their hearts. His name was Robert Llewellyn Bradshaw and he has been called "the Saviour of St. Kitts", "a great and good man", and "the only man who can put St. Kitts where it should be". And what St. Kitts is today, Bradshaw has largely made her through his own efforts.

Bradshaw, a man of humble beginnings, was born in St. Paul's, a small village. When he was 16 he went to work as a machinist in the island's only sugar factory. He became interested in trade unionism and played an active role in the St. Kitts Workers' League. By 1943 he was the Vice-President. The following year he left to found the St. Kitts-Nevis Trade and Labour Union.

In 1946 he entered politics, formed the St. Kitts Labour Party out of the Union, stood for the Cayon constituency, and won a seat in the Legislative Council. The same year he became member of the Executive Council. He was chiefly responsible for a thirteen-week strike by sugar workers in 1948, and later served on the Soulbury Economic Commission which inquired into the strike. But he refused to sign the report of the Commission and submitted a minority report of his own.

Tall, lean Bradshaw is always the epitome of sartorial elegance. He affects immaculately tailored suits, wears old-fashioned high wing collars, and usually has a flower in his buttonhole. His handlebar moustache is the pride of the island.

He travelled widely both as a sugar conference adviser and a Parliamentarian between 1948 and 1956 and that year he was appointed Minister of Trade and Production for St. Kitts, Nevis and Anguilla. A strong believer in Federation, Bradshaw threw the support of his party behind the newly-formed West Indian Federal Labour Party—WIFLP—and stood down from the St. Kitts legislature to enter Federal politics. He was elected to Federal House on 25th March, 1957, became the second Vice-President of the WIFLP in May and the Federal Minister of Finance in April, 1958.

But when he left the island for the larger political field, he promised the people of St. Kitts that he would return when he had done what he could to see the new Federation along on the road to independence and Dominion status.

When he left St. Kitts for Federal House and Trinidad Bradshaw handed the reins of Government over to C. A. P. Southwell, a big, bluff, bearded union man who had been in St. Kitts politics since 1952.

Caleb Azariah Paul Southwell was born on 13th July, 1913, not in any of the three islands of St. Kitts, Nevis and Anguilla, but in Dominica, the mountainous neighbour which lies between the French islands of Martinique and Guadeloupe. He became a pupil teacher at the age of 13, gained his 3rd Class Teacher's Certificate and taught in local schools until January, 1938.

He was a policeman in St. Kitts from 1938 until 1944 when he resigned to take a job as assistant stock clerk in the St. Kitts sugar factory. This brought him into contact with Bradshaw and he became interested in union activity.

In 1947, Southwell—he resembles ex-King Farouk in his size, build and almost permanent dark glasses—became second-in-command to Bradshaw when he was elected Vice-President of the St. Kitts-Nevis Trade and Labour Union. He worked in the sugar factory until 1948 and four years later contested the election under the new constitution, winning the Legislative Council seat for the constituency of St. Anne's-St. Thomas in October, 1952. The next election was held on 6th November, 1956, and he was returned to the Legislative Council for the constituency of Sandy Point. Bradshaw became Minister of Trade and Production. Southwell became Minister of Works and Communications, a post he held for three years. The St. Kitts Labour Party had gained five of the eight seats, independents winning the other three.

When Bradshaw left St. Kitts politics for Federal ones Southwell took charge. He became a member of the Executive Council in February, 1960, and was made Chief Minister and Minister of Finance. Elections came under the new constitution and on 17th November, 1961, Southwell was returned to the Legislative Council and re-appointed Chief Minister and Minister of Finance.

Meanwhile the Federation was crumbling. Jamaica was to secede and Trinidad too was making behind-the-scenes plans to leave. When the Federation fell Bradshaw was out of a job. He decided to go back to St. Kitts. He was still—for the 18th year—President of his union.

"In 1958 I told the people of St. Kitts that if I was elected to the Federal Parliament I would try to make available to the Federation whatever experience I had gained in my eighteen years of public service," said Bradshaw. "And I promised that as soon as we achieved nationhood I would feel free to go back home. We have not achieved nationhood. But I am going back home anyway."

In August, 1962, he won a by-election for the constituency of Central Basseterre and went back to his old stamping ground, the Legislative Council.

But he is not Chief Minister. For Southwell still holds the position. Bradshaw is popular. So is Southwell. Probably, if he was prepared to endanger the party solidarity by a trial of strength, Bradshaw could oust his old colleague. But Bradshaw does not go in for that kind of thing. He will be Chief Minister again, but in his own time. When the new Eastern Caribbean Federation is launched, Southwell will most likely resign and go on to another job. Maybe he will be High Commissioner in London.

CHAPTER SEVEN

THE WINDWARD ISLANDS

DOMINICA

Edward Le Blanc

Mountainous, cloud-capped Dominica is the most under-developed and under-industrialized of all the British West Indian islands. It is also the largest of the Windward Islands—and the newest member of the group. For before 1940, Dominica, sandwiched midway between the French islands of Martinique and Guadeloupe, was part of the Leeward Islands group.

The island, 305 square miles of dense forests, precipitous mountains and deep valleys, is the home of 60,000 patois-speaking people, almost as French as the population of their neighbouring islands. It is also the home of the last remaining pure Caribs, the original inhabitants of the area, a tiny handful of whom live on a special reserve.

Columbus discovered the island in 1493 and Britain fought France for it until 1805 when she finally won it for herself. Sugar was once king in Dominica. Then came limes. Now bananas are fast taking over as the main export crop. And like bananas, politics are something fairly new to this brooding, wet island.

The Chief Minister is Edward Oliver Le Blanc, joint-leader of the Dominica Labour Party, a light-skinned Negro politician who has tried hard to do something for his backward country.

Dominica got a new constitution with full adult suffrage in 1951 and the Dominica Labour Party contested the elections. The ministerial system was introduced in 1956 and another election came the following year. On 15th August, 1957, Edward Le Blanc won the Portsmouth constituency and was one of the five Dominica Labour Party candidates to get into the Legislative Council.

He became Secretary/Agent for the party in November of the same year.

But Le Blanc was not to stay in local politics. For in 1958 he resigned to run for the Federal Parliament and was elected. He served for two years and then, when a new constitution was granted to Dominica in January, 1960, he resigned from the Federal Government and returned home to contest the elections which were held on 17th January, 1961.

This time he got in for Roseau South. The Legislative Council had been enlarged to eleven seats and the Dominica Labour Party won seven of them; three went to the Dominica United People's Party; an independent won the other one. Four days after the election Edward Le Blanc became Chief Minister and Minister of Finance.

Dominica has problems: illiteracy; not enough hospital beds; and, paradoxically, too many people but not enough labour for local industries. For many of the workers have emigrated to England. Others have gone to Guadeloupe seeking seasonal employment, sometimes making it difficult for the local industries to find labour at the times they need it most. It is the old story of an agricultural economy which can employ people for only so many months and then must lay them off.

The island is a beautiful one but badly lacking in roads, making it an expensive, and slow, business to get export products to the docks in the shortest possible time.

*   *   *

ST. LUCIA

George Charles

During the life of the defunct West Indies Federation the St. Lucian family of Charles played a conspicuous and busy part. For George Charles was—and still is—Chief Minister of the island. And his father, James Luc Charles, was Minister Without Portfolio in the Federal Government.

St. Lucia is a verdant little island of 238 square miles and is the home of some 90,000 people. The capital is Castries and 25,000 people live there. The island lies twenty-five miles north of British St. Vincent and the same distance south of French Martinique. And St. Lucia is a mixture of the languages and cultures of both European powers. Mountainous, densely forested St. Lucia grows bananas and sugar and produces fine rum. Like many of the Windward and Leeward Islands it was fought over by France and England in the battle for supremacy in the Caribbean. But it holds the record for exchanges, both in battle and in treaties. It was alternately French and British fourteen times before finally becoming British in 1814.

St. Lucia's Chief Minister George Frederick Lawrence Charles was born in the town of Soufrière on 7th June, 1916, and was educated at St. Mary's College. For a short time he worked in his uncle's business, and then went to Dutch, oil-rich Curaçao to work for an oil company. When he returned to St. Lucia he set himself up as a commission agent.

Like many other British West Indian political figures, trade unionism was the ante-chamber to politics. He joined the St. Lucia Workers' Co-Operative Union in 1948 and the following year became its General Secretary. The St. Lucia Labour Party was born out of the St. Lucia Workers' Co-Operative Union and George Charles is President of both the party and the union. A new constitution was granted to St. Lucia in 1951 and elections were held in October. There were eight Legislative Council seats to be contested by full adult suffrage and George Charles, running on a St. Lucia Labour Party ticket, won one of them.

A fiery speaker who does not lose his temper easily and is completely impervious to criticism, tiny George Charles—he stands 5 feet 3 inches in his socks—soon earned the tag of "Little Caesar" from opposition Legislative Council members. His patois-speaking supporters call him "'Ti Creche". And those who are neither for nor against him call him "The Egg".

In the election held on 23rd September, 1954, Charles was re-elected for South Castries, four seats going to the St. Lucia Labour Party and four to the conservative People's Progress Party led by Garnet (now Sir Garnet) Gordon, who was later The West Indies' Commissioner in London. Charles was elected to the Executive Council on 14th March, 1956, and became Minister of Social Services in the quasi-cabinet under the newly-introduced ministerial system of Government. The following year elections were held under a new constitution and he was re-elected on 18th September, 1957. This time the St. Lucia Labour Party gained seven of the eight seats and the People's Progress Party got the other one.

When the West Indies Federation was launched Charles allied himself and his party with the West Indies Federal Labour Party and was a staunch supporter of the Federal concept. His father, James Luc Charles, became Federal Minister Without Portfolio. In January, 1960, there were further constitutional advances and Charles became Chief Minister and Minister of Finance pending the elections. They were held on 14th April, 1961, and this time running for the cane-cutting constituency of Cul-de-Sac, George Charles got into the Legislative Council, now enlarged to ten seats. He was re-appointed Chief Minister and Minister of Finance at a salary of £1,700 a year.

A married man with five children, Charles enjoys watching cricket—a game not as popular in St. Lucia as it is in other neighbouring islands—and playing table tennis, bridge and billiards.

Hard-working and keen, Charles says that he aims to help "the small, oppressed worker", and certainly he has done much for the island. Wages are still low and conditions somewhat primitive compared with some of the larger islands. But St. Lucia is looking increasingly to diversifying the agriculture and to tourism to help solve the ever-present problem of budget deficits which plague the small islands with their expanding populations.

* * *

ST. VINCENT

Ebenezer Joshua

St. Vincent's Chief Minister started his political career in Trinidad, failed, returned home to St. Vincent and succeeded. Both he and his wife are Ministers of Government.

St. Vincent lies twenty-five miles south of St. Lucia and sixty-eight miles north-east of Grenada. Barbados is 100 miles to the east and Trinidad is 180 miles to the south. It covers 150 square miles, but this includes the St. Vincent Grenadines, a chain of sparkling islets administratively divided between St. Vincent and Grenada. The largest of St. Vincent's portion is Bequia.

Columbus discovered volcanic St. Vincent in 1498; France and England fought over it until 1783 when Britain finally got it; and Captain Bligh of H.M.S. *Bounty* took to the island the first breadfruit trees from the South Pacific. The Soufrière, St. Vincent's semi-active volcano, last blew its top in 1902 with results that were disastrous enough for St. Vincent, but not nearly as disastrous as in Martinique where Mont Pelée erupted at the same time.

St. Vincent produces most of the world's arrowroot and also grows bananas, sea island cotton and some sugar. The mainly-African population number some 80,000 of whom about a quarter live in the seaport capital, Kingstown.

Ebenezer Theodore Joshua, born in the island in 1907, became a schoolteacher and went to Trinidad. There he became an active worker in the union activities of a remarkable Negro politician-agitator Tubal Uriah "Buzz" Butler, a Grenadian who was living in Trinidad and organizing the oil workers in the southern part of the island. Joshua became chairman of Butler's union in 1938 and held the post for thirteen years.

Trinidad had constitutional changes in 1950 and in the elections that followed Joshua ran for election on a ticket backed by Butler's long-handled British Empire Workers' and Citizens' Home Rule Party. But he ran against Syrian Roy Joseph in San Fernando and was roundly beaten. Resigning from Butler's union in June, 1951, Joshua hastened home to St. Vincent to take part in the local elections which had also been brought about by a con-stitution change which had enlarged the Legislative Council and introduced universal adult suffrage.

The elections were held in October, and Joshua was elected on a ticket backed by the United Workers' and Ratepayers' Union which was led by G. H. Charles. The party won all the eight Legislative Council seats, and as all members wore beards their unsuccessful political foes immediately tagged them "The Tribe of Goats".

But Joshua's association with the United Workers' and Ratepayers' Union was not to last. Soon he and Charles fell out and Joshua quit the party. The Governor, Sir Robert Arundell, used his reserve powers to prevent a disruption of the Government and Joshua formed his own political party, the People's Political Party, and a union arm to go with it.

But Charles's party still held sway in the policy-making Executive Council, and they were able to secure the necessary two-thirds majority to recommend that Joshua be expelled from it. They said he was "an unfit and improper person to remain in the Executive Council", and charged him with hostility to the Governor, disrespect to the Royal Family and with being a member of undemocratic organizations. Again the Governor intervened on his behalf and allowed him to remain.

But it was soon clear that Joshua's political career was to be a stormy one. He was charged with sedition, but acquitted on 10th January, 1953. Later, on a public mischief charge, he was fined £20 and put on a bond to keep the peace for two years. He appealed to the Privy Council. Early in April, 1954, he was removed from the Executive Council, but was restored the same month following the demands of the Legislative Council.

In November, 1956, he was ousted from the Executive Council again, this time for alleged Communist tendencies. Fined for being in possession of banned literature—*Thunder*, the Left-wing journal of British Guiana's People's Progressive Party—he appealed and it was allowed.

St. Vincent received a new constitution the same year and elections followed on 12th September, 1957. The four-year-old People's Political Party proved their power by winning five of the eight seats and Ebenezer Joshua himself got back into the Legislative Council for Central Windward constituency. His wife, Ivy, got in for neighbouring North Windward. Joshua was re-elected to the Executive Council on 3rd October.

He sided with the opposition West Indies Federal Democratic Labour Party during the life of the West Indies Federation and became the party's Deputy Leader in January, 1958. Later he was Vice-Chairman.

The ministerial system was introduced in St. Vincent and Joshua became Minister of Trade and Production on 11th May, 1958. Three years later—on 20th April, 1961—there were fresh elections after further constitutional changes had added one seat to the Legislative Council and he became Chief Minister and Minister of Finance and Local Government. His wife, also successful at the polls, became Minister of Social Services.

St. Vincent's arrowroot industry, once the biggest export commodity, has now been passed by bananas.

*   *   *

GRENADA

Herbert Blaize

Grenada's Chief Minister is unique in the British West Indies in that he represents the planter class rather than the working people. But then Grenada itself is unique. For "The Spice Island of the Western World" has more landed peasants than any of its neighbouring islands.

Possibly the most beautiful of the small islands, Grenada lies ninety miles north of Trinidad and seventy-five miles south-west of St. Vincent. The island is densely wooded, was the scene of fierce Carib wars, and still retains in many of its place names vocal evidence of its French period of occupation. Britain and France fought over Grenada until 1783 when Britain finally got it. An island of smallholders who grow nutmegs and cocoa, Grenada is fairly prosperous and free from the dire poverty of other Eastern Caribbean islands. The population is about 90,000 of whom 6,000 live in the picturesque capital of St. George's. It covers 120 square miles and with its dependencies in the Grenadines—the main one is Carriacou—it is 133 square miles.

The political history during the past twelve years has been a stormy one with riots, burnings, arrests, allegations of malspending, gunboats sent, the constitution suspended and franchises taken away.

Now, after being a member of the first Federation of The West Indies, there is some doubt whether the island will take part in the new one, or whether it will be joined to independent Trinidad and Tobago as a unitary state.

Leader of the party which favours a unitary state and Chief

Minister of the island, is planter-class barrister Herbert Blaize who won the last election solely on the "join Trinidad" issue and who intends to see that he lives up to his promises. Blaize comes from Carriacou, largest of the Grenadines.

Soft-spoken, bespectacled Herbert A. (for Anonymous?) Blaize was born in 1918. His father was a carpenter, but the son had bigger things in mind. His ambitious mother scraped to keep him at the Grenada Boys' Secondary School until he had gained the prized matriculation certificate and an ambition to study economics. But the path was not smooth. A traffic injury interrupted his studies and was followed by almost two years of confinement. He was forced to terminate his formal studies after passing the intermediate economics examinations and when he was able to get about again—in 1946—he sailed for the oil-rich Dutch island of Aruba, off the coast of Venezuela. His left hand was still partially paralyzed.

By 1949 he had become one of the eight elected representatives of the Lago Employees Council, the spokesmen for 7,000 oil-field workers. Three years later Blaize, his wife Venetia and their children, Norma—born 1946—and Valerie—born 1950—returned to Carriacou. He became territorial representative for a Bahamas-based insurance company, an active Anglican lay worker and later a vestryman.

Opposing him politically is one of the British Caribbean's more colourful and demagogic figures: Eric Mathew Gairy. Handsome, suave, 41-year-old Gairy has been the leading political figure in the island since 1950 and, despite the fact that he is now out of office, he will probably be a driving force in Grenada politics—and a vocal one in Trinidad politics too, if the island joins its independent neighbour—for a good many years to come.

In 1950 Grenada, along with the other Windward Islands, received a new constitution and elections were announced. Gairy, who had organized labour while he worked in the Dutch oil island of Aruba, founded the Grenada Manual and Mental Workers' Union and soon afterwards the Grenada United Labour Party. He is President-General of both.

In February, 1951, seven months before the elections, there were disturbances, animal maiming and house burning by members of Gairy's union—ostensibly demanding recognition for organized labour—and the Governor sent for troops. A frigate dropped anchor in St. George's harbour and extra reinforcements were sent from Trinidad, St. Lucia, Barbados and Jamaica. Three people died in the rioting and Gairy was arrested on 22nd February. Put aboard a schooner, he was taken to Carriacou and held for eleven days before being released and allowed to return to Grenada.

The elections came in September and Gairy's Grenada United Labour Party—known as either G U L Ps or Gairyites—won six of the eight seats in the Legislative Council. Gairy was elected to the Executive Council in November and on 22nd of the month he was fined £8 for using obscene language. Exactly a year later he was suspended from the Legislative Council for being abusive to fellow members, and in March, 1954, he forfeited his seat in the Executive Council for overstaying his leave.

In the elections on 20th September, 1954, the G U L Ps won seven of the eight seats. Blaize, who had run as an independent, had been roundly trounced. Gairy was suspended again in March, 1955, this time for disrupting the House. He became Minister of Trade and Production in March, 1956, when the ministerial system was introduced, and in November of the same year a Commission cleared him of imputations of abuse of office after a Government deal involving some land. Three months later—in February, 1957 —the Legislative Council passed a vote of censure on him by six votes to four for "wanton waste of public funds".

The elections held on 24th September, 1957, proved that the G U L P had lost ground. They gained 51.9 per cent of the votes but won only two seats. The People's Democratic Party, the Grenada National Party—which Herbert Blaize had joined the previous year—and independents won two seats each. Blaize became Minister of Trade and Production in the coalition Government.

During the election campaign free-spending playboy Eric Gairy was with a steelband which marched through a meeting being held by the People's Democratic Party and on 20th November he was disfranchised for five years. His constituency—St. George's South—was held for him by businessman Joshua Thorn.

A new constitution was granted in 1960. Blaize became Chief Minister. Elections were held on 27th March, 1961. Gairy, still without a vote, saw his party, immensely popular again, win eight out of the ten seats in the enlarged Legislative Council. His nominee retained his seat; his friend, barrister George Cline, became

Chief Minister of the island; his wife, Mrs. Cynthia Gairy, became
Minister of Social Services; and Gairy took on the role of Adviser
to the Government. Blaize and one other G N P member were also
re-elected.

Grenada now has an Administrator instead of a Governor who
acts as head of the Executive Council and is largely responsible for
running the island. Holding the post was James Montieth Lloyd,
an able and tactful man whose brother was Minister of Health in
Norman Manley's government in Jamaica.

Gairy, who had bought the outgoing Governor's sleek Humber
Super Snipe car as part of his trappings of showmanship, persua-
ded Administrator Lloyd to try to get his franchise back and it was
restored on 23rd June. Joshua Thorn resigned from the St.
George's South constituency creating a by-election and Gairy
won it. George Cline ceased to be Chief Minister and Minister of
Finance and on 17th August the reins of Government passed into
Gairy's carefully-manicured hands.

Almost at once he fell afoul of Administrator Lloyd. He resented
the fact that the majority of the senior civil servants who headed
Government departments were not Grenadians. The Administrator himself was a Jamaican, and other top posts were held by
Barbadians, St. Lucians, St. Vincentians and Trinidadians. Gairy
tagged Government House "The Foreign Office" and began
a campaign against the Administrator and the non-Grenadian
civil servants.

Things went from bad to worse and allegations of malspending
by the Gairy Government were bandied about with increasing
frequency. Eventually they reached such a pitch that Administrator Lloyd requested a Colonial Office investigation and a team
was sent out.

Gairy refused to testify before the Commission of Inquiry and
fought them every inch of the way. He sought to have the whole
inquiry prevented through court action, and when an injunction
to stop the proceedings getting under way was refused by one
court he carried it to another one. The extensive litigation dragged
on for months after the inquiry had been completed, published,
the constitution suspended and elections held.

Gairy—his supporters adore him and call him "uncle"—was
in London attending a conference on the formation of an Eastern
Caribbean Federation a few days before the Commissioners' Report

was published and had a great deal to say to the Press about what
he described as a "bogus" inquiry. Presenting himself as more
sinned against than sinning, he said that the whole thing was the
work of Administrator Lloyd and a few opposition politicians and
called it "political blackmail".

When the Report came out it was a shattering indictment of
the Government. Among other things which they reported was
that Gairy had spent £4,000 on furnishings for the Chief Minister's residence, including a £700 piano and a £300 radiogram;
that the morale of the civil service had been destroyed by "an
undesirable interference with administrative duties and by
improper threats against the security of office"; that they had
been induced by threats to "commit or condone improprieties or
irregularities in the expenditure of public funds"; and that Gairy
had "disregarded and contravened the laws and regulations
governing the control of expenditure".

Gairy returned to Grenada and a hero's welcome. Thousands
of supporters sang "We Shall Never Let The Leader Fall, For
We Love Him Best Of All". It is the party song.

Gairy's answer to all the charges was simple: "It's all lies." And,
of the piano, he retorted: "The Administrator's wife has a piano
—and my wife can play better than she can."

Soon afterwards, Reginald Maudling, then Colonial Secretary,
cut off all grant-in-aid funds to Grenada. On 19th June, 1962, he
suspended the constitution altogether making the affairs of the
island "the sole responsibility of the Administrator" pending an
election. Grant-in-aid monies were restored.

Said Mr. Maudling: "I have taken this action with very great
regret and only because the Chief Minister of Grenada left me
with no alternative. Not only did he do all in his power to prevent
the inquiry being held; but his comments on the report also
showed that he completely failed to appreciate the seriousness of
its findings."

Rain had kept Gairy away from his normal afternoon of tennis
and he was at home when the news came. The following day he
said: "The people are behind me, and I am using my influence to
prevent an uprising. The matter will eventually resolve itself."

He spoke long-distance to Dr. Cheddi Jagan, Leftist Premier of
British Guiana, and later announced that "the people of Grenada
may have to give careful examination to some other doctrine."

The implications that it would be Communism were strong and the powerful voice of the Roman Catholic Church in Grenada warned Gairy—he is a Roman Catholic himself—that this was a line of talk he had better not pursue.

Gairy, his Minister wife Cynthia and their two daughters, were told to leave Mount Royal, official residence of the Chief Minister. They moved into £350-a-month minimum splendour accommodation in the island's most expensive hotel.

Politicians in the neighbouring islands protested at the Colonial Office action. But Herbert Blaize merely said: "Grenada has been humiliated. It is sad, but it was necessary to humiliate Grenada to help remove the damage done."

As the pending elections drew near, both Gairy's Grenada United Labour Party and Herbert Blaize's Grenada National Party prepared for the fray. They announced their campaign platforms in plenty of time to let the 34,000 voters think hard about the situation. Gairy campaigned on what had become known as "The Squandermania Issue" and Blaize on the question of seceding from the proposed Eastern Caribbean Federation and joining with newly-independent Trinidad and Tobago. One Independent candidate, Clarence Fergusson, also announced that he would stand.

Gairy, in Trinidad for a hearing of one of his legal battles concerning the Commission of Inquiry, said blandly: "Support for me is gathering momentum outside of Grenada and it seems to be a question of me or Maudling. One of us will lose his job."

Soon afterwards British Prime Minister Harold Macmillan re-shuffled his Cabinet and Maudling was moved from Colonial Secretary to Chancellor of the Exchequer. Gairy was able to say that Maudling had indeed lost his job—he neglected to add that he had been promoted rather than demoted.

The election campaign hotted up towards the end into a straight fight on the "join Trinidad" issue put forward by Blaize and the Grenada National Party backed by white collar workers, businessmen and planters, and the unfairness of the Squandermania Commission as presented by Gairy's G U L PS.

At the last moment Gairy may have got cold feet over the "join Trinidad" campaign of his opposition. For while in Trinidad for one of his legal hearings, he applied for an interview with Prime Minister Eric Williams. When this was refused—Dr. Williams

did not want to influence Grenada's election one way or the other
—Gairy went home and soon his supporters were telling people:
"Vote for uncle because he must take us into a unitary state after
the elections. He isn't saying anything about it now, but he will
go unitary."

Few doubted that the immensely popular Gairy would win.
Much of his support comes from middle-aged women who adore
the handsome, free-spending leader, and from men who admire his
knack of kicking the bosses and smiling at them at the same time.

Gairy was talkative about the past and future.

"When I win it would be stupid for those civil servants closely
attached to Administrator Lloyd and who have sworn allegiance
to him, to remain in office and be asked by me to go," he said.

Of his malspending: "The furniture they talk about, that they
made so much about, is in Mount Royal. It's all there. It's Gairy
versus Squandermania in this election."

And, in an unintentionally prophetic remark, he said: "Through
the years my record at the polls shows that people are coming to
understand me better and better."

On the eve of the election he held a final candlelight, revival-
style meeting of 3,000 loyal supporters on the quay of St. George's
and hymns were sung.

It was obvious that if Blaize was to win it would be a very close
thing indeed. Few expected it, anticipating that Gairy would be
returned to power, but with a decreased majority. Blaize's own
constituency, Carriacou, was not contested by the Gairy party as
the island—along with its neighbour, Petit Martinique—was solidly
behind Blaize.

Election day was 13th September, 1962. The constituency of St.
George's Town which had always eluded the Grenada United
Labour Party, did so again and voted for the Grenada National
Party candidate. But Gairy himself retained his seat in St. George's
South, and his wife Cynthia retained hers in St. David's. Both,
however, had decreased majorities. Four of the floating constitu-
encies changed hands. The final result, after a high poll of 70 per
cent, was a defeat for Gairy. His eight seats were reduced to four.
Blaize's Grenada National Party made four complete gains,
finishing up with six seats.

But while Blaize's party had polled 11,632 votes against the
GULP's 9,927 votes, the actual result was only a hairbreath away

from being a dead heat which would have put the Administrator in the position of having to decide who had the Government.

For in the constituency of St. John's where Independent Clarence Fergusson was running, the Grenada National Party was declared the winner with a majority of only thirty-three votes after two recounts. The Blaize candidate had polled 1,003 votes to the Gairyite's 970; Fergusson's own poll of sixty-one had tipped the balance.

Said Blaize: "The people of Grenada want to join Trinidad and Tobago. The election asked if they did through my party's campaign and the answer is very clear. Now official and formal negotiations will follow."

The new Legislative Council was opened on 4th October, 1962, by Administrator Lloyd who was himself to leave shortly to take up a post in Jamaica. Soon afterwards Chief Minister Herbert Blaize announced that the various luxuries which Gairy had bought for Mount Royal would be disposed of. The radiogram went to the House of Refuge, and after the Executive Council had decided that the Chief Minister's office was no place for a drink trolley, ice bucket and drawing-room suite, they were handed over to the Minister of Social Services to dispose of to Government institutions.

But while Gairy is an opposition member not a Government one at present, Grenada will not have heard the last of the suave, immaculate union leader. Blaize has pledged himself to work to bring about a unitary state with Trinidad and that country's Prime Minister, Dr. Eric Williams, has given semi-official favour to the scheme. But he has warned that it will take at least two years and that Grenada will have to accept certain proposals of the Trinidad and Tobago Government.

One of these will be the ending of the Grenada Legislature and this will mean that when the unitary status negotiations are completed that there must be another election in Grenada.

"We have always said that at the conclusion of the negotiations we are going to have elections to select representatives of Grenada to the new Parliament of the unitary state," explains Blaize.

As Trinidad will probably allow Grenada only six seats in her Parliament, the ten existing constituencies will have to be broken up, and enlarged to make six electoral districts.

And Gairy is almost bound to win one of them.

CHAPTER EIGHT

BARBADOS

Errol Barrow

In the dark, grim days of 1940, when Britain was fighting for her life against the Germans and the Battle of Britain was at its height, a slim 20-year-old youth from Barbados arrived in London to fight for king and country.

It had been a particularly bad crossing from Barbados to Britain, twenty-nine days of pitching and tossing in seas as rough as only the South Atlantic can be in November, and the twenty-four West Indians were shivering and apprehensive as they were driven through blitzed London to meet the then Colonial Secretary Lord Lloyd at Number 13 Downing Street before being transferred to their training camp.

The slim young Barbadian was posted for training, and became number 1383402 Aircraftsman Second Class Barrow, E. W. Today, after a distinguished career with the Royal Air Force and an equally distinguished political career in his homeland, he is Premier of Barbados, the most English of Britain's Caribbean territories.

The son of an Anglican priest, Errol Walton Barrow was born in Barbados on 21st January, 1920. He has one brother and three sisters. Educated at the island's top school, Harrison College, he was a medium scholar, quitting school in 1939 to volunteer for service in the Royal Air Force.

Thousands of West Indians fought for Britain during the Second World War, mostly in the Royal Air Force but also in the Army and Navy. But Errol Barrow has the distinction of being one of the first group—there were twenty-four of them— to volunteer for aircrew service with the R.A.F.

After his initial training, Leading Aircraftsman Barrow was commissioned Pilot Officer Barrow, number 191485, and posted for flying training. He began flying in 1943 and by the time the war ended in 1945 he had made forty-nine operational flights over enemy territory and been promoted to Flying Officer.

Choosing to remain in the R.A.F. Barrow—"Dipper" to his friends—married in 1945 and the following year was posted to occupied Germany where he became personal navigation officer to the Commander-in-Chief of the British Army of the Rhine, a post he held for two years. A secondment to the Colonial Office took him back to London in 1947 and the same year he became a student at the London School of Economics, transferring later to study law at the Inns of Court. His Air Force discharge came the same year and in 1949 he took his bar finals at Lincoln's Inn, returning home and being called to the Barbados Bar in 1950.

Thick-set, jovial Barrow became interested in politics almost at once. Certainly he had the background for it as he is the nephew of Dr. Charles Duncan O'Neale, one of Barbados' earliest agitators for political status and recognition.

The tightly-packed island—there are 1,400 people per square mile in Barbados, one of the highest population densities in the world—lies in the Atlantic some hundred miles east of St. Vincent and 200 miles north of Trinidad and the South American mainland. The triangular island of 166 square miles, has a population of 237,000, the vast majority—some 78 per cent—of African extraction.

Nicknamed "Little England" because of its traditional loyalty to Britain and its wealthy ruling upper-crust white or light-skinned minority, Barbados has a history of its own Government which is the second oldest in the British Commonwealth dating back to 1639. But the old rule by the landed plantocracy has gradually been broken down by a series of statesmenlike Negro politicians who have fought for universal adult suffrage and equal rights since the early 1920s.

Dr. Charles Duncan O'Neale, one of the earliest fighters for political reform, founded the Patriotic League in 1923 and fought the antiquated political system. He was elected to the House of Assembly in 1932. Shortly afterwards a brilliant young Negro barrister Grantley (now Sir Grantley) Adams was elected to the House of Assembly. He was to gain fame as the advocate—in every sense of the word—of the labour leaders in the Eastern Caribbean and also as a labour leader himself.

An early clash between Adams and Duncan O'Neale led to a long and sustained series of disagreements between the men, with Adams airing his views in the now-defunct *Agricultural Reporter* and also in the *Barbados Advocate*. Partly because of this old family clash Errol Barrow harbours a deep and abiding dislike for Grantley Adams to this day.

In 1937 Adams distinguished himself in the defence of labour leaders involved in the plantation riots and the following year he was instrumental in the formation of the Progressive League, another political reform party. He became President of the League in 1939 and later—in 1941—President of its labour arm, the Barbados Workers' Union.

The Progressive League ran six candidates in the 1940 elections and five of them got in. Two years later Sir Grantley was appointed to the Executive Council, presided over by the Governor and the real rule in the island.

By the time the next election came in 1944 the Progressive League had become the Barbados Labour Party and they won eight seats in the twenty-four-seat House of Assembly. The West Indian National Congress Party led by W. A. Crawford had also won eight seats and Sir Grantley engineered a coalition which gave them the advantage in numbers over the old-established Electors' Association which tended to represent planter rather than worker interests.

The coalition worked hard to break down the traditional money qualifications for voting and managed to get them reduced substantially. This raised the electorate from 6,000 to 30,000 but even so the remaining financial qualifications barred the majority of the island's peasant cane-cutters from voting. And in Barbados, where sugar has for centuries been king—47,000 of the 66,880 acres under agriculture are given over to it—the cane-cutters are a substantial number.

Little by little the Barbados Labour Party made inroads among the elected members of the West Indian National Congress Party and by the 1951 elections the Congress had ceased to have much political influence.

Errol Barrow returned to Barbados in 1950 and soon became

prominent as the legal adviser to both the Antigua and the St. Kitts Trade Unions as well as building up a flourishing private law practice.

In the 1951 elections Barrow ran on a Barbados Labour Party ticket and won. The Labour Party had secured sixteen of the twenty-four House of Assembly seats and were to be firmly entrenched for the next ten years.

By 1954 a system of responsible government was firmly established and a ministerial system was introduced. Sir Grantley Adams, who had steered his country successfully through the initial stages of political evolution, became the first British West Indian to become Premier of his island.

But all was not well with the Barbados Labour Party. For, in April, 1955, Errol Barrow broke away from them and helped found the Democratic Labour Party of which he soon became Parliamentary leader.

But the Barbados Labour Party was still in power—it was to be the Government in successive elections from 1951 to 1961—and Barrow decided to quit Barbados politics in favour of Federal politics when the West Indies Federation was launched.

Grantley Adams's Barbados Labour Party had thrown in its lot with Jamaica's Norman Manley and his People's National Party, Trinidad's Dr. Eric Williams and his People's National Movement and a number of smaller political organizations in the various soon-to-be-federated islands. They called themselves the West Indian Federal Labour Party. The Democratic Labour Party in Barbados had not sided to any extent with the West Indies Federal Democratic Labour Party formed by Sir Alexander Bustamante's opposition party in Jamaica, and Albert Gomes's opposition party in Trinidad along with some of the opposition leaders in the other islands. Nevertheless, Errol Barrow—a passionate Federationalist himself—decided to contest the Federal elections of 25th March, 1958.

He resigned from Barbados politics, contested the Federal election—and lost. For three months he was in a political limbo until a by-election in the St. John's constituency of Barbados gave him a chance to get back into local politics. He contested the seat and won. By this time Sir Grantley Adams had become Federal Prime Minister and Dr. Hugh Cummins was Premier of Barbados. The Barbados Labour Party then held thirteen seats; the Democratic Labour Party five seats; the Progressive Conservative Party three seats; and Independents three seats.

In October, 1958, Barrow was elected Vice-President of the powerful Barbados Transport and General Workers' Union and exactly a year later he became chairman of the Democratic Labour Party which he had helped to found and then briefly deserted for the Federal field.

The Federal idea gradually ground to a shuddering halt as first Jamaica and then Trinidad became disenchanted with the idea. Disputes between the leaders did little to help matters. Paradoxically there were disputes between the leaders of both the federal parties. Equally strangely in both parties there was a segment which was pro-federation and a segment which was anti.

In the West Indies Federal Labour Party Trinidad's Dr. Eric Williams fell out with almost everybody—Sir Grantley Adams especially. He accused Sir Grantley of being a "stooge of the Colonial Office". Sir Grantley accused him of allegations which were "inaccurate, misleading and untruthful". In the federal opposition camp, the Federal Democratic Labour Party, it was no more peaceful. Sir Alexander Bustamante of Jamaica took exception to remarks by Albert Gomes of Trinidad and said he would rather "associate with scorpions than stay leader of a party which includes Gomes". Gomes apologized but the situation remained strained until Bustamante pulled out of the party and launched his campaign to take Jamaica out of the Federation.

During the federal difficulties Errol Barrow was solidifying his party. Elections were scheduled for December, 1961, and he was determined to end the ten year rule of the Barbados Labour Party.

The staunch support of the well-liked and experienced W. A. Crawford, who has now been in the House of Assembly longer than anyone else, was a great help. And Barrow stomped the island campaigning vigorously that it was time for a change.

In his spare time Barrow indulged in his hobbies. He enjoys sailing and flying. He owns and pilots his own Piper light aeroplane. He also spent much of his time with his two children; his daughter was born in England in 1949 and his son in Barbados in 1953.

The elections were held on 4th December, 1961, and when the results came in the Democratic Labour Party were the clear winners. Premier Cummins and two of his Ministers had lost their seats. The Democratic Labour Party had fourteen seats; the Barbados Labour Party five seats; the much smaller Barbados National Party had four seats; and one had gone to an Independent.

Errol Barrow became Premier and Minister of Finance on 8th December.

To keep his Government in power Barrow must do startling things. He gained a degree of unpopularity with some strong taxation measures within a few months of taking office. But these will be outweighed if he can bring to a successful fruition the dream of a West Indies Federation of the smaller islands.

There have been setbacks. For the islands—eight units commonly called the "Little Eight"—are not all federation-minded. Under its last Chief Minister Grenada was pro-federation. But the new Chief Minister got in on a "join Trinidad" ticket and this will presumably mean that the "Little Eight" will become seven.

"Don't call us the 'Little Seven' if Grenada goes," Errol Barrow told me the day the Grenada election results came in. "Call us the 'Lucky Seven'. I shall be interested in Federation if only one other island wanted to join Barbados. After all two is better than one."

By the same token eight are better than two and ten are better than eight. But from the original ten-unit federation Jamaica and Trinidad have withdrawn and are now independent. Grenada will probably pull out too. And if they do so perhaps other islands will have the same idea. Fragmentation, it seems, is catching in the Caribbean. It is rather like the nursery rhyme of ten green bottles.

But Barrow is adamant about Federation: "We have a grim determination to present an image to the world of the West Indies, not as a calypso country where people sing and dance all day long, but as a democracy," he says.

And he is probably just the man to make such a determination become a reality.

CHAPTER NINE

TRINIDAD

Dr. Eric Williams

The thousands-strong crowd packed into Port of Spain's Woodford Square watched in hushed silence as the little man with the dark glasses and hearing aid threw the papers on to the large bonfire below the bandstand.

"I consign it to the flames," he shouted as each one went into the fire. "To hell with it."

And a great roar went up from the crowd as with one voice they shouted: "Yes, doctor."

Dr. Eric Williams—then Premier, now Prime Minister—of Trinidad and Tobago, smiled as the papers burned. Among them, in this symbolic gesture, were the country's constitution, the agreement on American military bases in Trinidad, and the constitution of the Federation of the West Indies.

Eric Williams is an extraordinary mixture of brilliance and naïvety. He is undoubtedly the best academic brain in the area; he is the most polished politician; the greatest thinker. Yet he is still unsure of himself. And because of this, say his opponents, he may be politically dangerous in the future.

Trinidad, the smallest member of the Commonwealth, is the most southerly of the formerly British islands in the Eastern Caribbean, covering 1,864 square miles. Its sister island of Tobago, lying nineteen miles to the north-east, has been linked with Trinidad since 1888 and covers 116 square miles. At its nearest point Trinidad is only seven miles from Venezuela on the South American mainland. The population is 825,000 some 400,000 of whom are Negro, 300,000 Indian, the remainder European, of mixed descent and Chinese. Tobago's population of 35,000 is practically all Negro. Rich in oil, asphalt—from the 114-acre natural lake—and citrus, Trinidad is a land divided in many ways within itself. The most obvious division is on race. Less obvious is class. Politics—pre-1950 disorganized, uninspired and dry— have taken on such a lease of life that they are the most dominant factor in the country. The ruling party at the moment is considered a Negro party. The opposition, an Indian one. The development programme for 1958-62 involved the expenditure of more than £51 million. Under Williams's guiding hand petrol exports are now £45 million a year, as opposed to £12 million ten years ago. Exports are £56 million a year, as opposed to £17 million.

Eric Eustace Williams, the man who would give his island's politics a much-needed shot in the arm, was born on 25th September, 1911. His father, Thomas Williams, a civil servant, had a cricket team of a family in his home on Port of Spain's Dundonald Street. Eric Eustace was the oldest of the five boys and seven girls. He was educated at Tranquillity Boys' School from which, at the age of eleven, he won a scholarship to Queen's Royal College. A brilliant student and able sportsman, Williams shone at the school. His studies were exceptional; he enjoyed cricket and was known as a slow and tricky practitioner with a cricket ball; as a football centre-forward he established a name for himself as a man who hated to part with the ball—a trait he was later to exhibit in politics.

In 1931, after a brief period spent in teaching at Queen's, he won the Island Scholarship, became the year's Gold Medallist, went up to Oxford and entered St. Catherine's Society to study Modern History. He got his B.A., in 1935, First Class Honours in Modern History. His D.Phil.—also First Class Honours—came three years later with a thesis on "Capitalism and Slavery". In 1939 he accepted the post of Assistant Professor of Social and Political Science at the Negro Howard University in Washington, D.C., which he held until 1944 when he became Associate Professor.

Between 1940 and 1942 he had a Julias Resenwald Fellowship for travel and historical research and visited Cuba, Puerto Rico, Haiti and the Dominican Republic. While at Howard he wrote three books: *The Negro in the Caribbean* (1942), *Capitalism and Slavery* (1944), which was his D.Phil. thesis expanded, and *Education in the British Caribbean* (1946).

Academically, Williams was streets ahead of his contemporaries. Socially, he found he was often unacceptable. To white Americans he was coloured. To American Negroes he was West Indian. He withdrew into himself and found solace in his studies. But he became bitter too. And because of the hostility and discrimination he encountered, a deep-rooted dislike for America set in which has been evidenced in many of his actions.

In 1943 he joined the Caribbean Commission as head of their Washington Office, still retaining his links with Howard University. Two years later he was based in Trinidad as Deputy Chairman of the Caribbean Commission's Research Council. He travelled widely in the Caribbean visiting almost every territory, immersing himself in their history and becoming a leading authority on the area. Probably nobody in the Caribbean—and very few outside it—could stand up to him in an argument.

A slightly-built, 5 feet 3 inches tall, light-skinned Negro, Williams is a dedicated man. He is intensely nationalistic, logical, receptive and discursive in private. When he has time he still enjoys a game of football. Listening to classical records, occasional visits to the cinema and reading detective stories are also among his off-duty occupations. He celebrates two birthdays every year: 12th October—the date on his birth certificate—and 25th September—which he says he was told was the actual date.

Williams—he suffers from weak eyesight and wears dark glasses, has defective hearing so wears a hearing aid—is also a chain-smoker. His friends call him "Little Eric" or just plain Bill. He was baptized a Roman Catholic—his school Queen's Royal College was Anglican—but believes that the Church should keep out of politics and that a man's religious principles are his own business.

Williams's married life has not been happy. He has had three wives—all part-Chinese. The first one, Elsie Ribeiro, he married in England just before going to Washington to take up his professorship at Howard University. She had been a student elocutionist. They had a son, Alistair, in 1944, and a daughter, Pamela, three years later. His wife divorced him in January, 1951, for desertion and still lives in the United States with their children. His second wife was Soy Moyeau who presented him with one of the great happinesses of his life, a daughter named Erica. Tragedy struck when Mrs. Williams died in May, 1953. His third

E

marriage—a secret one in November, 1957, at Caledonia Island, off Trinidad—was to British Guianese dentist Dr. Mayleen Mook-Sang, but they separated after a year.

Williams's first association with politics interested him immensely. In 1954 he was appointed adviser to the Trinidad Government at a conference in Port of Spain. The following year he was again adviser at high level meetings in London and Geneva. And it was in 1955 that the Caribbean Commission failed to renew his contract after twelve years' service.

Williams decided that he was interested enough in politics to take a serious look at them. He became the protégé of Albert Gomes, the vociferous, boisterous politician who was the island's Chief Minister in all but name.

In the early 1950s Trinidad was the most economically advanced of the British West Indian islands. Politically it was one of the most backward. There had been well-defined unions and political parties in many of the other islands for a decade. But Trinidad, despite having attracted some of the most able men in the country into politics, had never been able to achieve any properly organized political party.

There had been riots in 1937. Tubal Uriah "Buzz" Butler, a Negro politician from neighbouring Grenada, had made Trinidad his home and unions his business. At the time he was the best known politician in the island, if not the whole Eastern Caribbean. But even he had never been able to form a really solid party. Universal adult suffrage and a Legislative Council with nine elected seats had been granted under a new constitution in 1945. Elections had followed in 1946 and a rash of parties had formed, disintegrated and re-grouped.

In November, 1943, Dr. David Pitt, a Negro doctor now living in London, had founded the West Indian National Party which quickly gained a great deal of support, including that of many of the embryo unions. But popular and powerful "Buzz" Butler refused to be associated with it. The election in 1946 brought about the fragmentation of several of the small parties—which were merely political pressure and study groups—and a United Front of most of the remaining parties was formed. Only three of the West Indian National Party candidates—part of the United Front—managed to secure places in the Legislature: Roy Joseph, a Syrian; Patrick Solomon, a Negro physician; and Albert Gomes, a Portuguese businessman and able speaker who had been expelled from the WINP but had run for election with the United Front under the sponsorship of the Party of Political Progress Groups.

Another constitutional change in 1950 raised the number of elected seats in the Legislative Council to eighteen which were contested by 141 candidates, including ninety independents. The most successful party was "Buzz" Butler's unwieldly-sounding British Empire Workers' and Citizens' Home Rule Party which secured six of the seats and was joined by one of the independents. But the other successful candidates soon made an alliance which outnumbered Butler, ensured that none of his party were elected to the Executive Council, and put him in the position of Opposition leader. One by one his party men defected to other groups until only Butler and two loyal followers were left to represent his party. Gomes, as Minister of Labour, was Chief Minister in everything but title.

Eric Williams, as Gomes's protégé, watched the political working for a few months and realized that there were many things in the administration with which he did not agree. He decided to form a party of his own, sparking off the most remarkable political ascendancy in the British Caribbean.

On 24th January, 1956, Williams launched the People's National Movement (PNM) exactly eight months, to the day, from the general elections which would sweep him to power. It was a tremendous achievement. He started at grass root level and with planning, sound policies, drive and initiative, attracted an enormous following. His passionate nationalism helped. The party symbol became the balisier—a fleshy, orange, cactus-family plant. Soon people began to take notice of what he was saying. His party organization flourished. Learie (now Sir Learie) Constantine, probably the most famous cricketer ever to come out of the Caribbean, became the party's Chairman and later a Minister in its Government. He is now High Commissioner in London.

The going was not easy at first. The island is predominantly Roman Catholic and the Church took an immediate hand in matters. They opposed Williams at every turn, attacked him when he made a comment that birth control was up to the individual man and not a matter for Government action, and were quick to define PNM as "pre-natal murderers".

Elections were held on 24th September, 1956. There had been

trouble during the campaigns: cars had been stoned, meetings broken up, two people killed in pre-election clashes. More trouble was anticipated. The frigate *Bigbury Bay* stood off-shore; four thousand police were held in readiness. But the polling went off smoothly as Trinidadians went out to vote for their seventh Government since the British captured the island from the Spanish in 1797.

Williams's brand new People's National Movement staggered everyone—even Williams. They got 103,000 of the 239,000 votes cast, giving them thirteen of the twenty-four seats in the Legislative Council. His former benefactor Albert Gomes lost his seat. The Democratic Labour Party gained five seats, "Buzz" Butler's Home Rule Party got three, the Trinidad Labour Party two, and one independent got in.

On his 45th birthday—25th September, 1956—Williams was called to Government House to discuss the formation of his Cabinet with Governor Sir Edward Beetham.

Williams became Chief Minister and Minister of Finance, Planning and Development. He embarked on a vigorous programme of social reforms. Roads were built, workers' housing schemes inaugurated, schools, hospitals and public buildings sprang up. He laid emphasis on social services, private enterprise and foreign investment, offering tempting concessions to outsiders who were willing to bring their money to the island.

For years he had favoured a complete link-up of the British, French, Dutch and American West Indies—a Confederation of the West Indies. But he was realist enough to see that this plan was a long way in the future—if it could ever come about at all. Meanwhile plans had been laid for a West Indies Federation of the ten island units of the British West Indies. He became an enthusiastic advocate for the scheme and threw his whole untiring energies into it. He wanted to see a strong central government with wide powers and financial backing. He urged planned economy, and the minimum of Government expenditure for the individual islands, with plenty of power invested in the Federal Government.

But from the big plans and lordly speeches came a weak Federal Government with virtually no powers and little money. Williams was extremely critical. He said openly that petty jealousies, political immaturity and childish insularities were bringing into being a political entity which could never work.

Trinidad was named as the Federal Capital. New buildings sprang up. Federal institutions were established. Despite his misgivings, Williams worked within the scope of the Federation, doing his best to knit together something which would mean more than a flag, a motto and a lot of paperwork.

The Federation was born in April, 1958, to a glare of publicity and the loud trumpeting of small island politicians, inexperienced in the ways of big-time politics.

Two Federal parties were born to sit in the 45-seat Federal House of Representatives. Williams's People's National Movement aligned itself with Jamaican Premier Norman Manley's People's National Party, Sir Grantley Adams's Barbados Labour Party, Grenada's United Labour Party, the St. Lucia Labour Party, the St. Kitts Workers' League, the Antigua Labour Party, and the Montserrat Trades and Labour Union. They called it The West Indies Federal Labour Party. Manley's Opposition, the Jamaica Labour Party headed by Sir Alexander Bustamante, joined forces with Trinidad's Democratic Labour Party led by Bhadase Sagan Maraj, St. Vincent's People's Political Party, and several other Opposition parties from the small islands. They called their alliance the Democratic Labour Party of The West Indies.

But when the Federal elections drew near it was clear that neither Williams nor Manley would be prepared to turn their backs on their own islands' politics to take a chance in the Federal polls. It fell to Barbados's Sir Grantley Adams, Q.C., an able statesman, staunch labour spokesman and greatly respected barrister, to take the initiative for the W I F L P. Bustamante would not leave Jamaica to run in the Federal polls either and it was generally expected that if the D L P won, Ashford Sinanan of Trinidad would be Federal Prime Minister.

But when the results of the Federal elections in March, 1958, came in, it was the Williams-Manley-Adams party which had triumphed—but only just. The W I F L P got twenty-two of the House of Representative seats; the D L P got twenty; one independent from Barbados was elected; two successful Grenada United Labour Party candidates—who had been sponsored by the W I F L P—announced that their votes would be "fluid". Bustamante supporters captured seventeen of Jamaica's twenty-two seats. In Trinidad the Federal D L P got six of the nine seats. Sir Grantley Adams became Federal Prime Minister.

In 1959 another constitution change—unaccompanied by an election—gave Trinidad a cabinet and elevated Williams from Chief Minister to Premier.

Williams's attitude towards the Federation became distinctly cool as he watched the politicians from the smaller islands quarrelling among themselves. Instead of trying to make peace or guide them by his wider experience—not in politics, but in the world—he grew increasingly more hostile.

From the Federation's strongest advocate, he became its bitterest enemy. Eventually he launched fierce attacks on the whole set-up.

Eric Williams is a master in the art of human communication at all levels. His vocabulary is superb. He can hold his own with the world's statesmen—or slug it out in Creole dialect with Port of Spain's locals. Woodford Square in the capital's heart, traditionally a gathering place for politicians and their supporters, is the P N M meeting ground.

Williams calls it the "University of Woodford Square" and harangues vast crowds in it for hours. From the copper-canopied bandstand in its centre he has become adept at putting across dry-as-dust political and economic theory to his followers who understand little of it. But with a fine sense of timing he can tell, even before they know it themselves, the exact moment at which they will become bored.

And just before that moment he will slip in a local phrase or a Creole proverb and they roar with approval. And he is not above a bit of flattery. He tells the crowd that Trinidadians are "the most politically mature people in the Caribbean"—and they love it.

But despite their "political maturity" many of the poorly-educated country people believe that this talented doctor of history was once a medical practitioner.

"Look how the man good," they say. "He gave up big medical business to help us."

His strongly anti-American line came to the fore in the protracted wranglings over the U.S. military bases in the Caribbean—given by Britain in 1941 in exchange for fifty out-dated destroyers. In Trinidad the Americans held the deep-water harbour at Chaguaramas—wanted by the Federation as the site for their capital and by Williams for nationalistic reasons. They also had several large tracts of land officially styled "de-activated bases" which could have been used for growing food but which were under a forty-eight hours notice-to-quit restriction by the Americans.

Williams launched a campaign against the bases—especially Chaguaramas, a missile tracking station, where radio-active components were, he claimed, being used.

"I am going to break Chaguaramas—or it will break me," he thundered from the Woodford Square bandstand.

Eventually an Anglo-American-West Indian conference was held on the subject. The first stage was in London, the second in Tobago and the third stages were individual conferences held in the islands concerned and attended by the Federal Government. The outcome was the return of de-activated bases, American financial aid was promised, Chaguaramas was retained but made smaller.

By early 1960 Williams had become so thoroughly disillusioned by the Federal situation that he launched a campaign against it.

On 22nd April, 1960, before a packed crowd at Woodford Square, he publicly burned seven pieces of paper. Branding them "the seven deadly sins" he cast into a bonfire the Trinidad and Tobago Constitution, the agreement on the American military bases, a racial statement made by the Opposition party, the Federal constitution, the Mudie Report on the siting of the Federal capital, the Telephone Ordinance of 1939 (Trinidad had had a long telephone strike), and a copy of the *Trinidad Guardian* (which was always attacking him).

It was a symbolic burning, but it created the effect he wanted. His audience roared approval for the gesture and he had made new friends out of old enemies. For there is nothing that Trinidadians like better than a bit of colourful showmanship.

He said at the time: "We have beaten our heads in vain against the forces and agents of Colonialism; against the unswerving and often discourteous hostility of the British and American Governments."

Williams is a man who needs an "oppressor" that he can get his teeth into. It used to be the British; then it was the Federal Government; then the Americans. If they ever leave their base he will have to find someone else. For the Fire Eater of Woodford Square, a real or imagined "oppressor" upon whom to vent his wrath is not only a necessity but a way of life.

In the final stages of his war against the Federal Government, Williams declared that all Trinidadians in the Federal Civil Service were "traitors to Trinidad"—but he would have been the first to complain if none had joined it. He attacked other islands' Chief Ministers, reserving special attention for Sir Grantley Adams whom he called "a stooge of the Colonial Office".

"It is not the sea which has stood in the way of Federation," he said. "It is the opposition of local potentates; big bosses over small areas."

Britain came in for her share of criticism too—and, in the Federal context, not without just cause.

"The Federation is a Colonial Office imposition, a political abortion, an historical anachronism," he said. On another occasion he called it "one of the most disgraceful episodes in the history of the West Indies".

And when, in September, 1961, Jamaicans prepared to go out and vote in a referendum to see if they wanted to stay in the ten unit Federation, Williams was quick to make his own position clear. If Jamaica went, Trinidad would follow.

"One from ten leaves nine," he said. "Two from ten leaves nought."

Jamaica voted herself out and seceded. Trinidad left without the benefit of a referendum.

Williams then launched a vigorous independence campaign.

"We have freedom in fact, if not in law," he said.

Race—never seriously a factor in Trinidad's politics until the latter part of the 1950s—has become important in campaigns. The Negro population numbers some 400,000; the Indians—originally from the province of Agra—number some 300,000. And, largely due to irresponsible remarks by inexperienced politicians, the PNM is now considered to be the Negro party and the Opposition Democratic Labour Party, the Indian party.

Williams, who seldom stops campaigning for the PNM whether an election is imminent or not, has gone out of his way to try to ensure that no racial label can honestly be attached to the party. He regards Indians who vote for the PNM as brands plucked from the fire. Negroes who do not vote PNM are far more to be lamented. Often he has exhorted his followers not to bring race into the political arena.

For this is something which transcends parties. Williams is an ardent nationalist. The country comes first in his mind. Pride in Trinidad is what he aims for, not pride in any particular race. He wants people to think of themselves as Trinidadians first, West Indians second, and by racial origins third—if at all.

Trinidad's Negro-Indian question, not insurmountable if stable heads come to bear, but yet of sizable and potentially dangerous proportions, is in directly inverse ratio to the racial situation in British Guiana. In both countries it boils down to fears of domination of one group by another.

On 4th December, 1961, an election was due. Williams prepared for this by purchasing voting machines from America to replace the traditional ballot boxes in use in Britain and virtually every Commonwealth country. The House of Representatives had thirty seats under the new constitution providing full internal self government, the Senate had twenty-four.

Williams and the P N M swept back into power winning twenty seats. The D L P, at the time led by Indian barrister Dr. Rudranath Capildeo, cornered the other ten. The African National Congress and "Buzz" Butler's Home Rule Party failed to gain a seat. In its way this was a sad political end for Butler—he even lost his deposit—who had played a substantial part in the political evolution of his adopted country for nearly a quarter of a century. Williams became Premier and Minister of External Affairs at a salary of £2,688.

The D L P alleged fraud in the voting machines, intimidation of voters, and the gerrymandering of electoral divisions in the northern part of the island where Williams is strongest.

And, at the constitutional conference held in London to fix a date for independence, they warned the then Colonial Secretary, Reginald Maudling, that there was a distinct danger of Williams becoming a sort of Caribbean Nkrumah heading a one-party state. They said that they feared that the democratic safeguards written into the constitution would be disregarded as soon as the British left and that the constitution itself would be consigned to the flames as the previous one had been.

Williams is changeable in his views on many things. He is likely to say one thing one day and then do the exact opposite a short while later.

Some quotes illustrate the point: "We must be good democrats and allow for an Opposition of at least one per cent" (1957); "I

believe in the principles of Parliamentary democracy, in the two
party system and in human rights" (1961). "I do not oppose the
denominational school and have never done so" (1955); "I see the
denominational school as the breeding ground for disunity"
(1956).

Williams says that Trinidad and Tobago will remain in the
Commonwealth.

"No republic for Trinidad," he says. "We want to stay in the
Commonwealth, with the Queen as our head."

His slogan as the nation became independent on 31st August,
1962, was simple: "Discipline, Tolerance and Production."

What will happen in the future remains to be seen.

But one thing is certain: either in or out of the Commonwealth,
republic or not, Trinidad and Tobago will have Eric Williams at
the helm for quite a while.

Despite his dogmatism, his fanaticism and his intolerance, he is
the best they have got—and he has done much for his country's
economic and material welfare.

PART TWO

THE MAINLAND COUNTRIES

"Woeful the land where the man of arms becomes
the lawmaker."

ANTONIO JOSÉ DE SUCRE

CHAPTER TEN

BRITISH HONDURAS

George Price

A slim, sharp-featured man stands in the dusty street. He holds aloft a large umbrella sheltering a small knot of people who cluster around him out of the blistering sun.

Even in the umbrella's shade the temperature is well over 90 degrees. The olive-skinned, bespectacled man, a lock of hair cascading on to his forehead, is talking politics. His companions are asking questions. They are dressed alike: brightly coloured shirts hanging outside their trousers, no jackets. Eventually the knot of people disperses. The man walks on down the street, a cheery word for everyone he meets.

His name is George Cadle Price. At 44, he is First Minister of British Honduras, Britain's last tiny outpost on the Central American mainland. The place they call "The Forgotten Colony".

Price, who in the last decade has sprung into prominence as a stormy petrel in Caribbean politics, is not a politician by choice.

He was born in Belize, the colony's capital, of mixed African, Maya Indian, Mexican and European descent and was brought up as a Roman Catholic. His boyhood dream of becoming a priest began to materialize when he went to the United States and entered the Seminary of the Divine Word in St. Louis. But he was to be disappointed and never became a priest. In 1940, after trying to enter a monastery, he returned to Belize. His brother qualified as a doctor at Marquette University in the United States. His six sisters are all married.

Price went to work as secretary to British Honduras's multi-millionaire Robert Sidney Turton, a man grown immensely wealthy—no one knows just how wealthy—on mahogany, chicle (from which comes chewing gum), and property.

British Honduras, bordered by Mexico to the north, Guatemala to the west and south, and the Caribbean Sea to the east, covers 8,866 square miles—roughly the size of Wales. The population—of mixed European, African, Maya Indian, Carib and Spanish origin—numbers 95,000—less than that of Rhondda. More than one third of them live in the seaport capital of Belize. It is the second smallest political division on the American continent, (tiny El Salvador is smaller).

Unlike their Central American neighbours who have played power politics for more than a century, and West Indians who became politically active in the mid-1930s, British Hondurans were not really interested in the political arena until little more than a decade ago. At various times commissions visiting the territory or conditions affecting it had stirred up slight activity but that was all. Their Government was dominated by the Governor and his Council and there were no political parties to speak of.

But on 31st December, 1949, the British Honduran dollar—which, despite the Sterling devaluation during the war, had always enjoyed parity with the United States dollar—was devalued. And with the economic distress that followed came an upsurge of political awareness.

George Price, still working for Turton, turned his attention to politics and was one of the founders of the provisional People's Committee which rapidly became the People's United Party—the P U P.

The leadership was young—all the top men were in their late twenties or early thirties—and radical. Headed by John Smith and two journalists, Leigh Richardson and Philip Goldson, and supported by George Price and Nicholas Pollard (a Mexican citizen and therefore not then eligible to vote), they were a force to be reckoned with.

They quickly gained a majority in the Belize City Council and the *Belize Billboard*, Richardson and Goldson's newspaper, began championing the cause. Their main trouble was lack of funds and Price was said to have made overtures to neighbouring Guatemala to remedy this. The P U P campaign was anti-British but Guatemala at the time was under the Presidency of the pro-Communist

Jacobo Arbenz. Because of Guatemala's traditional territorial claim to British Honduras, it was alleged that Arbenz gave money to the P U P in the hope of rallying support for his country's claim. Foreign newspapers attached a Red smear to the P U P which their opposition took up when and as it suited them.

In mid-1950 the *Belize Billboard* published what were claimed to be seditious remarks about the Governor and the two journalists were nearly jailed. In mid-1951 the King, Commonwealth and Government came under fire and this time court action ensued. Richardson and Goldson were found guilty of publishing remarks "aimed at teaching revolution, the overthrow of the Government, and discontentment of the people towards the British in Honduras and the King". Despite a spirited defence—partly paid for, it was later alleged, by Guatemala—they were jailed for eight months. The same year Price, who was secretary of the People's United Party, became President of the powerful General Workers' Union. Pollard became the Union's secretary.

When Richardson and Goldson came out of prison they began campaigning to awaken further political awareness in the people. In 1952 they called a general strike and by the time a new constitution was granted two years later election madness was ready to begin.

On the eve of the poll came the publication of a report of an inquiry by Sir Reginald Sharpe, Q.C., into the allegations of pro-Guatemalan tendencies in the People's United Party. Sir Reginald alleged, among other things, that the defence for Richardson and Goldson had been paid for by Guatemala and that Guatemalan money had helped the struggling *Belize Billboard* as the official voice of the party. But he was unable, he said, to divulge the sources of his information. Both these charges were strenuously denied by Richardson and Goldson. Price, who may or may not have known the answers, remained silent.

Voters decided that the timing of the Report's publication was "a Colonialist trick" and went out to vote in their first-ever general election with the intention of installing the P U P in the driving seat.

The result was an overwhelming win—eight out of the nine elected seats in the Legislative Assembly. Richardson became Member for Natural Resources and Goldson Member for Social Services. Under their guiding hands British Honduras prospered economically. They were young men with young ideas and plenty of energy.

Two years later they split with Price over the Guatemala issue which he was supposed to favour and formed the Honduras Independence Party (HIP).

The West Indies Federation was being formed to link most of Britain's Caribbean territories and feeling ran high in British Honduras. Many feared that entry into the Federation would leave them overshadowed by Jamaica, only half the size, but vastly more important in terms of wealth and population.

There were accusations by Price and Pollard that Richardson and Goldson favoured Federation. Price made it a plank in his platform. Another event helped him. Pollard was suddenly expelled from the secretaryship of the General Workers' Union, joined Price and formed what was to become the Christian Democratic Union. Richardson and Goldson retained the support of the General Workers' Union and many of the PUP Assemblymen.

One of the odd things about British Honduras's politics is that almost every Opposition politician in the field today has been a member of the PUP at one time or another. There have been many splits.

Elections came again in 1957. Price went to the polls crying "A vote for the HIP is a vote for Federation". Richardson and Goldson countered with "A vote for the PUP is a vote for Guatemala". But Price swept the board, getting all nine elected Legislative Assembly seats.

Much of Price's personal success stems from his "man of the people" image. A talented and enthusiastic church organist and still just as staunch a Catholic as he was in his younger days, he is up at first light every day to attend the five o'clock Mass. Afterwards he walks through the Belize market chatting with stall-owners. He says good morning to everyone he meets. If the greeting is not returned he says it again every day until the wall of resistance is broken down. He has lived in the same two-storied wooden house in Pickstock Street on Belize's North Side all his life.

His uncompromising nature—even to the point of dogmatism—his good looks and considerable charm, his rigid Catholicism, the asceticism of his private life, have all helped him considerably. And the immaturity of his people's political thinking has been a powerful ally.

Many of the PUP's most ardent—and noisy—followers are middle-aged women, usually married, who feel that "Mister George" needs mothering. His ever-tumbling lock of hair adds to the "little boy lost" appeal he has for them.

Price placed himself in the key position of Member for Natural Resources in the new Government and later in 1957 he was ready to lead a delegation to Britain to negotiate financial aid for the colony. He had gained power but lost former colleagues.

Pollard had split with him and formed the Christian Democratic Party. He had taken out naturalization papers so was eligible to hold public office. Frequently and publicly he branded Price pro-Guatemalan.

The *Belize Billboard* had withdrawn its support from the party and championed the newly-formed, pro-British National Independence Party born out of the Honduras Independence Party and Herbert Fuller's older National Party.

Leigh Richardson, badgered by a mob until he had to pull a gun to protect himself, and later burned out of his house by political mobsters, had left the country. Today he is chief political correspondent for the *Trinidad Guardian*.

In November, 1957, Price arrived in London to begin talks on financial aid for British Honduras with the then Colonial Secretary Alan Lennox Boyd (now Viscount Boyd of Merton). In mid-session the talks broke up in dramatic confusion with an announcement in the House of Commons.

Lennox Boyd revealed that Price had been in secret negotiations with the Guatemalan Minister in London, Don Jorge Granados. He told the House: "A plan was put forward which involved severing the connections of British Honduras with the British Crown and associating in some form with the Guatemalan Republic."

The talks were broken off. George Price returned home. Don Jorge was recalled by his Government. Denbigh Jeffrey, who had exposed the whole thing, resigned from the PUP.

In Belize Price received a hero's welcome, bands, and cheering PUP supporters. The blue and white flags of the PUP—Guatemala's flag has the same colours—were everywhere.

Governor Sir Colin Thornley listened to pro-Guatemalan speeches for two days and then went into action. Answering Price's sabre-rattling with gunboat diplomacy, Thornley called for the military. A few days later the frigate *Ulster* dropped anchor off Belize.

Thornley removed Price from the Executive Council for "not immediately rejecting the suggestion of the Guatemalan Minister". He retained his seat in the Legislative Assembly. Enrique De Paz became Member for Natural Resources. In January, 1958, another British Honduras delegation—minus Price—visited London and took up the talks where they had broken off.

Events moved swiftly. In March, the same year, while addressing a political meeting, Price was alleged to have said that toilet paper and not ticker tape was dropped from New York skyscrapers on to the Queen when she visited the city the year before. Immediately he was charged with sedition. Acquittal came in May.

Charges of his continued pro-Guatemalan activities were bandied back and forth during the rest of the year. The Guatemalan Presidency had changed hands twice since the days of Arbenz and Communism was not now one of the smears attached to the P U P even by foreign Pressmen—a foolish label in the first place since the party is predominantly Roman Catholic and therefore fiercely opposed to Communism.

But the pro-Guatemalan charges continued to pour in. Now it was openly declared that Price's one aim was to see British Honduras become politically associated with Guatemala. The charges were fortified by the actions and speeches of President Miguel Ydígoras Fuentes of Guatemala and by that country's Press.

For more than a hundred years the neighbouring Guatemalans have claimed that British Honduras rightly belongs to them. They refer to the country as their "Lost Province" and call it "Belice". The claim is rejected by the British Government, Mexico—who have a stronger claim that they do not press—and most of the people of British Honduras.

It hangs on the most tenuous of threads, but is complex enough to exercise the minds of international lawyers. The Guatemalans claim that the Anglo-Guatemalan Boundary Convention of 1859 is null and void. Under Article 7 both countries agreed that a road should be built by Britain and Guatemala to provide a valuable outlet to the Caribbean Sea for Guatemala and to the Pacific for Britain. But the Guatemalans—due to negligence—never ratified Article 7 and because Britain did not then think it necessary to build the road, they claim that the whole Treaty is null and void and claim the territory. Offers by Britain to accept any decision handed down by the International Court of Justice at the Hague have never been taken up.

One of Guatemala's favourite claims is that as the successor to Spain in that part of Central America she is entitled to claim the country. Mexico could put up a far stronger case for claiming at least the northern part of British Honduras but has waived her claim in perpetuity—as long as the country either stays British or becomes independent. They have said, however, that they would press their territorial demand if ever there was a chance of Guatemala being able to assert sovereignty over the country.

The Battle of St. George's Caye on 10th September, 1798, celebrated in British Honduran patriotic songs and poetry, finally ended all Spanish attempts to unseat the British from the country. The anniversary of the battle is remembered by the British Hondurans as a day of holiday and carnival. The settlers, black and white, had rallied to a small British sloop of war, H.M.S. *Merlin*, and put to flight a vastly superior fleet of Spanish invaders. The Spaniards were under the command of Field-Marshal Arthur O'Neill, Captain General of Yucatan (now part of Mexico)— which should be enough to decide who has most right to British Honduras—Mexico or Guatemala. For the Captain General of Guatemala would have mounted the attack if the country had been under his protection.

Price said and did little or nothing to refute his alleged pro-Guatemalan activities.

One of his few utterings was: "This colony belongs neither to the United Kingdom nor Guatemala—it belongs to the people of this country under rights expressed in the United Nations Charter."

He told me once: "I am not anti-British, I am anti-Colonialist which is an entirely different thing. We have made it quite clear to the Guatemalans that our goal is independence within the Commonwealth and we intend to evolve as an independent nation in our own right. We shall expect our neighbours to guarantee our sovereignty and respect our complete and full independence in accordance with the Charter of the United Nations."

Back in 1957, immediately after the Don Jorge incident and Price's return to British Honduras, the Legislative Assembly had passed a resolution denouncing the Guatemalan claim and re-affirming loyalty to the Queen and Commonwealth.

A similar resolution was passed in January, 1960, on the eve of a constitutional conference in London aimed at taking British Honduras another step along the path to independence.

And the preamble to the new constitution contained a specific denunciation of the Guatemalan claim, recognizing "the grave affront to the people of British Honduras caused by the persistent propaganda of the Government of Guatemala in furtherance of their unfounded claim to Sovereignty over the territory of British Honduras." Another paragraph in the preamble stipulated that, while seeking to better economic ties with their neighbours, there must be a referendum before there could be any question of a change of political status in favour of a neighbour—be it Guatemala or the West Indies Federation. It was signed by George Price (P U P) and Herbert Fuller (N I P).

Price said after the conference: "I expect British Honduras to be nothing less than a bridge between the Commonwealth and Central America."

An election was due before the new constitution came into force and the Opposition N I P and C D P were determined to oust the Government. Denbigh Jeffrey, who had been with Price when the Don Jorge negotiations were exposed, and had quit and joined the N I P, now resigned and joined the C D P taking over leadership from Nicholas Pollard who stayed on as second in command.

This vote-splitting position gave Price all the scope he needed. In March, 1961, he romped home winning all the 18 elected seats in the Legislature. Price became First Minister and Minister of Finance and Development at a salary of £1,650 a year.

The C D P disbanded and amalgamated with the N I P and party leader Philip Goldson was invited by the Governor to be one of the nominated members in the Legislature. He is the only real Opposition voice in the chamber, extremely critical of Price, strongly opposed to any connection with Guatemala and painstakingly detailed in his attacks on the Government.

In total power, Price went ahead with his own plans. His party newspaper the *Belize Times* puts over propaganda, never referring to the country as British Honduras, always calling it Belize—an extension of the Guatemalan "Belice". The Battle of St. George's Caye was branded a "myth" and a National Day was established to replace the older celebrations. The blue and white P U P flag flies everywhere; P U P Assemblymen and party members regularly commute between British Honduras and Guatemala.

On 31st October, 1961, Hurricane Hattie roared into British Honduras bringing a tidal wave and winds of up to 200 m.p.h. with it. Destruction was severe and 263 people died. Industries were shattered and Belize reduced to a mass of shattered, broken houses. George Price played an active part in clearing up the city —even to the extent of digging in the odious sewage canals. The British Government granted £5 million to the stricken colony, part of it for the construction of a new capital some fifty miles south-west of Belize.

In April, 1962, talks between Britain and Guatemala were held in Puerto Rico to "reduce the tensions" between the two countries. They ended with an agreement to raise both countries' diplomatic missions to embassy status and reaffirming a desire for economic and cultural links. The traditional claim was not fully discussed. "The respective juridical and historical positions of the parties concerned remains unchanged," said the conference report.

But the most important of the agreements reached—and the most frightening for anti-Guatemalan British Hondurans—was the clause which allows free immigration from one country to another. The British Government agreed to this migration suggestion and the British Honduran observers did not challenge it—proof enough, say the Opposition, that they are pro-Guatemalan. The presence of large numbers of Guatemalan voters in the next election could ensure the success of any party with a pro-Guatemalan platform. It could also sway any referendum aimed at changing the country's political allegiance.

Ahead of him George Price has a gigantic job. He must rebuild the capital inland, get the shattered industries back on their feet, find jobs for the unemployed, and take his country towards independence.

The traditional markets for British Honduran exports are Britain, Jamaica and the United States. But he must now look to his Central American neighbours. The country is already an Associate Member of the Economic Commission for Latin America and will probably join the Central American Common Market—comprised of Guatemala, the Honduras Republic, Nicaragua, El Salvador, and Costa Rica—after independence.

This will provide an outlet for industries with a potential market of 13,000,000 people.

In addition he must make good his promises either to stay in the Commonwealth or invite the people to vote on joining Guatemala. Probably he will stall this issue off for as long as possible. For most of the population feel that independence from Westminster and membership of the Commonwealth is quite a different thing to subjugation by Guatemala City and political association with Central America.

And, by branding the Battle of St. George's Caye a "myth"—he has since watered this down by saying "other battles in this area were more important"—Price may have signed his political death warrant. For the N I P capitalized on this and many of the intensely patriotic British Hondurans—rightly proud of their Baymen ancestors' achievement in defeating the Spanish—have begun to re-examine Price's party and its doctrines. On many things it has been found wanting.

The Opposition party is gaining ground.

CHAPTER ELEVEN

GUATEMALA

General Miguel Ydígoras *

The eyes of *El Presidente* are bright behind his glasses. His left hand grips the microphone, his right bangs on the rostrum table. His lip trembles as he shouts: *"Belice es nuestro*. Belize is ours. The National Army will know how to regain, when the moment is opportune, that part of our national soil which is today in a foreign clutch."

His voice drops to a low growl: "People of Guatemala, rise up, stand, be worthy of the great task which the bones of your fathers and your grandfathers ask of you; prepare to carry out another of your missions; to recover that part of our territory called Belice which moans in the claws of a great Colonialist power."

At 68, General Miguel Ydígoras Fuentes is top man in Guatemala. He rules 42,042 square miles of some of the most beautiful country in the whole of Central America. His subjects, of Maya Indian, Spanish, German and Negro stock, number something over 2,750,000.

His Presidential rule, since March, 1958, when he swept into power, is anti-Communist and pro-West. His Presidency, shown by periodic rumblings, is precarious at times but probably no more unsafe than that of any of the other democratically elected leaders in Central America. And Ydígoras is the leader of the campaign—so far virtually non-violent—to unseat the British from Guatemala's eastern neighbour, British Honduras, Britain's last tiny outpost in Central America.

Fast-talking Ydígoras constantly speaks of the "thousands of prisoners in that horrible concentration camp which British gaolers call Belize."

* Since this chapter was set in type General Ydígoras has been ousted from his Presidency. But, as the Guatemalan situation is confused pending promised elections, and as Ydígoras is the most colourful and resilient of the country's politicians, I have decided to leave him in this book. He may yet make a come-back.—C.W.R.

Frequently he rattles his Presidential sabre, threatening to expel all Englishmen (they number some 3,000) in Guatemala; to ban all imports from the United Kingdom (some £2 million-worth annually); and to terminate the Guatemalan export trade with Britain (some £500,000-worth annually). At other times his delegate at United Nations makes protests that Britain exercises "an unlawful sovereignty" over British Honduras. His Envoy Extraordinary in London delivers similarly phrased Notes to an unheeding and oblivious Foreign Office.

Today, on the face of it, President Ydígoras could rightly be called "anti-British". Certainly all his actions since he came to power have earned him the tag.

But it has not always been so.

In May, 1945, Ydígoras, then a mere general from a country whose generals were almost as numerous as its coffee beans, was appointed Envoy Extraordinary and Minister Plenipotentiary to the Court of St. James.

He was 50, a much travelled and highly respected military figure. He was born José Miguel Ramón Ydígoras Fuentes on 17th October, 1895, on a coffee plantation 6,000 feet up in picture-postcard Guatemala. At the age of seven he travelled for four days alone in an ancient coach to Guatemala City to enter a boarding school run on militaristic lines. He topped the entry class for the Military Academy and then headed the leaving class of 125. Two years later, he was conspicuous during the disastrous earthquake which virtually demolished Guatemala City, the largest Central American capital, in 1917, and the following year was in Paris as the Military Attaché. He stayed on for the Versailles Conference and then returned to Guatemala as vice-principal of the Military Academy which he had graced so creditably as a student.

Ydígoras enjoyed flying his own aircraft until, in 1923, he force-landed a biplane in a volcanic region and smashed his kneecap. Unlike many of Guatemala's former presidents, he knows the country like the back of his own well-manicured hand. He has served as Governor of four Provinces, worked as Director of Public Roads between 1938 and 1944 building highways and bridges across the country. He is also an experienced diplomat. Before coming to Britain he was Military Attaché in both Washington and Mexico City.

When General Ydígoras moved into the Guatemalan Embassy in London he was a vegetarian, an Anglophile and a devoted sight-seer. Food was still rationed in Britain and potatoes in particular were often in short supply. An often unpalatable substitute was cabbage. Ydígoras was soon to discover that small quantities of meat were more desirable than large quantities of green vegetables.

"British cabbage seems to be your main vegetable," he complained. "It has certainly cured me of being a vegetarian. I eat meat now and I really enjoy roast lamb."

He indulged his sightseeing instincts by visits to all the tourist attractions of London, and in trips to almost every major city in the country, going round factories, talking with industrialists and earning a reputation for himself as one of the most socially active diplomats at the Court of St. James.

His beautiful young daughter, Carmen, married Ian McGarvie Munn, a Scotsman and former Captain of the Seaforth Highlanders, in 1947. Two years later Ydígoras was a grandfather, taking pride in the fact that his first grandchild was born in Britain. As a christening present he gave the baby—Michele Ydígoras Laparra—a pearl and diamond necklace. McGarvie Munn is now Guatemala's Roving Ambassador and his wife is Ambassador in Paris.

Much of Ydígoras's time as Envoy Extraordinary was spent in writing to newspapers correcting what he considered to be misstatements about Guatemala and the traditional claim to British Honduras. In 1948 he carried on a long and technical correspondence with an Oxford don, who happened to be an expert on international law, through the columns of the London *Times*.

In 1949 he sat in as an observer when the International Court of Justice at the Hague deliberated on French possessions in India.

The following year he went home with £7,000 borrowed from his Scottish son-in-law's mother—who subsequently went bankrupt in 1952 because of it—for investment purposes.

Guatemala was ripe for power politics. The country had been in a state of political uncertainty for several years. The capital seethed with intrigues and plots.

The corrupt and violent Jorge Ubico had been ousted in 1944 after several abortive attempts to overthrow him had failed. His successor, General Federico Ponce, was himself ousted after less than three months. The junta who took over held elections which put into power Dr. Juan José Arévalo who held office until 1950 when he retired. Into the Presidential seat stepped Jacobo Arbenz, tough, pro-Communist, and violently anti-American. He had polled 242,901 in the elections of November, 1950. Ydígoras got 68,146. The other eight candidates got 64,454.

Immediately Arbenz began a scheme of nationalizing foreign—particularly American—businesses and investments in the country. And by doing so he signed his own walking papers. For the powerful American firms who saw their property being snatched away from them without redress and with inadequate compensation, began to stir up the Central Intelligence Agency. Men who owed America favours were called in. Some were ready to form an insurgent force if the rewards were big enough.

One of these men was General Miguel Ydígoras, in exile in El Salvador. Another was Carlos Castillo Armas. Both were to rise to the Presidency.

The C.I.A. spoke nicely to President Anastasio Somoza of Nicaragua and Somoza, keenly pro-American, gladly made one of his numerous private estates available for the training of troops under Ydígoras and Armas. The Americans also supplied several ancient aircraft—later used to drop leaflets and small bombs on Guatemala City and supplies to rebels—and guns and detached an officer from duty to help train the rebels.

Just before they were ready for the attack on Arbenz' Government the Guatemalan President got wind of the plot and discovered where it was to be launched from. On 29th June, 1954, he accused Somoza of harbouring insurgents—which was strenuously denied—and complained to the Organization of American States.

A few days later the rebels were on Guatemalan soil fighting their way towards the capital. By the time they got there Arbenz had fled, first to Prague and later to Communist Cuba, from where he now broadcasts red propaganda to Guatemala.

By October, 1954, Carlos Castillo Armas was President. His companion in arms, General Miguel Ydígoras Fuentes, went to Colombia as his country's ambassador in 1955 and stayed there for three years.

But Castillo Armas was not to last. He was assassinated in July, 1957, by his own guard—Trujillo of the Dominican Republic had his hand in the arrangements—and Dr. Luis Arturo Gonzalez took over the Presidency pending elections. They were held four months later and Ydígoras, who had run on a National Democratic Reconciliation Party ticket in 1950, now ran on a Redemption Party platform. He lost, but immediately denounced the elections as fraudulent and accused his opponent, Miguel Ortiz Passerelli, of rigging the polls.

For a brief time there was gunfire and bloodshed in the streets of the capital and then a military junta seized power and began to work for new elections.

In January, 1958, they were held and Ydígoras came to power with a majority of more than 40,000 votes. He assumed the Presidency on 2nd March, and began to install his relatives in influential Government positions.

Unlike most of his predecessors, Ydígoras does not live in the magnificent marble Presidential Palace, built by Ubico with Indian slave labour. Instead he lives in the Casa Crema, in the suburbs of the city. From the outside it looks like a desert fort. Machine-gun-carrying soldiers are everywhere. And Ydígoras is the last of the once-numerous generals in Guatemala. For he has abolished the rank as a dangerous spur to ambition.

Since his assumption of the Presidency, Miguel Ydígoras, the Anglophile, has taken a back-seat. In his place is Miguel Ydígoras the arrogant, the bombastic, and the vociferous fighter for what he rightly or wrongly believes to be his.

In this case it is British Honduras, 8,866 square miles of fertile land east of Guatemala, a country which was occupied by Britons 201 years before Guatemala shook off Spanish rule and became a republic. The Guatemalans have spent something more than 150 years claiming the territory—it now supports 95,000 people in an area about the size of Wales—which they refer to as their "Lost Province" and choose to call "Belice" (say it Beleesay), a Spanish pronunciation of Belize (say it Beleez), the colony's capital.

When the Dons ruled the Spanish Main they made many attempts to unseat the British settlers in what is now British Honduras. These settlers, engaged in cutting logwood—for dye—and mahogany, lived under the threat of Spanish attack for the first 160 years of the colony's history. Then, in 1798, aided by a British sloop of war, the settlers decisively defeated a superior

Spanish naval attack and the Dons gave up their claims to the territory, ceding it to Britain for logwood cutting.

Guatemala was a new young republic in 1859 when a Convention set up by both Britain and Guatemala established the boundaries once and for all. The two countries agreed to build a roadway from Guatemala City to the Caribbean coast which would give Guatemala an outlet to the Caribbean Sea and Britain an outlet to the Pacific.

But the Guatemalans, in the best tradition of Latin American "mañana" politics, failed to ratify the treaty until it was too late. Britain agreed that she had something of a moral responsibility to build a road and this has virtually been done by the recent completion of the Hummingbird Highway. The Guatemalans still have to build their part of the unratified bargain though they did build a railway from Guatemala City to the Caribbean coast at Puerto Barrios.

But Ydígoras—like many Presidents before him—has claimed that the Boundary Convention is null and void and that British Honduras is rightfully Guatemalan.

The controversy was at its height in the years before the turn of the century, died down between 1900 and the 1930s and then grew in intensity until Britain offered to negotiate in 1940. Britain was then at war but offered the Guatemalans the chance to state their case to the International Court of Justice at the Hague. The offer was never taken up. In 1946 Britain repeated it. Again there was no Guatemalan acceptance. Occasional offers since have met with no response.

Ydígoras's election to the Presidency of Guatemala set him on a road which brought him into prominence in the claim.

Castillo Armas, when rewriting the democratic constitution in 1956, declared that British Honduras was a Province of Guatemala. Three seats marked "Belice" in the Congress are kept empty, circled with a blue and white ribbon, for the representatives of the Lost Province.

By this move, both astute—for the claim rouses the feelings of many Guatemalans—and dramatic—for when the Congress is full the three vacant chairs stand out prominently—Armas managed to capture a great deal of support for his Government.

Ydígoras was not slow to see the usefulness of the claim as a red herring that could be used to draw attention away from the country's own internal problems. He also saw it as a drum to bang for world publicity for Guatemala. And, not least, as a card to have up his sleeve which he could whisk out for play whenever the Left-wing opposition began to clamour too hard for reforms in Guatemala.

In April, 1958, General Ydígoras, with a twenty-two-man retinue, visited the most easterly of the Guatemalan provinces, El Petén, which borders British Honduras. While there he took the opportunity to try to enter British Honduras at the village of Benque Viejo and was greatly annoyed when a Negro policeman —and a mere corporal at that—politely turned him back.

Later he closed the border preventing any commuting between the countries and other sabre-rattling activities have kept the dispute bubbling ever since. The border has been opened and closed frequently and with no given reasons. British Honduras chicleros—the men who gather chicle from which chewing gum is made—have been arrested for alleged trespass on Guatemalan territory. Speeches have been made in the United Nations by Guatemalan delegates. Notes have been delivered by diplomats.

The 15th of September is a public holiday throughout Central America to celebrate the anniversary of the end of Spanish domination in 1821. And, six months after he assumed office, on 15th September, 1958, Ydígoras thundered from the platform in Guatemala in an Independence Day speech.

"Looking from our frontiers, let us cry out in all pride and claim that which is ours, that which has been stolen from us, that which has been grabbed from us by the injustice of force," he roared into the microphones. "Let us pray . . . for our brothers in Belice who moan in a black night of political slavery, in a time of privations due to unemployment."

He has also given support to a group of anti-British, pro-Guatemalan British Hondurans who operate out of Guatemala City calling themselves The Committee for the Recuperation of Belice. They have kept up a constant pamphlet and propaganda war since receiving the semi-official go-ahead of Ydígoras's patronage. And he boasts of the "strong Fifth Column" that he maintains in British Honduras for propaganda purposes.

In another speech he said: "We shall drive out the British imperialists whose arrogance and perfidious diplomacy have made us waste more than 150 years in talk and more talk."

Always with one eye on his Left-wing opposition and the other on world publicity Ydígoras hit on a stunt to mark the centenary of the disputed Anglo-Guatemalan treaty. On 30th April, 1959, he performed a symbolic ceremony with the "reoccupation" of British Honduras on a concrete map.

Later the same year he was to declare: "Within twenty-four hours of the start of a nuclear war in Europe, Guatemalan troops will be in Belice, prepared to die if necessary to liberate our territory."

But Ydígoras's own backyard has been far from quiet.

In November, 1960, he turned out troops in Guatemala City to put down a small rebellion, and eventually had to mobilize virtually his whole 7,000-man army as insurgent camps sprang up throughout the country. It took him seven months to run down one of the ringleaders, Captain de Leon, who died in a blaze of machine-gun fire on the outskirts of the capital. Fifty other senior officers and ten civilians were granted asylum in the neighbouring Honduras Republic. Their revolt, they said with some justification, had been aimed at overthrowing Ydígoras in order to put an end to the widespread corruption which is rife in his Government.

As the last few days of 1961 drew to a close a respectable military visitor called on Ydígoras at his home. They talked for two hours and then the visitor left.

Immediately the Guatemalans announced that Field-Marshal Lord Montgomery, for the visitor was he, had offered to "mediate" in the British Honduras dispute. Both Monty and the Foreign Office in London denied this.

Ydígoras said at the time: "We have the English by the neck. We are tired of fourteen years of platitudes from a Government that never negotiates. We do not need to continue diplomatic relations and to live in this stalemate. We will live another fourteen years without a single Englishman in Guatemala and without a single £."

He followed up this tirade with a New Year's radio broadcast in which, for the first time, he publicly admitted that he had allowed America to train volunteers on Guatemalan soil for the ill-fated, American-backed, Bay of Pigs invasion of Cuba.

In return for this, he said, America had promised to mediate in the British Honduras dispute. "It remains for President Kennedy to take responsibility for the obligation contracted with Guatemala," said Ydígoras.

The American State Department denied all knowledge of any obligation.

More recently there have been revolutionary rumblings on Ydígoras's marble doorstep. His secret police chief Ranulfo Gonzalez was machine-gunned to death in Guatemala City on 24th January, 1962. The President immediately declared a state of siege in the capital and enforced a curfew.

His strongly pro-American régime, coupled with the constant threat of Communist infiltration in Latin America, causes him to blame Cuba for almost every untoward happening not only in Guatemala but in the rest of Central America. Ranulfo Gonzalez' murder, Ydígoras declared, was "the work of Guatemalan and international gunmen in the service of Marxism directed from Cuba". Fidel Castro he calls "that perverse parrot who has sent gold to buy unpatriotic Guatemalans".

Castro strikes back by calling Ydígoras "a tool of Yankee Imperialism".

Following the state of siege he arrested Left-wing leaders Mario Mendez Montenegro, of the Revolutionary Party, and Manuel Colom Argueta, of the Democratic Revolutionary Union.

Events were moving swiftly. While Guatemala was restless within herself, the British Government offered to hold talks with the Government to discuss the stresses which had strained Anglo-Guatemalan relations during the previous year.

Before Ydígoras could even answer the Note delivered to his Foreign Minister by Britain's "man in Guatemala City", Mr. M. S. Williams, a ragged band of Guatemalan civilians, probably with Left-wing backing aimed at embarrassing Ydígoras at a crucial moment, crossed the border into British Honduras. They tore down photographs of Queen Elizabeth and Prince Philip from a village school and burned them. Then they pulled down the Union Jack, burned it, and ran up the blue and white Guatemalan emblem.

Troops captured several of them and the ringleader, a young Guatemalan named Sagastume, received ten years for armed invasion and two years for sedition. His British Honduran lieutenant received ten years and a number of Indians were put back across the border.

February brought a rash of incidents in Guatemala. A bomb was exploded in the Supreme Court building. . . . A minor revolt in Izabal Province was put down after the offices of the American-owned United Fruit Company had been broken up. . . . Armed men seized two government radio stations, broadcast anti-government propaganda, and fled.

Criticism that Ydígoras was "too old at 67" caused the President to book a half-hour programme on television during which, stripped to shorts and sweater, he gave an impressive display of press-ups and physical jerks.

Britain's offer to hold talks in Puerto Rico was taken up. But it was economic ties with Central America, rather than political ties with Guatemala, which were discussed. The most disturbing point of the conference was an agreement reached by Britain and Guatemala to allow free immigration from Guatemala into British Honduras. This could easily have far-reaching results on future elections in the colony.

Mexico—which has a stronger claim to British Honduras than Guatemala has—did not even participate in the talks.

Apart from traditional loyalty to the Crown, the 95,000 British Hondurans are of a predominantly Negro origin and do not look with favour on the possibility of joining the mainly Latin Guatemalans. Added to this they are committed to a referendum before any change in their political status and the majority of them are against the idea of being taken over on nationalistic grounds. And independence from Westminster is an entirely different thing to subordination to Guatemala City.

The talks' main result was to get the status of the diplomatic missions raised to the status of embassies.

By March the incidents had grown in size and number and on Tuesday, 13th March, there were serious demonstrations by students in the capital. The British Embassy, used to stoning, had installed shutters which they immediately lowered. Petitions from the students proclaimed Senate elections held in December, 1961, to have been fraudulent. Three days later the army took over the capital, banned public meetings, and ordered a speed limit of 18 m.p.h. in the streets. A general strike paralysed the city, eight rebels were killed in an engagement forty miles north of the city, and students barricaded themselves in the university.

Ydígoras enforced a rigorous Press and radio censorship and

issued a statement saying that 40,000 volunteers from the country were marching on Guatemala City to aid the army. Two days later the question of the fraudulent elections came up again with manifestos from the National Liberation Movement, the Christian Democrats and the Revolutionary Party demanding a civil-military junta to govern the country.

Ydígoras ignored the demands and put his own position perfectly clearly when he announced: "I will resign on 28th February, 1964, unless destiny decrees my death before."

In November, 1962, his palace was bombed by three rebel Air Force officers who escaped afterwards to El Salvador. The Army remained loyal to Ydígoras and arrested the 500-man Air Force until the situation eased.

Ydígoras said that the revolt was the work of Fidel Castro and called him "the bearded vermin", prophesying that there will be no peace in Central America while the Castro régime is in power.

Whether "destiny", hired gunmen, or time will end Ydígoras's reign remains to be seen. What is certain is that his continued rule depends on the Army.

If ever they revolt, or if the rebel officers of 1960 return from the Honduras Republic to overthrow Ydígoras, there is no doubt that Guatemala will have a new President.

On 31st March, 1963, Ydígoras was overthrown in a bloodless military *coup* headed by his Minister of Defence, Colonel Enrique Peralta Azurdia. The spark which touched off the revolt was the rumoured return of Left-wing ex-President Juan José Arévalo who had been in exile in Mexico. Arévalo had announced his intention to run in the elections later this year and was at first threatened with immediate arrest and imprisonment by Ydígoras if he crossed the border into Guatemala.

Later it appeared as if Ydígoras might be willing to let Arévalo return—for the satisfaction of seeing him roundly thrashed at the polls. Taking no chances, Colonel Peralta, backed by the Armed Forces, engineered a *coup* and sent Ydígoras himself into exile in Nicaragua.

Calling his revolt "a defence against Communism", Peralta quickly named his cabinet from among the country's most prominent anti-Communists, most of them civilians.

"We intend to eradicate Communism, totally, from Guatemala," he said. He has also promised elections, and tax, agrarian, and labour reforms.

From his exile in Nicaragua Ydígoras said: "It has been the same for both Napoleon and I. Only he was sent to St. Helena and I was allowed to go to my friendly neighbour." And he added that the revolt was "a good thing for Guatemala and for Central America".

Ydígoras mounted his 1954 invasion of Guatemala from Nicaragua. It is possible that he will do the same again in time.

F

CHAPTER TWELVE

HONDURAS

Dr. José Ramón Villeda

The Republic of Honduras is the most underdeveloped, unexplored and worst-off for internal communications of all the Central American countries. The tag of "banana republic"—often misapplied to most of the republics—fits Honduras to a nicety. For the republic lives from the banana. The holdings of the powerful United Fruit Company are vast. And in times of economic stress and strain the Government has borrowed from the Company to make up the budget.

But while it is the most backward of the Central American republics—air travel is just about the only link with most parts of the country—Honduras has a charm all its own and the cobbled capital of Tegucigalpa is one of the oldest and most picturesque cities in the New World. And Honduras, after a stormy history of political instability and a lengthy dictatorship, is forging ahead.

Tegucigalpa still has no railway; neither has Belize, capital of British Honduras. Together they are the only Central American capitals without rail-links. Illiteracy is still a problem. So is unemployment. And the budget is still dependent on bananas. But a progress-minded Government has established a limited scheme of social services and also a college of tropical agriculture which draws students from all over the Caribbean and beyond it as well.

In Honduras the Presidential term lasts six years as opposed to four in most of its neighbours. And the country has had its revolutions, recalcitrant Army officers, abortive uprisings and its dictators.

Lying at the fat part of Central America, Honduras covers

43,278 square miles and is divided into eighteen departments. It is the home of just under 2,000,000 people of Spanish and Indian descent as well as a large number of Negroes from the British West Indian islands who work the enormous banana plantations on the Caribbean coast. Guatemala lies to the north-west; El Salvador to the south-west; and Nicaragua to the south. A number of islands lie off the Caribbean coast and have predominantly Negro populations—the descendants of settlers from nearby British Honduras who fled at various times from Spanish oppression. One island—Swan Island—has been on loan to the United States since 1863 and the Hondurans are anxious to regain it.

The United Fruit Company is all-powerful, being the largest employer in the country and also, through its taxes, the greatest single contributor to the budget. More than 30 per cent of the Company's entire holdings are concentrated in Honduras and it controls railways, ports, harbour facilities and newspapers.

For sixteen years Honduras was the private domain of one of the old-style Caribbean dictator-presidents, General Tiburcio Carías Andino, a remarkable Indian who managed to gain the Presidency and then hold on to it until he was ready to give it up.

During the 1930s and 1940s people spoke of "The Three Generals" or "The Three Ts"—meaning the dictatorships in Honduras, Nicaragua and the Dominican Republic of Generals Tiburcio Carías, Tacho Somoza and Rafael Trujillo. But of the three it was Tiburcio Carías who was the shrewdest. For he knew when the days of dictators were drawing to an end. He stood down peacefully in 1949 and was allowed to remain in plushy retirement in his country. Neither Tacho Somoza nor Rafael Trujillo had the sense to follow suit. And both fell to assassins' bullets, the one in 1956 and the other in 1961.

In the past the banana companies ran the politics. Today their control is not as complete. The fact that in the 1922 elections the Liberals beat the Conservatives did not mean that the one party was stronger than the other. It merely meant that the Cuyamel Fruit Company which backed Liberal Miguel Paz Barahona was stronger than the United Fruit Company which backed Conservative Tiburcio Carías.

The same thing happened in 1928. But this time, while failing to gain the Presidency, Carías became Leader of Congress. And then, in the period between the elections, the United Fruit Company bought the Cuyamel Fruit Company. At the next elections, in 1932, Tiburcio Carías got in.

He was inaugurated President of Honduras on 1st January, 1933, and by the time-tested methods of political fiddling managed to stay in office for the next sixteen years. But before he could start making the necessary changes in the constitution he had to deal with rebels.

The year that he became President he commandeered the civil aircraft of TACA—Transportes Aéreos de Centro América—and used them to bomb insurgents, making history for himself as the first Central American President to take war into the air against enemies of his régime.

In 1934 shaggy-haired, heavily moustached President Carías amended the constitution to allow him to succeed himself at the next election. But that was still four years off and by 1936 he had decided to rewrite the whole constitution. His second term of office began in 1939.

Despotic, but in his own way, far from harsh, Carías was a stable factor in his country. Nevertheless he ruled with the constant fear of assassination foremost in his mind. And when devout, frugal-living, teetotal Carías went to Mass the machine-guns were set up *inside* the church to prevent any attempt on his life.

During the Second World War Carías was the first of the Central American Presidents to declare his stand with the Allies. He ordered the German Ambassador out of the country and declared war on the Axis the day after Pearl Harbour. Honduras's lead was followed by a number of other Caribbean American states.

Carías allowed only one political party to function—his own Partido Nacional. But a strong underground movement was maintained and various parties worked continuously for the overthrow of the dictator. The present President, Dr. José Ramón Villeda Morales, was a key figure in the clandestine politics.

Born in 1908, he was educated at the University of Honduras and in Munich, becoming a physician and surgeon and returning to Honduras. In 1932—the same year that Carías became President —Dr. Villeda Morales entered the political field. But his open interest in the Liberal Party was to be short-lived. For Carías clamped down on political activity.

Outwardly Dr. Villeda Morales wrote books on sociology

and medical subjects. Behind the scenes he was engaged in politics. In between times he married Alejandrina Bermudez Milla in 1936 and had five sons: Ramón Adolfo, Ruben Antonio, Alejandro, Mauricio and Leonardo.

In 1944, student and later worker uprisings and riotings gave Carías the hint that his days were numbered, as placard-carrying mobs seethed through the streets of Tegucigalpa waving "Down With Carías" banners.

Carías kept a keen eye on all developments in his country and by 1949 he could see that political awareness was firmly established in the people's minds. Shrewdly he realized that his long run was about over.

He announced elections, put up Juan Manuel Gálvez, a one-time lawyer for the United Fruit Company, as the candidate for the Carías-controlled Partido Nacional, and had him elected. But unlike Tacho Somoza, who from time to time put puppet nominees in the Presidential chair and then controlled them through the National Guard, General Tiburcio Carías was happy enough to retire into peaceful solitude. He kept an eye on the political situation for a while and then even gave that up.

President Gálvez soon broke with Carías. They had disagreed about allowing exiles to return, and allowing a degree of political freedom, and Gálvez resigned from the Partido Nacional to found his own Movimiento Reformista.

The Liberal Party came into the open with Dr. José Ramón Villeda Morales at its head. The same year he became chairman of the Party's Supreme Council and launched the newspaper *El Pueblo* as its official voice.

Gálvez, a sickly man, was not to see out his six year term of office, retiring through ill health and leaving Vice-President Julio Lozano Díaz to continue in office until the next elections.

Hondurans went to the polls in 1954 and Dr. José Ramón Villeda Morales who had led the clandestine political activity under Carías was one of the three candidates for office. He won the election but did not get the Presidency. Under the Honduras constitution the winning candidate must get 51 per cent of the votes cast. None of the three contestants did so. And Provisional President Julio Lozano Díaz used this as an excuse to prolong his own unelected term in the Presidential office.

On 6th December, 1954, he seized power, declared a "constitutional dictatorship" with himself as "Chief of State", and hounded Villeda Morales into exile. He fled first to Guatemala and then to Costa Rica. Lozano managed to hold on to the Presidency for just under two years but there were rumblings of unrest and charges of corruption in high places during the greater part of his administration.

An abortive attempt to unseat him was put down on 1st August, 1956. But it was a taste of things to come. On 7th October, the same year there was an election for the fifty-eight-man National Constituent Assembly and minor electoral violence was suppressed at the time only to reappear on 21st October in a full-blooded—but bloodless—*coup* which tossed Lozano from office.

General Roque Rodríquez of the Military Academy, Air Force chief Colonel Héctor Carracioli, and Minister of Development and Local Government Major Roberto Gálvez engineered a highly efficient revolt which snatched the Presidency from Lozano and established a junta to govern the country.

The reason for the revolt, said the junta, was that they "did not want to be placed in a position whereby they had to enforce the laws of a Government which did not represent the will of the people."

Dr. Villeda Morales, still in exile, was appointed Ambassador in Washington in January, 1957, while the junta restored order in Honduras and laid plans for the promised elections. He returned home in June to organize his campaign and on 12th December, he won the election and became President of Honduras and moved into the vast palace with its turrets, battlements and spires.

But since coming to power President Villeda Morales has not had an easy passage. Having changed his position from being clandestine leader of underground politics to actual President, it is ironic that he should now be forced to suppress clandestine politicians and military men united to oust him.

Rebel groups are always active in the mountains of Honduras and 1959 was a particularly busy year for them.

At the end of January a radio station broadcasting "from somewhere in the mountains" sent out a call to overthrow "the tyrannical Government". The rebel slogan was "First the mountains of Honduras, then the valleys and then the capital".

A few days later some 250 rebel troops under the command of former Chief of Staff Colonel Armando Velazquez Cerrator swooped from the mountains on the town of Santa Barbara in the hills behind the Caribbean coastline, some 150 miles from Tegucigalpa. After stiff fighting which cost the rebels 130 captives and kept Santa Barbara under shellfire for three days, Colonel Velazquez withdrew.

Another, and this time more serious, attempt to unseat the Government came in May when two of Velazquez' followers, Colonel Maximo Bejarano and Colonel José Iglesas, made an attack on the valley township of Gracias in the western part of the country. The 500 rebels held out for four days against Government troops and then retreated to the mountains.

One group of rebels had set up their headquarters in a disputed tract of land in eastern Honduras which both Nicaragua and Honduras claimed and this made location of their hideouts considerably more difficult. The border dispute has since been settled by the judgement of the International Court at The Hague and Honduras now is established as the rightful ruler. There are still territorial claims against the United States which has virtually taken possession of Swan Island, some 100 miles out from Honduras's northern coastline—and from which they beam Radio Swan to Cuba in an attempt to stir up revolt against Castro—and with the neighbouring republic of El Salvador whose eastern boundary is also Honduras's western boundary.

The third phase of Colonel Velazquez' "from the mountains, to the valleys to the capital" campaign was well organized and led by the Colonel himself. In July he led a bold attack on Tegucigalpa, persuaded the National Police to join him, and was only beaten because the Army remained loyal to the President. After a grim thirteen-hour battle which left parts of Tegucigalpa in smoking ruins and cost the police headquarters which was set on fire, the rebels realized that their revolt had failed. Colonel Velazquez was granted asylum in the Costa Rican embassy and the rest of his troops either surrendered or fled to the hills again.

President Villeda Morales is due to end his term of office in December, 1963. If he manages to do so, and if he is replaced by a man of courage and ability such as himself, Honduras will prosper. But if, after a tradition of military dictatorship, another is established the country will stagnate and remain the most backward of the Central American republics.

CHAPTER THIRTEEN

NICARAGUA

Colonel Luis Somoza

Giant pictures of a chubby-faced, middle-aged man in a medal-bedecked uniform smiled benignly down at shopping crowds in almost every store in every town in Nicaragua until a few years ago.

Beneath the photographs was written: "General A. Somoza, man of peace, work and progress. His name is cherished in the hearts of the working people of Nicaragua, in the hearts of the peasants, in the hearts of the agricultural labourers, and because they admire and love him they have voluntarily made him President."

Today only the picture, the rank and the initial are different. For it is Colonel Luis Somoza's smiling face which now watches over the populace—"Big Brother" style. Succeeding his father and establishing a Somoza dynasty, Colonel Luis represents the only hereditary dictatorship to have been pulled off this century.

The tough old tyrant who first put up his picture and asserted that the people loved him and had "voluntarily made him President" left no loophole unguarded in his efforts to make the happy-go-lucky people of his troubled country realize just who held the power in the land. He gave his name to Port Somoza, Villa Somoza, Avenida Somoza, the Somoza Stadium and countless other public edifices to add weight to his claim.

His daughter's picture appeared on the banknotes. She is now Ambassador in Washington. His two sons controlled the Army and the Congress. His grandchild was a colonel in the National Guard—on full pay—two days after he was born. Relatives held high-up Government positions. And, from his hilltop fortress overlooking Managua, the capital, he ruled—and his son now rules—with an iron hand.

More than anything else Anastasio Somoza managed his country like a cross between a feudal baron and a director of a large modern business firm. His efficient sons took over. From the time he first settled his ample rear into the Presidential chair in 1936 until his assassination twenty years later, Somoza saw to it that money, money and still more money went into the family coffers. Some of it went into the country in a roundabout way but much stayed in the family.

His people called him Tacho—or Satanasio—when they talked of him. He enjoyed being called simply The General.

Today his son Luis runs Nicaragua, with his brother Anastasio —called Tachito—as his able and ruthless right-hand man. Tachito is now The General. Luis has stood down from the Presidency— but he is still the man in power, the strong-man of the country. And Tachito will probably be President next time round.

But to understand the sons one must look back to the father and to the early 1930s when American Marines were stationed in Nicaragua and the elder Somoza was beginning to stir restlessly as he tentatively stretched out his hands to grasp his country.

The largest—and most sparsely populated—of the Central American republics, Nicaragua covers 57,145 square miles of lakes, plains and mountains. It is about the size of England and Wales. Its 1,500,000 people live mainly from coffee, bananas and cotton and are virtually divided in their country by the mountainous Pacific range. To the west is coffee country and three-quarters of the people live in it. The flood plains of the Caribbean—banana country—are only sparsely settled by about one quarter of the population. One eighth of the Nicaraguans are of Spanish descent. The rest are either Zambo or Mosquito Indians, with a sprinkling of Negroes—who work the banana plantations—originally from Jamaica.

The country is bounded to the north by the Honduras Republic, the south by Costa Rica, the east by the Pacific, and the west by the Caribbean Sea. The vitally important Panama Canal is only 275 miles away.

American Marines were sent into Nicaragua in 1912 to "protect American property and citizens" as the State Department put it. They were withdrawn in 1925 only to return the following year after an outbreak of political violence.

Anastasio Somoza, who had done a two-year commercial course

in Boston and then sold motor-cars for a living, quit his job with the Rockefeller Foundation's anti-malaria campaign in Nicaragua to become an interpreter for the Marine Corps. The Americans liked the 36-year-old Somoza who wrote poetry in his spare time. They liked his taxi-driver English, his zest for life, effervescent personality and erratic humour. They made him Under-Secretary for Foreign Affairs, and when they began their second withdrawal in 1932 Somoza was already a power in the National Guard.

By the time the last Marines had left he was Commander of the Guard, a full general, and well on his way towards his ultimate goal—the Presidency.

Somoza was a family man. His eldest child Luis Anastasio Somoza Debayle had been born in 1922. A second son, named Anastasio after his father, arrived in 1926. And there was a daughter. Luis was sent off to school in the United States. Between 1936 and 1945 he attended the Universities of California, Louisiana and Maryland, and later the La Salle Military Academy in New York. The other children were also schooled in the United States. Having got his children safely out of the country Somoza went ahead with his revolutionary plans.

Dr. Juan Sacasa—Somoza was his nephew-in-law—had been left as President when the Americans went home and Anastasio Somoza meant to succeed him. But first he had others to deal with.

A popular rebel guerilla, Augusto César Sandino, had harried the Marines during their occupation but had laid down his arms when they left. He was number one on Somoza's list. At a celebration party in Managua on 21st February, 1934, Somoza's National Guardsmen assassinated the guerilla chief. Immediately afterwards they rounded up and dealt with Sandino's men.

Two years of plotting and scheming later Somoza struck in open rebellion early in 1936—in the name of democracy. President Sacasa had made a pact between the Liberals, of which he was the leader, and the Conservatives to nominate joint candidates in the forthcoming elections. The aspiring Somoza immediately claimed that this would deprive the people of a democratic election and went into action. His forces soon held four departments of the country and he set up provisional governments.

When President Sacasa issued proclamations outlawing Somoza's administration The General knew the time had come for the final overthrow, and in May, 1936, he sent one force of his National

Guardsmen against the heavily-guarded Presidential Palace on the hill of La Loma which overlooks Managua. At the same time another force attacked Fort Acosasco, near León, in an effort to gain control of two more departments.

The revolution was a success and on 1st January, 1937, after several months during which he had provisionally controlled the country's affairs, General Anastasio Somoza was inaugurated President of Nicaragua.

From that day he never looked back.

His salary was fixed at £20,000 a year. His relatives—and he had legions of them—clamoured for public office. Their cries were not in vain and soon Somoza kinsmen were packing every Government department.

He set about turning the country into a vast private business. Soon he exported cattle to Peru, Panama and Costa Rica; his own gold mine brought in vast revenues; his monopoly in milk pasturizing plants netted another fat profit; so did his cement factory. He acquired ranches and coffee plantations. He purchased *haciendas*, factories and land. In a short time he was the country's greatest landowner, biggest employer, and the richest man in Nicaragua with an income of nearly £500,000 a year. And still he expanded his interests.

A vast sugar plantation called "Montelimar" on the Pacific coast became his second home. He commuted between it and the Presidential Palace in an armoured limousine with bullet-proof windows. Preceding it, heavily armed, went an open truck of hand-picked National Guardsmen.

Tacho ruled without a break for ten years but he could not hope to do so for ever and still preserve the façade of democracy so important to his extremely amicable relations with the United States. He had to let someone else take over the reins—nominally at least. His country's stamps proclaimed "Nicaragua Believes in the Triumph of Democracy" and this had to be preserved.

His son Luis, after a final year as Nicaragua's Military Attaché at the embassy in Washington, returned home in 1945.

On 1st May, 1947, he stepped aside in favour of Leonardo Argüello. But he had chosen the wrong man. The new President had no intention of being a puppet nominee and within a few days of taking office after an overwhelming win in a carefully-rigged election, he ordered a shake-up of the highly-disciplined

5,000-strong National Guard which Tacho considered his own personal and very private responsibility. He objected at once. In reply Argüello gave him twenty-four hours to get out of the country.

The crafty Somoza begged for three days to clear up his affairs, was granted them, and used them to overthrow Argüello and re-install himself as President after being out of the office for exactly twenty-six days.

"That old fool thinks he was elected," he growled. "He didn't get more than 10,000 honest votes."

Three months later Somoza put his uncle, Victor Román y Reyes into the Presidential chair. Uncle Victor proved more tractable and this gave Tacho a chance to devote more of his untiring energies to his business interests and to travel. He was still virtually dictator of Nicaragua and it was as a Head of State that he went visiting in 1948, taking a risk that few Central or South American dictators in office had ever dared take before or have since. His goodwill tour took him to every neighbouring republic—including the Honduras Republic with whom he was squabbling over disputed boundary rights—and the United States.

His greatest idol, President Franklin D. Roosevelt, met him on arrival in Washington and Tacho's happiness was complete.

"I want to treat everybody good," he confided to Roosevelt. "Democracy in Central America is like a baby—and nobody gives a baby anything to eat right away. I'm giving them liberty—but in my style. If you give a baby a hot tamale you'll kill him."

And, much to the annoyance of the Nicaraguan Opposition—today there are seven Opposition parties, all of them impotent—Roosevelt agreed with him. Of all the things that America has done to Nicaragua, her troop landings, her filibusters, her Marines, the one thing that can never be forgiven by the Opposition is the recognition and support that has been given to the Somoza family and their régime.

On the same visit a high-ranking diplomat asked Tacho how he dared to leave Nicaragua. Was he not afraid that someone would take over the country in his absence?

"They're all fools," The General laughed. "There's no one who could do it."

And he was right at that.

His two American-educated sons had returned home and had

their fingers well in the family pie. Luis was President of Congress
—he had been elected in 1950—in which the Opposition were
present but powerless. Tachito, having graduated from West
Point, was head of the National Guard.

Tacho's intense Americanness came out in his favourite sport—
baseball. He established scores of baseball parks, which at least
gave slum children somewhere to play. And, as another illustration
of his pro-American régime, he decreed that the Fourth of July
—American Independence Day—be a National Holiday in
Nicaragua.

Back home from his travels Tacho's acquisitiveness asserted
itself with a renewed burst of business acumen. He bought more
land, more factories, more businesses and soon had the country
virtually sewn up.

Every businessman wishing to import raw materials into Nicaragua knew that a very large percentage of his expenses would
find their way into Somoza's hands. He would fly about the
country making arrangements for his deal in aircraft owned by
Somoza. When his raw materials arrived they would come in
ships owned by Somoza, and be transferred to lighters owned by
Somoza. They would be cleared through the family port of
Somoza by a Somoza-owned customs brokerage firm, put into
lorries owned by a Somoza trucking company and delivered to the
factory—itself built with Somoza cement and Somoza equipment
on land for which he paid taxes to Somoza.

His militaristic side asserted itself when he sponsored an invasion of neighbouring Costa Rica in a brief and unsuccessful
attempt to overthrow his old enemy President José—"Pepe"—
Figueres in December, 1948.

By early 1950 Tacho owned fifty-one ranches and forty-six
coffee plantations. Gold mining companies paid him a personal
allowance of £70,000 annually in addition to the taxes to the
State—a percentage of which went to Somoza. He was the richest
man in Central America.

In May the same year Uncle Victor died and Tacho was
"elected" to hold office until 1957.

But for all his personal gain and immense riches Tacho Somoza
was a fairly benevolent dictator—as dictators go. He built schools
—not enough of them, but schools nevertheless. When he came
to power there were 622 schools in the whole country. Twenty

years later there were 2,000—although 60 per cent of the population were still illiterate. He planned roads—in 1956 there were four times as many miles of all-weather roads as there had been in 1936. He diversified the agriculture. In 1940 exports stood at £1¼ million and imports at £2½ million. Twelve years later exports had risen to £14 million and imports to £13 million. Regularly, 39 per cent of the budget was spent on economic development. Coffee and cotton exports doubled between 1950 and 1954. Four times as much was put aside for health services in 1956 as in 1950.

The Opposition, instead of being stood against walls and shot, as happens in dictatorships, were for the most part sent into exile where they plotted his overthrow unsuccessfully.

There were only two serious attempts to remove the Somozas. Of them, one was unsuccessful; the other merely exchanged Tacho for his son.

On 3rd April, 1954, as he drove along a road sixteen miles from Managua, rifle fire riddled his car but failed to touch the President. In the skirmish that followed two National Guardsmen were killed and the country was put under martial law until the excitement had cooled off. There was no proof, but Tacho blamed Costa Rica's President José Figueres for sponsoring the attack and in reprisal he assisted two ousted Costa Rican Presidents to launch an invasion in January, 1955. It was a week-long, pocket-sized war which ended with the Costa Rican insurgents returning to Nicaragua thoroughly whipped. Tacho even challenged Figueres to a duel on the border before the trouble fizzled out.

By mid-1955 Tacho had the prospect of an election coming up on the horizon and was anxiously looking for some way to stay in power while preserving a democratic front. He found a way in April by amending the constitution, set the election date and accepted nomination for President.

Then disaster struck.

On 22nd September, 1956, a second attempt was made on his life. This time it was at a reception at León. An idealistic young student—a poet like Tacho—got close up to the President, pulled a revolver from the front of his shirt, and pumped four bullets into him. The General sank to the floor desperately hurt and the party-goers tore the assassin to pieces.

President Eisenhower sent his personal surgeon to Managua on the first available plane but President Anastasio Somoza died in the American hospital at Balboa, Canal Zone, eight days after he was shot.

Pending an election—a mere formality—Luis Somoza became Provisional President. His brother Tachito used the state of emergency declared to round up some 3,000 potential enemies and fling them into jail. Relatives in influential Government positions, and there were many of them, gathered around the brothers, preserved the dynasty and created the first hereditary dictatorship this century.

They managed to do what the sons of the Dominican Republic's dictator Rafael Trujillo tried unsuccessfully to do five years later when their father also fell to assassins' bullets.

The enormous wealth built up by their father was the Somozas' millstone. To preserve it they needed to hold absolute sway. And to hold sway they needed to be at the top of the power ladder. Nicaragua moved into a new régime, one far more ruthless and brutal than that of Tacho. Political executions became everyday affairs. Tachito's National Guard scoured the country for potential troublemakers and settled a number of personal grudges in the process.

Nicaraguans began to say that nobody was really anybody until they had seen the inside of the prison at La Avacion. Forty-five of the 132 members of Nicaragua's bar association have been in jail—including four of the seven-man governing body. Doctors have been tossed into cells, engineers have been taken from their homes and jailed, erring Army men have fled across the borders into Costa Rica and Honduras seeking asylum.

And in the meantime the brothers carried on adding to their father's fortune and empire.

President Luis Somoza, now a fleshy man of fourteen stone plus, already sporting a double chin and with the lustre gone from his troubled eyes, looks considerably older than his 41 years. He works a long day, often till midnight or later, keeping tabs on the family fortunes.

His brother Tachito, who holds nearly as much power as the President, is lithe, charming and iron-hard. He looks younger than his 37 years. But then his is not the constant worry of the family finances.

The brothers have a monopoly in the cattle export trade; own a match factory (therefore there is an embargo on cigarette lighters); and sell liquor at reduced rates from an illegal still. They control a sugar factory, coffee plantations, the Mercedes Benz Agency, ships, aircraft, a gold mine, and 279 *haciendas* in the Department of Managua—one of the smallest Departments. Their fortune in Nicaragua is estimated at 200 million Cordobas (£ 10 million) plus assets salted away overseas for a rainy day—or a hurried departure.

President Luis coyly admits that they own 200,000 acres of land. In fact they own 400,000 acres in one Department alone. He modestly says his personal fortune does not exceed £ 3½ million. Managua bankers, totting up assets in Nicaragua and overseas, put it at nearer £ 14 million, cash.

But since their father's death and Tachito's repressive measures which followed it, the Somoza brothers have lost a great deal of their former influence.

In 1959 the country was in a virtual state of siege for nearly the whole year. The most serious threat came when insurgents under the command of Dr. Lacayo Farfan, an eminent exiled gynaecologist-turned-rebel, crossed the border from Costa Rica and gave Tachito's National Guard a hard time before they were chased out. President Luis blamed everybody he could think of for the attack: Cuba's Fidel Castro for sponsoring it, Venezuela's Rómulo Betancourt for giving support, Costa Rica's former President José Figueres for supplying guns. He complained bitterly to the Organization of American States about the whole thing. Figueres, regarded as one of the ablest statesmen in Central America, denied having anything to do with the business and left it to Dr. Lacayo to do the rest.

"We have had nothing but moral support from the Venezuelan Government," Lacayo said in Costa Rica's capital immediately after being chased out of Nicaragua. "The Costa Rican Government is quite properly neutral. This is a Nicaraguan affair. The rebel movement represents every section of Nicaraguan opinion which is against dictatorship. Time is our ally. The current of history is running against dictators and the Nicaraguan people won't be left out."

Having chased out the rebels—Dr. Lacayo Farfan has since taken refuge in Mexico—President Luis Somoza went on record as saying: "Any other invasion will definitely be under Communist leadership." And he accused Castro of "a cold-blooded master plan" to help future rebels.

Castro and Figueres—the two men could not be farther apart, one a Moscow pawn, the other a democratic voice with few peers—were again blamed for a major revolt in 1960 which sent Tachito's National Guardsmen rushing to a college south of Managua where rebels were holed up after a skirmish with Government forces. Other rebels struck in the town of Jinotepe but the revolt was eventually crushed.

Between 1959 and 1961 there were twenty-three revolts in the country varying from quite serious uprisings to minor rebellions by peasants or groups of students.

How long the brothers Somoza can hold power in Nicaragua depends to a large extent on their remaining friends. It is possible that neither one could hold power without the other, but of the two Tachito would have a slightly better chance of doing so independently than Luis. He holds such complete power over the National Guard that he would be able to hold most of the country by force if necessary. But Tachito is not the brain of the family. Neither is he so steeped in the complex ramifications of the family estates as is Luis. Tachito holds the gun, Luis the purse strings.

But even more important to their power than their brotherly relations is the patronage of the United States. Now that the Dominican Republic's Trujillo has fallen there are only two dictatorships left in Caribbean America—in Nicaragua and in Haiti. Both of them are supported by the United States at the moment—Nicaragua by tradition and Haiti from fear that Communist Cuba, only a few miles across the water, might get a hold if America completely relaxes its grip.

But America could find herself in an embarrassing position if ever a really strong anti-dictator *bloc* were to assert itself in the Organization of American States.

President Luis, following in his father's footsteps, announced that he would hold elections for a new leader. He decreed that no member of the Somoza family might run for office; promised the first-ever secret ballot in Nicaragua; reduced the Presidential term from six to four years—and named the candidate for his Partido Liberal Nacional.

The man he chose was 53-year-old Dr. René Schick Gutierrez,

one-time personal secretary to Anastasio Somoza Snr., later Minister of Education and at the time of his nomination Foreign Minister.

Parties were permitted to organize and soon Dr. Fernando Aguero Rocha's Partido Conservador Tradicionalista emerged as the dominant Opposition group. Dr. Diego Manuel Chamorro also announced that he would contest the Presidency as the candidate of a break-away group from Aguero's party.

President Luis Somoza refused to permit the Organization of American States to supervise the elections and Dr. Aguero withdrew in disgust. Rioting broke out in Managua, three men and a child were killed and eight people wounded, and Dr. Aguero was placed under house arrest.

Polling day was 3rd February, 1963. And the following day, while admitting that the full results would not be known for ten days, Somoza candidate Schick announced his victory by a ten-to-one margin over Dr. Chamorro.

This self-effacing lawyer, diplomat and former university professor became President of Nicaragua on 1st May, 1963. A deeply religious man, he was concerned over the scathing tags of "Somoza puppet" with which the Opposition labelled him. He suggested—to no avail—that the Somozas should part up with between 20,000 and 40,000 acres of land to aid his new agrarian reform plans.

And he went on record as saying: "I would not sell my dignity for all the power in the world"—meaning he will not let the Somozas dominate him.

But Tachito has made no secret of his determination to be the next President of Nicaragua—this would be in 1967—and however well-intentioned Schick may be, the brothers will continue to pull the strings.

Luis will control from behind the scenes; and Tachito will head the National Guard. It is merely a front of democracy.

CHAPTER FOURTEEN

COSTA RICA

Francisco Orlich

The 62-year-old President of Costa Rica, Francisco José Orlich Bofmarcich, can proudly claim to be the only Central American President in power who has bombed his country's enemies.

It happened back in 1955 when Orlich, then Minister of Public Works under President José Figueres, was ordered into the field at a moment's notice to direct operations against rebels who had invaded the country from Nicaragua, the northern neighbour.

In Costa Rica Ministers of Government lead their troops to war in much the same way that Princes did in the Middle Ages in Europe. For there is no Army in the country, only a police force. But then, in democratic Costa Rica, wars are rare. And the 1948 civil war which cost some 2,000 lives—most of them Government supporters—and overthrew a pro-Communist dictatorship, is regarded as The War of National Liberation. The battles against Nicaragua, its many-medalled dictator Anastasio Somoza, and two ex-Presidents of Costa Rica, were mere skirmishes in the name of the protection of the Motherland.

Costa Rica, sandwiched between Nicaragua to the north and Panama to the south, is the pleasant, democratic and peaceful home of just over a million people. The country—it covers 19,653 square miles of mountains and coastal plains—produces some of the best coffee in the world and millions of bananas on the vast 250,000-acre United Fruit Company holdings on the Caribbean coast. San José, the 3,800-feet above sea level capital, has a population of 100,000 people who value their country's democracy above all else. Even its National Anthem is not martial—its name is "Long Live Work and Peace."

One of the reasons for the lack of strife in Costa Rica is that the country has the highest proportion of small landowners in Central America. And land is one thing that peasants will fight for in most of the Central and South American republics where agrarian reform is urgently needed. For in most of them a tiny per cent of the uppercrust population own the vast majority of the agricultural land.

Politically more mature than any of their neighbours and with a history of democracy behind them, the happy-go-lucky Costa Ricans were the only Central American people who were not under a dictatorship or a series of dictatorships during the turbulent 1930s. It was not until the late 1940s that the totalitarian-minded managed to get a foothold in the country.

Costa Rica has no Army; the small National Guard is used for ceremonial, rather than military, purposes—such soldiering as has to be done falls to the police and the coastal guard; there are ten times as many teachers as there are National Guardsmen; and three-quarters of the population are literate.

In the past the Presidency of Costa Rica was a family affair. Ricardo Jiménez Oreamuno held Presidential office three times— but never in succession. Both his father and his grandfather had been President. Dr. Rafael Angel Calderón Guardia, the President who plunged his country into civil war when he aided Communists to hold the Presidency by force, and later launched attacks from Nicaragua, was the grandson of a former President.

It is also an intensely personal business. For the President feels himself to be at the disposal of every one of the country's citizens and makes himself available for interviews at certain hours of the day.

Low paid by the political standards of their neighbours—in 1940 they got £648 a year, today it is £3,500—the Presidents of Costa Rica traditionally stood down in favour of duly-elected sucessors at the end of their four year terms of office. Prolonging a Presidential term by means of the accepted formulas common to most other Central and South American states was unthinkable in Costa Rica. Gentlemen just did not do that sort of thing. And as for graft . . . well Costa Rican Presidents never even gave it a passing thought. Two Presidents went bankrupt soon after leaving office, another fought a legal action over slanders about him when his incumbency was finished.

President Cleto Gonzalez Viquez was so short of money when he completed his Presidential term in 1932 that he had to sell his house. But when Congress, recognizing his services to the country, offered a pension, the ex-President was incensed. Instead Congress created a post for him and he became a historical research worker earning his beans and tortillas legitimately. Today Presidents get a one-third pension.

Professor León Cortés Castro, who was President from 1936 to 1940, was accused of taking a Government-owned lamp from La Casa Presidencial when he moved out. Enraged at this slur, he produced a bill for sale from the appropriate Ministry and the matter was closed. Soon afterwards he took a Government official to court after it had been alleged that the President accepted some chickens as a bribe while in office. The official was fined £2 for slander. But the question of a pig he was also alleged to have received was not gone into, the President explaining that the agricultural school who gave it to him were as much at fault as he.

In May, 1940, Belgian-educated physician Dr. Rafael Ángel Calderón Guardia became President of Costa Rica and a new phase in the country's politics began. Supported by the Catholic Party, Calderón Guardia had a promising start in the office his grandfather had also held. He made many changes in the country, the most notable being an extremely progressive labour law.

But sinister parties were working behind the President's back. Costa Ricans had never persecuted Communists, believing that political beliefs should be allowed to flourish. And since 1925 it was the only country which had an organized Communist Party. It was to Costa Rica that the young student Rómulo Betancourt fled from the harsh Gómez régime in his native Venezuela. And it was in Costa Rica that Betancourt, now the fiercely anti-Communist President of Venezuela, had his first taste of Communist doctrines which he accepted and later shrugged off.

Calderón Guardia's term of office expired in 1944. An election was held and his friend Teodoro Picado became President. Half-Polish Picado was a Communist through and through and he rapidly went about making sure that he or his nominee could hold on to the Presidency when his term was up. He packed Congress with timid yes-men, disregarded the advice of experienced Ministers, and tried to hold all the reins of Government himself.

The resulting financial chaos plunged Costa Rica into dire

money troubles. The inept dabblings of Picado brought the whole economy to the brink of ruin and by the time the 1948 election came along the Costa Ricans were thoroughly sick of him and looked forward to a new President who would unravel the mess left by Picado.

But such was not to be the case.

Costa Ricans went out to vote in February, 1948, decided that newspaper publisher Dr. Otilio Ulate of the Oposición Nacional was a better bet than ex-President Calderón Guardia who was also running, and accordingly voted for him. But between the voting and the inauguration things were to happen, and it was not until a civil war, a dictatorship, and two invasions later that, in November, 1949, he was able to move into La Casa Presidencial.

Immediately after the election which Calderón Guardia had lost, President Picado went before his yes-men Congress, told them what he wanted them to do and obligingly, on 1st March, the election result was nullified and Picado "requested" to remain President.

President Picado and ex-President Calderón Guardia got busy. In the absence of a regular Army the police and coastal guards doubled up as the military and Picado sent two coastal guards to arrest Dr. Ulate. In a shooting incident they were both killed. Picado had just the excuse he needed and on 2nd March, he had Ulate arrested and imprisoned on a charge of complicity in the double killing.

But at this juncture a remarkable thing happened: a once-exiled farmer-turned-politician went into the mountains, recruited a fifteen-man "army", handed out the six rifles he had and declared war in the name of democracy.

This unexpected Liberator was José Figueres Ferrer, one of the most remarkable men in Central America, and he was to lead his country out of Communist-dominated dictatorship and back along the well-trodden road of Costa Rican democracy.

The same year that Cleto Gonzalez Viquez—he who spurned the pension—became President of Costa Rica, slim, dark-haired José Figueres returned to the country from studying engineering in the United States. The son of a Catholic, Spanish immigrant doctor, young José—"Pepe" to his friends—decided not to practise in the capital but to go instead to the mountains and put his knowledge to practical use.

He went into the hills, ripped a vast plantation from the virgin land and christened it *La Lucha Sin Fin*—The Endless Struggle. He became immensely wealthy, treated his workers better than most other plantation owners, and built a loyal group of peasants around *La Lucha Sin Fin*. In 1941 he married Alabama-born Henrietta Boggs but the marriage was dissolved.

A great believer in democratic rule, "Pepe" Figueres had made a broadcast in 1942 in which he had called upon President Calderón Guardia to resign. But he never finished the broadcast. For in mid-sentence, listeners heard shouts, bangs and the sounds of a struggle. And moments later a voice announced that the broadcast had been stopped by order of the chief of police. Figueres was jailed and then exiled, but President Picado allowed him to return and he became head of the Social Democratic Party.

"Pepe" Figueres had been watching the Picado administration for some time. The events immediately following the February elections had confirmed his worst fears. And when Congress nullified Dr. Ulate's Presidency he knew that something had to be done.

The same day he launched the Liberación Nacional Party, began recruiting fighters and declared war on the Government. Six men walked into San Isidro del General airport and stole three civil aircraft belonging to the civil airline TACA. Later they stole three more. These, six smooth-bore rifles, and a selection of sporting shotguns were the nucleus of his military arms.

"I had previously done a little shooting as a hobby, but never had any military training," he says today. "The tragic thing was that after close on a hundred years of peace we should have found it impossible to make any changes by peaceful means. We were forced to take up arms. We had for some time had a well-organized underground movement and everything was thought out and planned in detail."

Figueres's rebels soon occupied Cartago and several isolated towns, and then the Caribbean seaport of Puerto Limón. "Don Pepe" never had more than 600 untrained men against the well-armed 2,000 police, National Guards and coastal guards, but they fought like true patriots. The bloodiest fighting came midway through the six-weeks-long War of Liberation when the rebels fought the Government at San Isidro del General. Nearly two hundred men were killed. Not many perhaps. But it was a pocket-sized war. And for Costa Rica the death-in-war of two hundred men was a major tragedy. Messages from the front in most rebel-Government clashes did not report the number dead in day-long battles: instead, the losses were reported by name.

It took "Don Pepe" just six weeks to show the Government that they were messing with a dangerous man. Then with 1,900 dead on the Government side and fifty-six on the rebel side, Calderón Guardia and Picado threw in the towel.

On 20th April, 1948, they surrendered to José Figueres who gave them time to get out of the country. A plane flew the arch-collaborators to Managua, capital of neighbouring Nicaragua, where they were gladly received by business-associate Anastasio Somoza.

Santos León Herrera became President and held office until 8th May, when he turned over the Government to "Pepe" Figueres and a military-civilian Founding Junta of the Second Republic. Figueres became Minister of Justice and Foreign Affairs. The Communist Party was outlawed.

"The uprising in 1948 was a true popular rising and only thanks to that were we able to win," he says.

He disbanded his own rebel army—as a "gesture of peace"—turned the barracks into a Museum of Fine Arts and settled down to run the country. On 8th December, 1948, elections were held and Dr. Ulate's party won thirty-three of the forty-five seats in Congress.

But two days later came more trouble and Figueres remained at the head of the Government, this time as Provisional President.

On 12th December, 1948, the President of the United Nations Security Council in New York was handed a telegram which read: "On Friday, Dec. 10, at 23.15 hours, the territory of Costa Rica was invaded by armed forces coming from Nicaragua."

Within a few days the invaders, mostly Nicaraguans but led by exiled Costa Ricans, had penetrated sixty miles into Costa Rican territory. Figueres received reports that ex-President Calderón Guardia was waiting on the border to fly to San José when his troops were in command. The thousand-strong Costa Rican police force and the 700 men of the coastal guard went into action.

After some stiff fighting in the mountains the rebels were beaten and hastily withdrew to Nicaragua. The revolt was over. But it was not to be the last time that Nicaraguans invaded Costa Rica.

And a personal enmity grew up between José Figueres and Anastasio Somoza.

Figueres's policy was public ownership and he announced an intention to do some nationalizing. He also favoured the workers which made him less than popular with many of the large and wealthy landowners who had hoped that he would repeal Calderón Guardia's progressive labour laws.

Says Figueres: "Philosophically I am a hell of a Socialist. I believe in the prosperity of the masses. We have an appallingly large number of poor people here. Free enterprise has done more harm than good in Costa Rica, dividing the people into a few rich and many poor. I want increased prosperity for the poor."

This policy was unpopular with the staunch old-time landed class and they worked on the National Guard. In April, 1949, President Figueres had to crush Colonel Edgar Cardona, Minister of Public Security, who headed a small rebellion aimed at ousting him.

"Our plantation owners hoped that I would repeal the Communist workers' code," he said. "The gentlemen have become used to leading a soft life at the expense of their workers—moreover, with the irrational methods used by their fathers. I'm a landowner myself and I have done more for the workers on my property than the law compels me to do and it still pays because I take the trouble. Others have got to do the same."

But "Pepe" Figueres had not got himself into power merely to hold on to the reins of Government. He had announced that he would step down in favour of the constitutionally elected President when Costa Rica was back to normal and on 8th November, 1949, he kept his promise. Under a new constitution, prepared by Figueres, Dr. Otilio Ulate became President of Costa Rica.

But Conservative Ulate was soon in trouble. He was impeached and then acquitted by the Congress, Dr. Alberto Oreamuno Flores acting as President during Ulate's suspension.

At the election "Pepe" Figueres ran for office and won hands down. He became President in June, 1953, appointing as his Minister of Public Works a good friend and well-to-do farmer named Francisco Orlich, Costa Rica-born son of Yugoslavian immigrant parents. Ultimately Figueres would back him for the Presidency.

The nationalization of banks and the 10 per cent property tax he imposed let Costa Ricans know that President Figueres was not just talking when he said he was "a hell of a Socialist". He prepared to do battle with the powerful United Fruit Company who already paid 15 per cent of their profits to the Government—an amount equal to half the national budget which brought home forcibly to Figueres the realization of what tremendous tax dodgers the majority of his own wealthy countrymen were. He also became interested in Moral Rearmament. In February, 1954, he took time off from his Presidential duties to marry blonde Karel Olsen, American-born daughter of Danish parents.

But he had not had the last word with Anastasio Somoza. Far from it. For in April, 1954, Somoza's car was shot at near Nicaragua's capital. The dictator escaped injury but he immediately accused Figueres—who may indeed have given it his blessing —of engineering the assassination bid. In revenge he planned a better-organized attack on Costa Rica and gave ex-Presidents Picado and Calderón Guardia the green light for more activity.

On 11th January, 1955, the attack was launched and Nicaraguan troops led by West Point graduate Teodoro Picado, Jnr., crossed the border and seized the Costa Rican town of Villa Quesada, some fifty miles deep into Costa Rican territory and about the same distance from the capital, San José. Figueres rapidly complained to the Organization of American States and an immediate investigation was made. The 1947 treaty provided for a mutual defence agreement providing that a minimum of eleven of the twenty-one OAS members agreed on the course of action.

A Costa Rican spotter plane reported that some seventy men with bulldozers and tractors appeared to be constructing an airstrip for reinforcements. Figueres guessed that they had reached Villa Quesada by boat. He mobilized his own fighting men at once.

Francisco Orlich, Minister of Public Works, flew to the front in a commandeered civil aircraft, bombed the rebels and flew back to report. Within hours he was in the air again with a second load of bombs. Rebels soon held ten Costa Rican towns and a small aircraft strafed Figueres's home before it was shot down and crashed into a river. The war was hotting up.

Figueres went on the radio and announced to his people that the Nicaraguans were busy in the revolt. This drew an immediate denial from Somoza but the dictator could not contain himself when he heard Figueres's voice coming over the air a few nights

later attacking Somoza and branding him as the head "of a family
of gangsters".

He challenged Figueres to a personal duel on the border.

"If Figueres has so much personal hate for me, let us put it on
a man-to-man basis," he said. "There is no reason for bloodshed
between our countries. Nobody has ever called me what that man
called me. The least he said was that I had a family of gangsters.
But I will not reply to Figueres. Why should I? I will not go that
low."

The war assumed a momentary comic-opera touch when Señora
Figueres, asked by newsmen if her husband would fight the duel,
replied: "My husband does not shoot that low."

But while Francisco Orlich was leading air raids from ancient
Dakotas with machine-guns poking out of the side doors, and
the rebels were being supported with fighters from Nicaragua,
the O A S was busy. They decided that there was aggression and
support must be given. The war was just over a week old when
four American Mustang fighters were delivered to Figueres who
signed on the dotted line and bought himself an air force for "a
nominal sum".

The war was as good as won. Rebel-held villages were recap-
tured by the Costa Ricans. Prisoners were taken to San José. The
invaders fled back across the border. Heroes of the war Figueres
and Orlich returned to the capital in triumph.

President Figueres finished his term of office without further
fighting—despite an attempt by that other arch-dictator Rafael
Trujillo of the Dominican Republic who sent two would-be
assassins to kill him. Unfortunately for them and for Trujillo,
Figueres's police captured the gunmen on the streets of San José
before they had a chance to kill. He was more fortunate than
Guatemala's President Castillo Armas who would fall to a bullet
in another Trujillo-inspired assassination bid in 1957, and Venezuela's President Betancourt who would emerge badly scarred
from a bomb attempt of Trujillo's killers in 1960.

Elections came and went. Mario Echandi Jiménez, who had
been a Minister under Ulate, became President of Costa Rica. The
people would have been pleased to have Figueres remain in office.
But the constitution which he himself had written forbids the
re-election of a President until two full terms of office have
elapsed.

In 1962 Echandi stepped down from office and Costa Ricans went out to vote again.

The Liberación Nacional Party—Figueres's party—put up war hero Francisco Orlich, the bombing Minister of Public Works. And politics in Costa Rica being what they are—gentlemanly— two former Presidents ran for office. One of them was Dr. Otilio Ulate who had been in the thick of the 1948 troubles and had been impeached after having held the Presidency for less than three years. The other, more surprisingly, was Dr. Rafael Ángel Calderón Guardia, pro-Communist, pro-Somoza, and instigator of two invasions of his native land. But then that is politics in Costa Rica.

The people went out to vote on 6th February, 1962. When the returns came in Francisco Orlich had more than 50 per cent of the votes and forty of the fifty-seven seats in Congress. Calderón Guardia got nine seats and Otilio Ulate eight seats.

During the campaign President Francisco Orlich was called "Figueres's tool". Certainly he has had the backing of his friend and every possible bit of help the ex-President can give him. And almost certainly he will carry on the work that Figueres started in 1953. Equally, it is more than probable that Figueres will be the next President of Costa Rica. For the two full terms of office clause will enable him to run in the 1966 election.

But it is equally certain that Francisco J. Orlich will make his own mark on the Presidency. Like Figueres he believes that the days of vast foreign-owned enterprises on another country's soil are gone. The United Fruit Company may well be shuffling their well-shod feet in nervous anticipation.

CHAPTER FIFTEEN

PANAMA

Dr. Roberto Chiari

In its sixty years as an independent country Panama has had forty-six Presidents. But despite the fact that the constitutional term of office is four years only two Presidents have been able to see it out. The average length of a President's tenure of office has been only fifteen months.

The current President, 58-year-old millionaire business tycoon Roberto Chiari, is now in his second term of office. His first term, in 1949, lasted exactly four days. And in those four days Panama had three Presidents—a record even for the politically-stormy, strategically-vital, republic at the point where Central and South America are joined.

Panama is a paradox. For the long, narrow republic—covering 31,890 square miles and the home of just over a million people— is both extremely rich and extremely poor. Divided in two by the American-controlled Panama Canal, lifeline of the world's shipping, Panama produces coffee and bananas on its immensely fertile soil, yet only about half of the country is cultivated. A small minority of the people live in comparative luxury in Panama City, the majority in destitute conditions throughout the country. And only a matter of an hour's flying time from the capital primitive Indians live in virtually impenetrable jungles covering one quarter of the country, hunting with bows and arrows, and living much as their forefathers were living when the Spanish conquistadores first came to the Isthmus.

Turbulent Panama owes its existence—in every sense of the word—to America. For without America the country would be poor. And without America there never would have been a

Panama. The Canal brings money to the Government and to the people. For America maintains a large staff to run the 648-square-mile Canal Zone. And it was America who—in President Theodore Roosevelt's imperialistic tenure in the White House—brought the country into being, fomenting a revolt and helping the people to break away from Colombia, of which what became Panama was the ninth Department.

That was back in 1903. A French company under the formidable Ferdinand de Lesseps of Suez Canal fame had an agreement with Colombia to build a canal across the Isthmus. But after years of trying at a cost of thousands of lives in the malaria-ridden jungles, the French sold out to American financiers and the birth of a nation began. At first America tried to buy the Canal site for £2 million and a yearly rental but the Colombians thought it was worth more. The Americans refused to pay and began looking for another way to gain control of the region.

Philipe Buneau-Varilla, agent for French and American capitalists interested in the Canal project, hurried to the United States seeking financial backing for a revolution. He called on President Roosevelt, was given a tacit go-ahead, and returned to Panama to lay his plans.

Curiously, the revolt was reported in Washington before it took place in Panama. On 3rd November, 1903, only hours after the U.S. warship *Nashville* arrived off Panama, the American State Department cabled their Consul: "Uprising on Isthmus reported. Keep department promptly and fully informed." The Consul cabled back: "No uprising yet. Reported will be in night. Situation critical." A few hours later he cabled: "Uprising occurred tonight, 6, no bloodshed. Army and Navy officers taken prisoners. Government will be organized tonight."

American troops were landed, Buneau-Varilla and the revolutionaries declared independence the same day. Washington recognized the new country within three days. It was all a very smooth operation. A treaty was negotiated between the Panamanians and the United States for the building of the Canal and President Roosevelt remarked smugly to Congress: "I took the Canal Zone."

The £8 million America paid out in compensation to the French canal company went largely to American financiers who had bought up the company's shares for a song. Colombia demanded that they too should receive compensation but their demand was rejected out of hand. It was not until some twenty years later, when American businessmen wanted a share in the newly-found oil in Colombia, that the U.S. Congress reversed their decision and rushed a belated £5 million in compensation for the loss of the Canal. Such are the ramifications of international skulduggery.

The Panama-U.S. Canal Treaty—signed on 18th November, 1903—gave the new republic £3,570,000 for the Canal Zone— a site ten miles wide and covering 648 square miles, cut through by the Canal, completely bisecting the country. It gave America the Zone and all the "powers, rights and authority to the exclusion of the exercise by the Republic of Panama of any such sovereign rights, power or authority". And it gave to them "in perpetuity", for an annual rental of £90,000 which has gradually been pushed up by a succession of statesmanlike moves by Panamanian Presidents until today it stands at £690,000. And it caused in Panama a bone of contention which rankles to this day. For no nation likes to know that another holds part of its land "in perpetuity"—and makes nearly £2 million a year clear profit in doing so.

The Canal was completed in 1914 after thousands of Chinese, West Indian Negro and Spanish immigrants, working millions of man hours had ripped a passageway across the Isthmus. By the time they had finished the fifty-one-mile-long canal more than 400 million cubic yards of earth had been moved—enough to make 119 Egyptian pyramids or fill a hole 16.2 feet square right through the Earth.

But while the Canal Zone was quietly ruled by the Americans— a Major-General is Governor of the Canal Zone and President of the Panama Canal Company—in much the way any colony or virtual-colony is ruled, the political history of the split-in-two republic was far from happy.

Despite the fact that the President is supposed to fill a four year term of office only two have managed to do so. There have been three constitutions since 1903. On thirty occasions Panamanians have gone out to vote for a President. And forty-six Presidents have taken the oath. Only President Belisario Porras (1912-16) and President Ernesto de la Guardia (1956-60) have managed to complete their terms of office. The forty-three other Presidents have averaged out terms of only fifteen months. But, surprisingly, only one has been assassinated.

The Presidency in Panama is a family concern—as it was in the not-too-distant past in neighbouring Costa Rica whose border lies to the north of Panama. Largely it is a power-struggle between the wealthy aristocratic families and some of them have had several generations of Presidents.

In recent years it has been the Arias family who have dominated the Presidential scene. Its members have revolted, invaded, plotted, schemed—and rarely been elected—in their frantic efforts to claw their way to the top of the political heap.

President Florencio Harmodio Arosemena was overthrown on 2nd January, 1931, by Harmodio Arias, brother of another President-to-be, father of an unsuccessful invader, and father-in-law of world-famous ballerina Dame Margot Fonteyn who was flung into jail when her diplomat husband tried to overthrow another President.

In 1940 Dr. Arnulfo Arias, a Harvard Medical School graduate with a shrill voice, impeccable tailoring and fluttering eyelashes, became President and unleashed a reign of Fascism on troubled Panama. Arias, violently pro-Hitler, was a strong believer in white supremacy. His constitution raised the term of the Presidency from four to six years and opened the way for racial warfare. Thousands of Chinese, the descendants of the original Canal builders, were dispossessed and left the country after Arias nationalized their shops and forced them to sell out their thriving businesses—usually to his friends—at rock-bottom prices. He considered the many thousands of Negroes, descendants of the British West Indians—mostly Jamaicans—who had helped build the Canal, to be "a cultural blot". Rapidly depriving them and their locally-born children of their Panamanian nationality, he made them stateless persons. A sizable number of Hindus, along with the West Indians, were deprived of their jobs under a law which forbade either race to be employed in any capacity other than that of domestic servants.

But Arnulfo Arias was not the first to bring racial feeling to Panama. He had been beaten to the post by many years by the Americans who offered cut price racial discrimination in the Canal Zone.

In the early days the American Canal Zone workers were paid in gold. The immigrant workers and the Panamanians were paid in silver. And from this financial difference, based on the comparison of wages, has grown a rigid caste system of "Gold Men"

GEORGE PRICE
First Minister of British Honduras

GENERAL MIGUEL YDÍGORAS
President of Guatemala

DR. JOSÉ RAMÓN VILLEDA
President of Honduras

COLONEL LUIS SOMOZA
Strong-man of Nicaragua

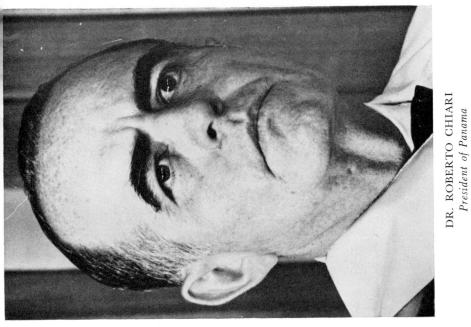

DR. ROBERTO CHIARI
President of Panama

FRANCISCO ORLICH
President of Costa Rica

DR. GUILLERMO LEÓN VALENCIA
President of Colombia

RÓMULO BETANCOURT
President of Venezuela

DR CHEDDI JAGAN
Premier of British Guiana

and "Silver Men". Today all wages are paid in U.S. dollars, but
the caste system and the phrase from which it was born are almost
as binding as they were in the past. Post offices have "gold"
windows and "silver" windows—meaning Americans and non-
Americans, often meaning black and white, and sometimes creating ridiculous situations when American Negro workers find
themselves barred from the American window.

The highly paid jobs in the Canal Zone still go to the 3,000
Americans who are the key-men in the Zone. The 8,000 Panamanians and others who do lesser jobs draw vastly lower pay—
about a quarter of the pay of U.S. employees. Americans average
out at £2,500-a-year, plus 25 per cent overseas allowance, and
are able to shop in the Canal Zone shops at low prices. The
Panamanian employees get around £650-a-year and are not free
to make use of Zone facilities.

This, along with the American "in perpetuity" clause and the
annual rental of the Zone, has caused countless hours of sometimes acrimonious wranglings between a series of Panamanian
Presidents and a series of U.S. Presidents. For the Panamanians
want a parity in wages, more Zone jobs—particularly responsible
ones—for locals and more money for the Canal.

But racemongering Arnulfo Arias, though he did untold harm
to the ethnic groups in Panama in a remarkably short time, was
not long in office. For in September, 1941, while the Americans
fumed at the pro-Hitler viper in the bosom, a bloodless revolt
was being planned. Given the old heave-ho, Arias fled, first to
Colombia and then to Cuba, Mexico and points north. The new
President Ricardo Adolfo de la Guardia's first move was to revoke
completely the Arias constitution.

Panama elected fifty-three Representatives to its National
Assembly, including a President and two Vice-Presidents. And on
15th July, 1945, they installed President Enrique A. Jiménez in
the country's highest office. He sponsored a new constitution and
was followed in the office by President Domingo Díaz Arosemena.

But Panama has never been noted for its political stability and
forces were on the move against the new President. The election,
held in 1948, had been hotly contested and Arnulfo Arias, returned from his wanderings, had run for office. He had been
defeated but had claimed that fraud and behind-the-scenes wranglings had deprived him of the Presidency.

G

In Panama a large number of illegal activities at election times are loosely classified as "fraudulent". It is a word which covers a multitude of sins. It is "fraudulent" to drive voters to the polls with a pistol at their heads. It is "fraudulent" to steal ballot boxes and burn their contents. It is "fraudulent" to intimidate counting officials and to inscribe in electoral registers the names of dead or imaginary voters. It is also "fraudulent" to sell your vote—but it is done, and on a grand scale.

President Domingo Díaz Arosemena's two Vice-Presidents—Daniel Chanis and Roberto Chiari—were both to be President for a short while in 1949 and Chiari is President today.

Dapper, greying Roberto Francisco Chiari—"Nino" to his friends—is the millionaire owner of Panama's biggest sugar factory. Born in 1905, he now controls a vast dairy herd, a sugar empire and a newspaper, *La Nación*. A soft-spoken man, he is a master of the tactful diplomatic discussion and a skilful negotiator. His father, Rudolfo Chiari, was President in 1924.

President Díaz Arosemena died, of natural causes, on 23rd August, 1949, and Vice-President Daniel Chanis stepped into his place. Roberto Chiari became first Vice-President. But the sinister hand of Arnulfo Arias was working behind the scenes.

The powerful and ruthless chief of police José "Chichi" Rémon was his friend—incidentally he was also Roberto Chiari's cousin. And these two men, representing as they did both wealth and power, were determined to install Arnulfo Arias in the Presidential chair. The first steps in their campaign came less than three months after Chanis became President. They also bore fruit faster than either Rémon or Arias could have hoped.

On 20th November, 1949, police chief Rémon and two high-ranking officials defied an order made by Chanis and surprised themselves when he resigned. Roberto Chiari became President, was sworn in by the Supreme Court, and planned to move into the Presidential Palace. But four days later the same Supreme Court ruled that Daniel Chanis was still President.

Hours later police chief Rémon announced that Arnulfo Arias was President and that Chanis would be deposed.

Edinburgh-educated Chanis replied stoutly: "I shall remain President until I am killed"—a bold assertion which could have been asking for trouble.

But the following day—25th November—the Electoral Grand

Jury surprisingly ruled that Arnulfo Arias had been right all along when he said that the 1948 elections had been "fixed" and proclaimed him President of the Republic.

Police chief Rémon was on hand to see that everything went off smoothly in the change of office. He was also on hand to see that police chief Rémon did not do badly out of the deal either. Subsequently he worked up a nice monopoly in meat packing. Three ex-Presidents—Ricardo Adolfo de la Guardia, Enrique Jiménez and Daniel Chanis—fled to the Canal Zone for protection and Panama waited to see what Arnulfo Arias, his sartorially-elegant bottom now firmly in the Presidential chair, was going to do.

He soon made it abundantly clear. The 1940 constitution was immediately brought back and in the two years he managed to hold on to the Presidency racial conflict was again the order of the Panamanian day. He appointed four of his relatives—and he has legions of them—to high positions in the Cabinet. Big business suffered at his hands. So did the country's newspapers. An old-established firm of private bankers closed their doors and fled rather than let the President get control of it. The highly-respected newspaper *El Pais* attacked him in their editorial columns and he closed them down. Workers who struck in protest were machine-gunned and beaten by police chief Rémon's efficient officers. When six ex-Presidents—including the three who had fled to the Canal Zone and then re-emerged to fight Arias—went into action against him, Arias had them flung into jail. Ricardo Adolfo de la Guardia—who had ousted Arias back in 1941—was severely beaten for this sin of nine years standing.

But by 1951 the Panamanians had had enough. A series of strikes and minor riots convinced chief of police "Chichi" Rémon that this time the people meant business. Deciding that he did not want to be on the receiving end of whatever they handed out he rapidly changed sides and became violently anti-Arias. When the lid finally blew off and the people revolted, Rémon sent troops to arrest the President who had barricaded himself in the Palace with some supporters.

Major Lescano Gómez and Lieutenant Juan Flóres went after him and succeeded in breaking in the door of his study. But as they rushed in a fusillade of bullets literally shot them to pieces and when other troops reached the room they found it a shambles.

Blood and broken furniture was everywhere. Arnulfo Arias—popularly supposed to have personally killed at least one of the officers—was arrested, jailed and later tried by the National Assembly and deprived of his rights.

The President of the Court, Alcibiades Arosemena, was made President of the republic on 10th May, 1951.

Exactly a year later police chief Rémon who had done very well for himself out of the overthrow of his former friend, became President in an election. His National Patriotic Coalition won resoundingly over other candidates. President-for-four-days Roberto "Nino" Chiari ran against Rémon at the head of a five-party coalition called the Civil Alliance but he lost. Arnulfo Arias stood for election but withdrew his Panamista Party at the last moment.

To everyone's surprise President Rémon's régime got off to a promising start. He quickly strangled earlier bribery and corruption in high places and managed to balance the country's budget after several years which had left the finances in a very shaky state.

And he took himself to Washington to dicker with the Americans over the old bogey of the Canal Zone. "We do not want charity," he told them. "We want justice."

These were the good sides of his régime. The obverse of the coin came out when the high-living ex-colonel was found to have added some £3 million to his own personal and not inconsiderable fortune.

On 2nd January, 1955, President Rémon and a party of wealthy friends went to the racecourse. After watching a race, which one of his horses won, they retired to the well-lit, but shadow-surrounded bar to celebrate. Suddenly, from the murky fringe came a sustained burst of machine-gun fire. President Rémon half rose from his chair and then collapsed. He died in hospital a few hours later.

Vice-President José Ramón Guizado became President, arrested Arnulfo Arias for complicity in the assassination, and sat back. Twelve days later he was himself arrested for complicity after lawyer Rubin Miró made a confession that he was the trigger-man but added that Guizado had known about the plan for some months. Both men were tried and jailed.

Again the Vice-President took a step up. This time it was an

Arias, Ricardo Arias Espinosa—no relation to Harmodio, Arnulfo and all the other President-prone Ariases. He held office until the election in 1956 which put Ernesto de la Guardia—he is related to ex-President Ricardo Adolfo de la Guardia—into the Presidential office.

His incumbency was notable for two things: he managed to do what no other Panamanian President since 1916 had been able to do—complete his term of office; and he successfully put down an armed invasion by Roberto Arias, son of Harmodio Arias, nephew of Arnulfo Arias, and husband of ballerina Margot Fonteyn who stole most of the headlines and was jailed for her part in the revolt.

In April, 1959, a small ship with eighty-five armed men aboard slid ashore and the Roberto Arias revolt had begun. After only a few days it ended with Roberto seeking what was to become a sixty-two-day asylum in the Brazilian embassy and Dame Margot sitting in one of President de la Guardia's jails.

Elections came again on 8th May, 1960. Roberto Chiari, the four-day President of 1949, and leader of the Conservative opposition under President de la Guardia's outgoing régime, ran for office. So did Ricardo Arias Espinosa who had preceded President de la Guardia and who was backed by him in the election.

Several days after the election, when most of the outlying area votes were in, both candidates claimed victory. Chiari's paper *La Nación* screamed from its headlines: "Chiari Elected—Hydra-Headed Monster Crushed", and it published a set of figures supporting the statement. Meanwhile, *Hoy*, owned by Ricardo Arias, shouted: "And now To Work", going on to outline Arias's policy. It also published figures, very different from those of *La Nación*. It was some days before the final results were published and Chiari's victory finally and irrefutably established.

But between the election of 8th May, and Chiari's inauguration on 1st October, things were to happen. Feeling had been running high against the United States during the election campaign over the Canal Zone and their "in perpetuity" clause. Irate mobs stormed the Zone and the Panamanian flag was run up while people yelled for sovereignty and the withdrawal of the Americans.

In September President Eisenhower decreed that the Panamanian flag might fly in one place beside the American flag as "visual evidence of Panamanian titular sovereignty". But this was not enough for the Panamanians, their nationalist feelings thoroughly aroused.

Roberto Chiari took office on 1st October, and on 25th November he went on record as saying: "The people of Panama want more economic benefit from the Canal. Furthermore we want more Panamanians in top jobs in the Canal Zone."

A year later he made an impassioned plea in his annual State of the Nation address to the National Assembly demanding Panamanian sovereignty over the Canal Zone. At the same time he wrote to President Kennedy asking for sovereignty, an end to the "in perpetuity" clause and the substitution in its place of a lease clause.

He followed this up in June, 1962, with a visit to Kennedy on which he got off on the right foot by telling the American President: "I believe that frankness is the only way two friendly nations can attempt to solve their problems."

He asked for more employment and higher wages for Panamanians in the Canal Zone; for a U.S.-enforced system to withhold income taxes from Panamanian employees and then turn it over to the Government; for the right to fly the Panamanian flag next to the United States flag everywhere in the Zone; and for a larger rental. Backing the last demand he claimed that the charges for ships using the Canal are out of line with present shipping conditions. He asked that the tolls be raised and that Panama be given 20 per cent of the revenues.

While Kennedy was thinking it over, President Chiari turned his attention to the problems of Latin America, in particular the threat of Castro's Cuba.

He told the Council of the Organization of American States: "We are seeing, not without disturbing thoughts, the basic principles of non-intervention and self-determination of peoples drifting towards a new 'eyes shut and hands off' formula, which were not exactly their original meanings."

Then he went back to see Kennedy.

Some of the .Panamanian requests were met. The question of more money for the Canal was not. Kennedy pointed out that the presence of a large American contingent in Panama made a great difference to the national economy. Some 40,000 United States citizens live in the republic. For Panama is the head of the United

States Caribbean Defense Force and the Americans—including wives and families—living within the boundaries of the republic spend some £24 million a year. The country's national budget is only £21,428,000—of which £7,970,000 comes from exports, and the rest from the Canal. Americans spend the £2 million annual profit of the Canal on upkeep and maintenance.

President Chiari was sent on his way with Kennedy's promise that when the Canal reaches its capacity—sometime between 1980 and 2000—a new canal will be built, probably in Panama.

So the Canal Zone continues to be a bone of contention with the Panamanians. And it will remain so unless the American Government changes its policy regarding it.

For, as President Chiari has said: "Panama will always insist it has sovereignty over all our territory, and this is something we will never surrender."

CHAPTER SIXTEEN

COLOMBIA

Dr. Guillermo León Valencia

The Liberal member was speaking from the floor of the chamber. His deep voice intoned the crimes of the Conservatives, itemizing them in lengthy, emotion-packed accusations.

Suddenly from the Conservative benches came a burst of gunfire. Several members leapt to their feet, pulled guns and began pumping bullets across the floor of the chamber into the packed Liberal ranks.

Gustavo Jiménez, who had had the floor, fell with a bullet in his heart. Jorge Soto del Corral, up-and-coming Liberal member, was badly wounded. Other Liberals were wounded as more than a hundred shots echoed through the chamber.

The newspapers ran a screaming headline: "Liberals shot by Conservatives"; pro-Conservative students paraded through the streets carrying Falangist banners; Liberals went into hiding.

The place: Bogotá, capital of Colombia. The date: 8th September, 1949. The setting: A year after the start of a bloody, senseless, vicious, dictator-inspired civil war which cost something like a million lives—one fourteenth of the population of the country.

Today the majority of Conservatives and the majority of Liberals are united into one party and democracy has been restored in Colombia, the spot on the map where Central and South America are joined.

A fiery orator and crack pistol shot, Guillermo León Valencia, sits in the Presidential chair and there is peace in the country after two dictatorships and killing on a grand scale which—because of Press censorship—was one of the least-reported slaughters since the Second World War.

For decades Colombia considered itself the most democratic of the South American republics. The people prided themselves on being three things: Devout—the Roman Catholic Church is the most powerful in Latin America, education is Church-controlled to an extent unknown outside Spain, and Bogotá is called the "Citadel of God"; Cultured—Bogotá, also called "The Athens of South America", is a city of bookshops with a population of poets; Democratic—the Conservative-Liberal wars of the last century were forgotten until the dictators gripped the country in the late 1940s.

The country, 460,000 square miles of mountains, valleys and plains, supports some 14,000,000 people of mixed Spanish, Indian and European immigrant stock. It produces the best coffee in the world and is largely dependent on the price fluctuations of the one crop. Cattle are raised by the Indians. Foreign adventurers tear vast fortunes in emeralds and other precious stones out of the mountainsides. The only South American country to have both a Caribbean and a Pacific coastline, Colombia is the fourth largest republic in South America.

It is bounded to the north by the Caribbean Sea; the east by oil-rich Venezuela; the north-west by Panama—once part of Colombia—with its strategically vital Canal; the west by the Pacific Ocean; the south-west by Ecuador; the south by Peru; and the south-east by Brazil. It is divided into sixteen departments all administered centrally from the capital Bogotá which is poised on a plateau 9,000 feet up in the western slopes of the Andes, the farthest from the sea of all the South American capitals.

The political wars between the Conservatives and the Liberals in the nineteenth century were also holy wars. For the Conservatives were violently pro-Church; the Liberals violently anti-Church. Some seventy wars, large and small, were fought in the name of God. In one 80,000 Colombians died. In another the death roll was 100,000. But by the end of the century the religious fighting had died out. The Liberals had ceased to be violently anti-cleric. And the Conservatives were in power. They held office continuously from 1886 until 1930. By tradition, it was said, the Archbishop nominated the next President and the politicians fell into line.

And then, in 1930, the Archbishop made some untimely, off-the-cuff remarks on the eve of an election, the Conservative ranks were split, Dr. Enrique Olaya Herrera became the first Liberal President for forty-four years and a new pattern was set for the political rulers: a pattern of Doctors and Generals. For every leader—constitutional, usurper, or dictator—since has been one or the other. But, by mere force of numbers, the Doctors have it.

The Presidential term in Colombia is four years. And in 1934 Liberal Dr. Olaya handed over to Liberal Dr. Alfonso López Pumarejo who four years later handed over to Liberal Dr. Eduardo Santos. Liberal Dr. López was back in the Presidential chair again four years afterwards.

But new forces were at work in democracy-minded Colombia. For on 10th July, 1944, a military group led by Conservative Dr. Laureano Gómez captured President López near Pasto with the intention of forcing him out of office. Only public pressure brought about López' release. Arch-plotter of overthrow, Laureano Gómez, fled to neighbouring Ecuador. A year later President López fell out with Congress and resigned in a huff leaving the Presidency in the hands of his able Foreign Minister Alberto Lleras Camargo—soon to head the Pan American Union in Washington—who held the office until the elections in 1946.

After a Doctor-ridden campaign the Conservatives won through disunity among the Liberals. It had come about through the actions of a great Liberal, Dr. Jorge Eliécer Gaitán, champion of the Indians, who disagreed with his party's line on agrarian reform and ran against the Liberal Presidential candidate. Gaitán's cry of "Liberal Oligarchy" captured a substantial number of the Liberal votes, cleanly split the party down the middle and ensured Conservative victory.

Dr. Mariano Ospina Pérez for the Conservatives polled 565,489 votes; Liberal candidate Gabriel Turbay polled 437,089; and Dr. Jorge Eliécer Gaitán polled 363,849 votes. On 7th August, 1946, Dr. Mariano Ospina Pérez was inaugurated President of Colombia. Guillermo León Valencia became Vice-President.

He immediately invited the Liberals to form a coalition cabinet, a system which worked well for two years. Then Dr. Laureano Gómez, the man who had plotted the overthrow of Liberal Dr. Alfonso López, returned from Ecuador to become Foreign Minister. A Fascist-extremist, pro-Hitler during the war, friend and admirer of Spain's Franco, Dr. Gómez was violently disapproved of by the Liberals who thought to show their displeasure by resigning from the coalition cabinet.

But instead of toppling the Ospina Pérez régime the move merely left the Liberals without a voice in the cabinet. And Dr. Laureano Gómez immediately began a series of anti-Liberal moves aimed at destroying the party and bringing about the kind of totalitarian state he had always dreamed of.

Soon after the Liberal-Conservative coalition split, the powerful and popular Dr. Jorge Eliécer Gaitán was assassinated on his way to his down-town Bogotá law office and enraged mobs put the capital to torch. Colombians speak with a horror of the events of 9th April, 1948, the day of the assassination. Mobs ran through the streets firing everything that was not already alight, looting, beating, killing. The troops refused to leave the barracks. The recipe for Molotov Cocktails was given out over the radio—and used with devastating effect.

When the day was over the capital lay in ashes.

President Ospina Pérez clamped down on everything. The Press was censored. A state of seige was declared. Dr. Laureano Gómez fled to Spain and his friend Franco. Eventually Ospina invited the Liberals to rejoin him in forming a coalition cabinet. They did so, but resigned in early 1949 when Laureano Gómez returned to Colombia.

Then came the gunfire and killing in the House of Assembly and when, soon afterwards, it was time to put up candidates for the Presidential elections, the Liberals refused to do so and announced that they would boycott the elections. Only two days before the polls it seemed that they might change their minds and Laureano Gómez, the Conservative candidate with the dictatorship-plans, went into action. Liberal leader Dario Echandia, his brother, and a group of students were walking on the streets when policemen appeared and opened fire on them. Dario Echandia escaped death by inches. His brother and four students went down in a blaze of gunfire. On polling day, when President Ospina Pérez heard that the Senate intended to summon him to judgement, the Congress was forcibly suspended and the police were publicly congratulated for the Echandia attack by the President.

On 27th November, 1950, Dr. Laureano Gómez became President of Colombia. His Fascist tendencies immediately came to the fore. The worst fears of the Liberals were well founded. For

Laureano Gómez unleashed a reign of terror on the land. Liberal politicians were hunted into exile. Liberal supporters were beaten and shot. In outlying areas Conservative villages with Government-supplied arms fought Liberal villages with pitchforks. Men were forced to sign pledges of loyalty to the Conservative Party in order to be given identity cards which would give them freedom from persecution. Conservatives who spoke out against the Fascist régime were persecuted and often hunted into exile along with out-and-out Liberals.

While Liberals took to the hills and became adept guerilla fighters, President Gómez was busy. Whole areas, usually Liberal strongholds, were proclaimed "militarized zones" and notice to quit was given. Those found there after the deadline were shot. All homes were destroyed. Even in the capital the purges went on. Many of ex-President Ospina Pérez' moderate Conservatives found themselves tossed from office and their jobs given to Fascist-minded, Gómez-supporting, yes-men. One of the first to be purged was Chief of Staff, General Gustavo Rojas Pinilla. And it was a mistake that Laureano Gómez lived to regret.

It will never be known exactly how many people died in the Laureano Gómez anti-Liberal régime. Only a year after Gómez came to office Alfonso López, the old-time Liberal ex-President who somehow managed to keep in the picture, possibly through his close friendship with Gómez, said in a censor-passed report that 50,000 people had been killed. Colombians reasoned that if President Gómez admitted to that number it was safe to think that probably about six times as many was a more realistic figure. And that was after only one year.

In September, 1951, Gómez suffered a heart attack which kept him from active politics for a short time. And soon after he returned he had another. This time he was confined to his bed. Roberto Urdaneta Arbeláez became Acting President but Gómez continued to rule from his home.

Government tanks continued to roll into the countryside, level-ling villages, hunting down Liberal guerillas, destroying crops and farms as Gómez' troops shot, raped and hanged their way across the nation.

But Colombians at the top had had enough. Deposed Chief of Staff General Rojas Pinilla still had friends in the armed forces. And on 13th June, 1953, ten tanks surrounded Dr. Laureano

Gómez' home as Rojas marched into the house and deposed the tyrant at gunpoint. Soon afterwards Laureano Gómez left for Spain.

But General Rojas had no intention of restoring democracy to troubled Colombia. Instead he saw himself as a powerful military dictator. The Army was strong. Nearly a million peasants had been ruthlessly killed by Gómez' troops and the population was cowed. Rojas thought that he could stay in power by force of arms. As head of the military junta he poised himself for power. In mid-1954 the Congress he had virtually hand-picked named him "constitutional President" despite protests from some members.

A brisk and energetic campaign against such members of the public as objected to the move solidified his position. Some student demonstrators who protested too loudly were machine-gunned. The famous newspaper *El Tiempo*, a free voice always, attacked Pinilla in its editorials and he closed it down. His position was further strengthened when Jorge Eliécer Gaitán's widow formed the Independent Liberal Party and threw in her lot with Rojas. Soon afterwards the smaller Popular Socialist Party followed suit. Only the Communist Party raised a voice in public and Rojas dealt with them by outlawing the movement on 4th March, 1956.

But while General Rojas was complacent in his Presidential chair, plotters were busy. Liberal journalist-diplomat-politician Alberto Lleras Camargo who had been Acting President for a few months in 1945 after Alfonso López had resigned, was a leading light in the moves to restore democracy to Colombia. A former *El Tiempo* editor, Lleras Camargo had spent seven years in the United States as the head of the Pan American Union and had virtually drafted the constitution which changed the weak and ineffectual Union into the far stronger Organization of American States.

Democracy-minded politicians and leaders, among them Guillermo León Valencia, gathered round Lleras Camargo and persuaded him to be their spokesman in a meeting with Laureano Gómez, still in Spain, but still nominal leader of the Conservative Party. Lleras Carmargo flew to Spain to see Gómez, presented him with a plan to draw up a Conservative-Liberal front which would agree to alternate Presidents, got his reactions and flew back to Bogotá to confer with his fellow conspirators.

A second flying visit to Spain resulted in a Conservative-Liberal agreement which Gómez signed for the Conservatives and Lleras

Camargo for the Liberals at the Spanish resort of Sitges. The
two parties agreed to form a National Union and alternate the
Presidency until 1974.

Meanwhile Rojas Pinilla had ordered the arrest of Dr. Guillermo
León Valencia. Surrounded in a friend's house, he refused to give
in. And when troops arrived with orders to take him by force, he
appeared at a window brandishing a .32 calibre revolver.

"You will have to take me out either dead or tied up," he
yelled. "You know the kind of fight I can put up."

The troops withdrew.

When Lleras Camargo returned to Bogotá the plotters went
into action. Luck was with them. The blustering Rojas Pinilla
had offended the Roman Catholic Church—a dangerous thing to
do in devout Colombia. A series of strikes in the capital and other
major cities brought the situation to crisis-point. And then the
troops revolted and refused to back Rojas Pinilla.

On 10th May, 1957, he was ousted and a five-man junta of
Army, Navy and Air Force officers under the leadership of Major-
General Gabriel Paris took over. Rojas was tried by Congress and
deprived of his civic rights.

A national referendum, in which women voted for the first
time ever, ratified the Pact of Sitges and an election date was set.
But the Conservatives, who should have had the first term under
the alternating Pact, were unable to agree on a candidate. The
only man acceptable to both sides was Liberal Alberto Lleras
Camargo. He fought and won the election and was inaugurated
President on 4th May, 1958.

The problems in Colombia were tremendous. After twelve
years in which little had been accomplished, Lleras Camargo had
his work cut out. Back in 1949 a World Bank report had spot-
lighted illiteracy. The Ospina Pérez régime had done little for
education. The previous Liberal administrations had also been
lacking. The report found that the majority of the population
were under-fed, under-clothed and under-housed. Some 44 per
cent of the population were illiterate. There were more adult and
school-age illiterates in 1947 than there had been in 1937. The
situation since the Bank's report had, if anything, worsened.

A bad coffee crop added to the immediate financial troubles of
the country and the unsettled state of the politics had frightened
off many much-needed foreign investors. Lleras Camargo institu-

ted tax and land reforms, built schools, and tried to present a smiling face to the outside world.

He had done much by the time his four-year term of office drew to a close. But there was still much to be done. Colombians waited tensely to see whether the Pact of Sitges would be adhered to in the elections, and if so how much support the National Union candidate—a Conservative this time—would get.

Power-hungry Liberals and Conservatives waited on the side-lines to snatch the Presidency. And when the National Union nominated 54-year-old Dr. Guillermo León Valencia, pro-West and anti-Communist, as their candidate, the "dissidents" of both sides were quick to nominate their own men.

Dr. Alfonso López Michelsen, son of ex-President López, stood for the "dissident Liberals"; Dr. Jorge Leyva for the "dissident Conservatives"; and ex-Dictator General Gustavo Rojas Pinilla ran for the Popular National Alliance, despite the fact that he was still deprived of his civic rights and his election would have been invalidated.

When Dr. Guillermo León Valencia went to cast his own vote a vast crowd surged behind him shouting, "Viva Valencia! Viva the President of the Poor!"

And when the results came in he had won overwhelmingly. The people, pleased with the work of Lleras Camargo and the National Union, wanted them to stay in office. Guillermo León Valencia got 1,643,020 votes; "dissident Liberal" Dr. Alfonso López got 617,950; "dissident Conservative" Dr. Jorge Leyva got 307,858; and General Rojas Pinilla only 5,011. Valencia, with 60 per cent and over a million votes more than his nearest rival was President of Colombia. The "dissidents" captured only ninety-seven of the 282 seats in Congress.

Diplomat, holder of doctorates in law and political science, son of a poet, Guillermo León Valencia was now President of Colombia.

Alberto Lleras Camargo handed over the Presidency on 7th August, 1962, after the first completed term of office since Ospina Pérez handed over to Laureano Gómez twelve years before.

"The most important thing my successor will possess is having gained office in a true and open election," Lleras Camargo said.

And he warned of future outside dangers and influences which Valencia will have to face when he added: "The new Cold War theatre is clearly this Hemisphere."

CHAPTER SEVENTEEN

VENEZUELA

Rómulo Betancourt

When Rómulo Betancourt was four months old his proud father wrote a poem about him. It summed up his character and was strangely prophetic.

The first verse ran:

> There is much of the fighting bull
> In this little fellow,
> For he begins his life knowing
> That although he smiles
> He must act as fierce as ten.

Today, fifty-five years after little Rómulo inspired his grocer's accountant father to verse as he gurgled happily in his cot, President Rómulo Betancourt is fighting—and barely winning—a battle for democracy in Venezuela. If he fails the country will fall either to the Communists or to a military dictatorship.

His is the classic story of the Latin American revolutionary, the dedicated idealist fighting dictatorship, corruption, suppression and poverty. He has overthrown constituted authority—and has himself been overthrown. Three times this quiet, pipe-smoking revolutionary has been forced into exile by dictators. And three times he has returned to fight for democracy. Twice the chubby-faced, greying grandfather has been President of his country and has achieved much. He has survived revolutions, military coups, and assassination attempts. His brown eyes still sparkle behind his horn-rimmed glasses when he talks of battles past and plans to come. More than anything else—apart from his all-consuming patriotism—Rómulo Betancourt's resilience is his outstanding quality.

Venezuela, the most northerly republic in South America, was the birthplace of Simón Bolivar, "The Great Liberator", who wrested it, along with half the continent, from the Spaniards. He was also the first of its long line of military dictators. Divided into a Federal District, twenty States and two Territories, the country has the highest *per capita* income in Latin America, supports nearly 7 million people, and covers approximately 352,051 square miles of coastal plains, snow-capped Andean mountains and virtually unexplored Amazon jungle. Bounded in the north by the Caribbean Sea, the west by Colombia, the east by British Guiana, and the south by Brazil, it is a country of untold wealth, great riches and dire poverty.

Rómulo Betancourt, who has spent the greater part of his life fighting dictatorships, and has spent twenty-one of his fifty-five years in jail or exile for doing so, was born on 22nd February, 1908, in poverty-stricken Guatire, in the state of Miranda, some forty miles from Caracas, the country's capital.

The same year General Juan Vincente Gómez became President of Venezuela, a position he was to hold through force of arms—and despite Rómulo Betancourt—for the next twenty-seven years. He regarded Venezuela as his private ranch, amassed a fantastic private fortune, countered all opposition with torture, prison and exile and earned for himself the nickname of "The Tyrant of the Andes".

Young Betancourt was an avid reader, an amateur poet like his father, and, it would seem, a born revolutionary. At the Caracas Liceo, one of the principal high schools, he came under the influence of Rómulo Gallegos, Venezuela's most famous novelist, who was to become a life-long friend and political companion. Between high school and university he was a bill collector for a wholesale tobacco firm. Then, in 1927, he enrolled at the Central University to study law and began to meet other students, many of whom were to be at various times political allies or enemies.

A good speaker and keen political agitator, he established in February, 1928, while still at university, what he calls "the first exclusively liberal movement" in Venezuela, and helped sponsor a week-long series of student protests. He affectionately remembers those days and his followers as "the Boys of '28". Supporting him at the time were two men who would one day be politically opposed to him: Jóvito Villalba and Gustavo Machado.

Betancourt made a violently anti-Gómez speech in a cinema, and was immediately arrested and tossed into a dungeon with a 96 lb. leg iron shackled firmly to his ankle. Three weeks later Gómez had him released. It was a mistake. For in April the band of determined students led by Betancourt changed their tactics from protests to open revolt, seized the Miraflores Palace—the President was away at the time—and stormed the San Carlos Barracks.

But the Army held out. The revolt was put down. The students fled. Gustavo Machado escaped to found in exile the Venezuelan Revolutionary Party. Betancourt made the first of his three dashes for freedom hotly pursued by troops. He reached Colombia, stayed there lecturing until 1930 and then headed for Central America, winding up in Costa Rica.

There he met lovely school teacher Carmen Valverde, veered towards Communism—which he later renounced—and prepared to settle down until he could chance returning to Venezuela.

"It was an era of radicalism. Sinclair Lewis. Dreiser. John Dos Passos. In Costa Rica we formed a group. We called it the Worker and Peasant *bloc*," he says today explaining that part of his life.

Gómez died on 17th December, 1935, enormously rich, full of years and surrounded by more than a hundred illegitimate children —an achievement of which he was not unjustly proud. His Minister of War—and son-in-law—General Eleázar López Contreras confiscated some £70 million of Gómez' personal fortune, took over the Presidency and immediately relaxed many of the dead dictator's harsh laws and rulings.

Exiles returned to Venezuela rejoicing. Rómulo Betancourt married Carmen and went home. López Contreras allowed political activity, a degree of freedom to the Press, and a partial restoration of civil liberties. He also reduced the term of the Presidency from five years to four.

Betancourt gathered together a band of kindred spirits and formed the Venezuelan Organization (OREV) and won some seats in the Congressional elections held in January, 1937. But the traditionalist party, the Bolivarian Civic Group (ACB), still held most and the newcomers' hands were fairly tied. OREV began pressing for better housing, free Presidential elections, and agrarian reform. Oil had been discovered under the murky waters of Lake

Maracaibo in 1922 but Venezuela had not felt the full benefit of it as most of the profits the foreign companies made were sent out of the country. Betancourt urged a new petroleum policy. He stumped the country rallying support for his party from peasants, industrial workers and businessmen.

But after a year López Contreras cracked down on political activity. Many of Gómez' laws were resurrected and the new President added a few of his own. At first Rómulo Betancourt merely went "underground" and continued working for his party. But soon the President's secret police were searching for him everywhere. When they did not find him and his party was gaining an even bigger following, López Contreras decided it was time for a showdown.

He exhibited a shrivelled human ear and announced that the grisly relic belonged to Betancourt. He promised that soon he would have the rest of him.

Betancourt quickly disowned the ear—it had belonged to a gardener who had had it bitten off in a brawl with a policeman— and announced that his party would fight for freedom in Venezuela as long as there was oppression in the country. Enraged, López Contreras ordered an all-out hunt for Betancourt and eventually he was forced to flee again. This time he went to Argentina and then Chile. O R E V was outlawed.

In February, 1941, López Contreras prepared to hand over the Presidency to his hand-picked nominee General Isaias Medina Angarita and again exiles were allowed to return home. Again political parties and unions quickly formed. Betancourt's O R E V became the Partido Nacional Democrático, but later, after expelling Gustavo Machado and the Communist element, they called themselves Acción Democrática (A D). They quickly gathered a large following. Moscow-trained brothers Gustavo and Eduardo Machado formed the Partido Comunista and set about collaborating with the new President-designate. In the next three years Acción Democrática became the major political force in Venezuela and their demands for free elections were louder than ever.

But despite his partial democracy Medina refused to allow the free election of his successor, wanting to hand the Presidency to a hand-picked nominee in the same way that he himself had received it. Military strongmen had controlled Venezuela almost from the beginning and long-serving senior Army officers did not want a change. But they reckoned without the junior officers who saw the way to promotion blocked by many aged generals.

The junior officers formed a secret organization calling themselves the Patriotic Military Union and began to discuss ways and means of overthrowing the Government. Recognizing AD as the major political entity, they invited Betancourt to join them in a coup. At first he refused. He wanted power through a free election, not through a military revolt. But elections under Medina were impossible. Eventually he joined with the officers. A secret council of war was held in the home of the mother of Major Carlos Delgado Chalbaud and the final plans drawn up. Speeches were made about democratic government, an end to tyranny and free elections.

"The loudest voice in the military group was that of the then Major Marcos Pérez Jiménez," Betancourt wrote later.

On 28th October, 1945, the rebels struck. Within twenty-four hours the Government had toppled, forty-eight people lay dead in the streets, and two ex-Presidents were in custody. López Contreras, Medina and some twenty of their close followers were put on a plane for Miami. Each was given a cheque for £280—the minimum requirement under American immigration laws.

"The power was off in the Presidential Palace and gasoline lamps lighted the memorable scene," Rómulo Betancourt recalls. "Civilians and military side by side, all with tense expectations, we signed the constituent act of *de facto* Government."

Rómulo Betancourt was named Provisional President and a seven-man junta was set up. It consisted of the President, three AD members, two military members—Major Carlos Delgado Chalbaud and Captain Mario Vargas—and one independent civilian. They went to work immediately.

Pledged Betancourt: "We will make the defence of our human resources the centre of our preoccupation. We will not construct ostentatious skyscrapers, but men, women, and children will eat more, will pay less for clothing and rent, will have better public services, and will be provided with more schools."

In the two years that Betancourt was Provisional President he made remarkable changes in Venezuela. All bans were removed on political parties, freedom of the Press and personal liberties. There was political reform. New parties sprang up. One of "the Boys of '28", Jóvito Villalba, formed the Unión Republicana

Democrática (URD), similar to AD in its aims, but not in agreement
with its leadership. Rafael Caldera formed the Social Catholic
COPEI. A new agreement was negotiated with the oil companies
providing that petroleum profits be split fifty-fifty with the companies and the Government; teacher training colleges were
established; houses, schools and hospitals were built. Agrarian
reform was urgent as 5 per cent of the property owners held 78
per cent of the land and only 10 per cent of the agricultural
farmers had any land at all. In 1945 there were 300,000 children
in schools; in 1948 there were 400,000. In 1945 only 319 towns
had electricity; in 1948 it was in 606 towns. In 1945 only 1,000
children ate state-supplied dinners at school; in 1948 more than
38,000 ate them. In 1945 Venezuela exported 323,400,000 barrels
of oil—a barrel contains 42 gallons; in 1948 they exported
490,000,000 barrels.

Free elections had been promised and free elections were held.
The first, in October, 1946, was for a constituent assembly. Of the
1,385,000 votes cast, AD got 1,100,000 (37 seats); COPEI, 180,000
(19 seats); URD, 54,000 (2 seats) and the Partido Comunista 51,000
(2 seats).

The Presidential election was held in December, 1947. Rómulo
Betancourt prepared to stand down from his Provisional office.
The AD put up his old teacher and ally Rómulo Gallegos as their
candidate.

The parties chose colours to represent themselves to the illiterates as they prepared for Venezuela's first free election—and
also the first-ever under universal adult suffrage. AD ballots—
candidate Rómulo Gallegos—were white; COPEI—candidate
Rafael Caldera—green; and the Partido Comunista—candidate
Gustavo Machado—red. The URD did not contest the Presidency.
When the results came in Rómulo Gallegos had won overwhelmingly: AD 871,752 votes; COPEI 262,204 votes; Partido Comunista 36,514 votes.

Rómulo Gallegos was inaugurated as President on 15th February, 1948, and Betancourt was at his side. In April the same year
he went to a Pan-American conference at Bogotá, Colombia,
delivered an impassioned speech demanding the end of British,
French, Dutch and American colonialism in the Caribbean and
then returned home to settle down to the serious work ahead as
Gallegos's right-hand man.

Corruption was stamped upon. Some 150 former officials were charged with illicit self-enrichment and £40 million confiscated —López Contrera and Medina had accumulated £1¼ million each.

The new President continued with the policies of Betancourt, building democracy on the firm foundations that his able student had laid. But democracy in Venezuela was young and there were many forces working against it. The Army had ceased to be the dominant factor in the political field and they did not like it. Several minor uprisings between 1945 and 1948 had been put down. More were on the way.

Major Marcos Pérez Jiménez—he who had had "the loudest voice" in the plans to overthrow Medina Angarita—called on Gallegos and presented him with an ultimatum: exile Rómulo Betancourt and give more power to the Army—or get out. Gallegos did neither. Pérez Jiménez went back to the barracks to complete his already prepared plans.

On the night of 24th November, 1948, Pérez Jiménez overthrew the Government, tossed Gallegos into jail along with eight Cabinet Ministers, a Supreme Court judge, the Governors of Caracas and Aragua, five Congressmen and sundry other senior politicians and officials loyal to the régime. Rómulo Betancourt first went underground and was then forced into exile for the third time. He went to Costa Rica again to his friend José Figueres. Later he spent some time in Cuba—where, in April, 1951, a man attacked him on the street and tried to plunge a hypodermic full of poison into his arm. Then he went to Puerto Rico. His first book, *Venezuela: Politics and Oil*, was published in 1950.

Pérez Jiménez set up a junta composed of Carlos Delgado Chalbaud—who had changed sides rapidly—Major Luis Felipe Llovera Páez and himself. Betancourt's AD was outlawed, the development programme lapsed, and new oil concessions granted to outside companies in return for large cash settlements to the top men in power. Two years later shady business surrounded the assassination of junta-head Delgado Chalbaud who was waylaid and murdered on 13th November, 1950, by Rafael Simón Urbina, a friend of Pérez Jiménez. The police caught up with Urbina and killed him the following day so whatever the political ramifications were they died with him. Marcos Pérez Jiménez became the key figure in Venezuela.

In his exile Rómulo Betancourt was busy. He wrote a second

book, *Rómulo Betancourt: Thoughts and Action*, which was published in 1956, and he analysed the things that had brought about
the *coup* and cut short his work. He decided that AD had made
"psychological errors".

"There was a certain arrogance, a certain intolerance with
minorities," he says. "Some say we tried to do too much too fast.
But there was so much to be done."

Meanwhile Pérez Jiménez was preparing to make his *coup* look
democratic. Elections were held on 30th November, 1952. Both
the URD and COPEI were allowed to nominate candidates. The
Government nominee was running on a new party ticket, that of
the Frente Electoral Independiente (FEI). At the last moment, the
AD, who had maintained a strong "underground" despite stringent
measures taken against those captured, let it be known that they
would back the URD. People who would not otherwise have gone
out to vote went to the polls to support the URD because of their
AD backing. As the results came in it was clear that the party was
going to win and that COPEI would come second; the Government's FEI was only getting some 20 per cent of the votes.

Pérez Jiménez immediately suspended the counting and two
days later announced that the FEI had scored "an overwhelming
victory". In January, 1953, Pérez Jiménez was inaugurated
President of Venezuela.

Now Venezuelans who had grown up in fear of Gómez' régime
remembered it with nostalgia. For Pérez Jiménez unleashed a reign
of terror on the country the like of which even hardened,
dictator-ridden Venezuela had seldom seen. The URD was outlawed—for it had won the election showing itself to be a potential
threat. The COPEI was vigorously persecuted—for they had come
second and could also be a danger. The infamous Seguridad
Nacional—Secret Police—was established under sadistically
efficient Pedro Estrada who enlisted spies throughout the country,
tossed former friends and enemies into torture chambers with
equal impartiality, and launched an all-out attack on the AD
"underground" movement. Their leaders were betrayed by spies,
tortured by professional pain-givers, stood against adobe walls
and shot.

Pérez Jiménez and his close henchmen amassed fantastic personal
fortunes in an incredibly short time—his own was estimated at £80
million. Lesser lights near the top made proportionately less.

The Army had seized power in 1948 and stalled elections until 1952, but Pérez Jiménez, attempting to keep up his pseudo-democratic front mainly to keep in with the United States, knew that he must hold elections in 1958. He could not risk another fiasco election like the 1952 one and put his mind to the problem of how to stay in power without going to the polls. Finally he came up with an answer: the country would hold a plebiscite on whether or not they wanted the Pérez Jiménez régime for another term of office. Voting cards would just state "yes" or "no". The plebiscite was held in December, 1957, and a circular was sent to civil servants requiring them to show cards marked "yes" when they reported for work on polling day. The heads of many of the larger business houses were approached by the Seguridad Nacional and told to make sure that their employees were likewise instructed. The Government was unanimously "re-elected", getting 85 per cent of the votes.

But it was too much for many Venezuelans to stomach. On New Year's Day, 1958, the Air Force, one of the largest and best-equipped in Latin America, rose in protest almost to a man. Their revolt was ruthlessly crushed but many of the top men and virtually all the aircraft took off from their airfields and flew across the border into neighbouring Colombia. Shortly afterwards the military leaders, seeing the writing on the wall, forced Pérez Jiménez to expel Pedro Estrada and the Minister of the Interior who flew out to Trujillo's Dominican Republic, haven of the sadistic, the deposed and the politically undesirable.

Of the four political parties only COPEI had been allowed to operate in the country—and then only according to the whims of the President. But the three others maintained "underground" movements and they immediately made contact with each other. A Junta Patriotica was formed consisting of two members each of the outlawed AD, URD, Partido Comunista and the legal COPEI. A general strike was called for 22nd January, fighting broke out in the streets as the military were ordered to break the strike, and the following day Army officers called on Pérez Jiménez and told him that they would support him no longer. He fled, in the wake of Estrada and his Minister, to the Dominican Republic.

Now a new junta took over composed of one representative each from the Navy, Army and Air Force and two wealthy businessmen. Admiral Wolfgang Larrazábal was put at its head.

Rómulo Betancourt returned home as he had done on the other occasions. Elections were promised and parties re-organized. The AD, URD, COPEI and the Communists were very active. So was a new party formed by businessmen and called the Integración Republicana. The junta agreed that they should honour the debts left by the Pérez Jiménez régime, were staggered when they amounted to nearly £70 million, and went ahead with Government business trying to restore the country's crippled economy. Minor revolts by the ex-President's supporters were put down in July and September and the election was set for December, 1958.

The AD put up Rómulo Betancourt; the URD supported junta-head Wolfgang Larrazábal; the COPEI candidate was Rafael Caldera. Neither of the other parties put up candidates but the Communists backed Larrazábal and the Integración Republicana backed Caldera.

Rómulo Betancourt tallied 1,284,092 (49 per cent) of the 2,610,833 votes cast, getting most of his support from the country. Admiral Larrazábal won overwhelmingly in Caracas. Caldera came third. Betancourt announced that he would form a Government with a coalition cabinet composed of the AD, URD, COPEI and independents. He was inaugurated President on 13th February, 1959, and took up where he had left off.

Ten years of exile, age and contact with men like Costa Rica's José Figueres and Puerto Rico's Luis Muñoz Marín had mellowed the Leftist Betancourt. No longer was he a fiery revolutionary. He was now a man with a burning desire to get back to the work he loved best. He championed Fidel Castro the Liberator, took a long look at the Communists as they took over Cuba, and denounced Fidel Castro the Dictator. Frequently he attacked the tyrannical Trujillo régime in the Dominican Republic, and, having seen enough of dictators to last him several lifetimes, he denounced every dictator, would-be dictator and Communist who arose in Latin America.

"The philosophy of Communism is not compatible with the development of Venezuela," he said.

Internally Venezuela had big problems. The debts of the Pérez Jiménez Government had to be paid off. Too many people were leaving the land to try to get work in the oilfields on Lake Maracaibo. They would go to the area, fail to get jobs, and sit in

almost starving misery in tin-can-and-cardboard shacks, idle and
hopeless. Betancourt pushed forward an agrarian reform scheme
aimed at settling some 60,000 landless peasants on two million
hectares of land. He plans to settle another 40,000 by the end of
1963. Roads had fallen into disrepair under other régimes—many
had not been touched since Gallegos had been tossed from power
in 1948—so he set about repairing 2,100 miles of them. Another
1,900 miles of road were paved, 600 miles re-paved and 625 miles
of highways built. There were too few schools—and 56.8 per
cent of the population were illiterate—so he set about building
more and training more teachers. He has built more schools since
1959 than had been built in the previous fifty years. State con-
tribution to universities was upped from £3 million a year to £10
million a year. More than 25,000 students are now registered in
the universities. Exports of petroleum rose from 950,057,000
barrels in 1958 to 1,011,450,000 barrels in 1960, Venezuela pro-
ducing one seventh of the world's petroleum.

But while more jobs were created, more amenities made available—electricity now reached all but the most remote villages—
and more money was coming into the country, the people were
gathering near Caracas.

The capital city lies at the foot of the Andes, a great sprawling
metropolis of steel, glass and concrete, with fly-over roads, vast
bridges and huge skyscrapers. Nearly 4,000 feet above it, perched
on Mount Avila, the floodlit Hotel Humbolt, reached by a cable
railway, pushes a fiery pencil into the sky on nights when the
mountain is not shrouded in cloud. And between the huge hotel
and the magnificent city are the slums, thousands of them, row
upon row of tightly-packed, tin-and-cardboard shacks without
electricity, water or proper drainage. Here live 500,000 people, the
workless, the starving and the hopeless.

Betancourt has tried to get jobs for them, to create low-cost
state housing, to re-settle them on the land. Much of the £469
million annual government revenue—petroleum revenues bring in
£1 million a day—has been spent on schemes for the working
population. But it is a huge job. To some, Betancourt has not done
enough, to others—many of the middle class—he has done, and
spent, too much.

Between his inauguration in January, 1959, and mid-1962, there
were seventeen attempts to topple his régime, some by friends of

ex-President Pérez Jiménez, many by Communists. All have been put down. Far more serious was the assassination attempt sponsored by the Dominican Republic which nearly cost Betancourt his life.

On 24th June, 1960, the President was on his way to attend Army Day celebrations when a bomb was set off by remote control near his car. His chief aide-de-camp, a guard and a traffic officer died in the explosion but Rómulo Betancourt emerged from the blazing inferno which seconds before had been his car with nothing more than facial burns—he is badly scarred on his upper lip as a result—and a bad temper.

He immediately accused the Dominican Republic of complicity in the attempt on his life, and carried his complaint to the Organization of American States who found that the plotters had had "moral support and material assistance from high officials of the Government of the Dominican Republic". Diplomatic relations were broken with Trujillo at once.

In March, 1961, Betancourt went to the classical-domed, pseudo-Grecian Parliament Building to deliver his annual message to Congress and suggested that the Organization of American States should rule that only countries in which freely elected Governments held power should have membership of the Organization, and that members should withdraw political asylum and diplomatic privileges from deposed dictators.

But while he has made Venezuela the most industrialized state in Latin America, Betancourt is still under fire from all sides. The Army thinks it should have more power—the same problem that Gallegos faced in 1948.

Of the seventeen risings since he came to power, the two biggest occurred during the first half of 1962. The first of them, by 450 Marines based at Carupano, was led by a former Army officer who transferred to the Navy and served as aide-de-camp to Admiral Larrazábal, now Venezuela's Ambassador in Chile. Betancourt despatched ships and the Army to put down the Communist-inspired revolt. The second attempt was more serious. It broke out, again in the Marines, at Puerto Cabello, the country's largest Naval base, seventy-five miles west of Caracas. Pro-Castro officers released anti-Betancourt civilians from a detention centre and they united with a band of well armed students. The first National Guards who tried to break up the revolt were chopped to pieces with machine-guns and Betancourt had to despatch tanks, field-guns, paratroops and 3,000 regular troops to the area before the revolt was quelled. During the Cuban crisis of October, 1962, Castro sympathizers blew up oil installations on Lake Maracaibo and Betancourt had to declare martial law.

Much of violently anti-Betancourt propaganda comes out of the universities, particularly the Central University in Caracas— ironically, the very place from which he led "the Boys of '28" in their abortive attempt to overthrow Gómez thirty-five years ago. Under the universities' constitutions the police may not enter the areas and many of the teachers are preaching Communism to their students. Betancourt has been compelled to suspend the activities of the Machados' Partido Comunista and the Movimiento Izquierda Revolucionario, an offshoot of dissatisfied A D members. But they still flourish in the universities. In the Central University is a twice-as-large-as-life papiermâché dummy of Betancourt, scowling grimly, a Swastika arm-band prominently displayed, and with the dollar-sign decorated tentacles of a huge octopus (the United States) tightly encircling him.

Despite all his plans Betancourt is having trouble making any headway with his country. Venezuela has been called "the richest under-developed country in the world" and much has been done to break the back of the main problems. But there is still about 11 per cent unemployment; there are still half-a-million people living in the slums above Caracas; there is still only one hospital bed per 500 people. Illiteracy has dropped from 56.8 per cent in 1959, to less than 20 per cent. But literacy does not mean that the people are well fed, well clothed or well housed.

When, in January, 1960, Rómulo Betancourt completed his first year in office he made history as the first freely elected Venezuelan President ever to do so. His term of office is due to end in February, 1964, and if Betancourt gets through it he will again be the first President ever to do so. He still smiles, but "the fierceness of ten" that his father wrote of may no longer be enough.

For Venezuela the question will be: should the country be governed by a Civil-Military junta? Or should free elections be held again? Whatever their answer is, it will be of the utmost importance not only to Venezuela, but to the whole of Caribbean America.

CHAPTER EIGHTEEN

BRITISH GUIANA

Dr. Cheddi Jagan

The famous smile was gone. So was the tranquillity. The Caribbean's most elusive and evasive politician was visibly ruffled. A ripple of anticipation ran through the watchers. At last Cheddi Jagan, Premier of British Guiana, the man who had for nearly a decade answered reporters who demanded "Are you a Communist?" with "You define Communism, then I'll tell you if it fits", was in a tight corner.

As he sat in the box answering questions before the Commission of Inquiry into the riots of February, 1962, Jagan must have known that he was to meet his Waterloo. Evasion would not be enough.

"Are you a Communist?" demanded cross-examiner Lionel Luckhoo.

"You will have to explain what you mean by a Communist," countered Jagan. It was the old line.

"Would you say that Fidel Castro was a Communist?" demanded Luckhoo.

"That is for him to say," said Jagan.

Minutes of challenge and evasion followed until Committee Chairman Sir Henry Wynn Parry insisted on a direct answer from the smooth-talking Jagan.

"If he continues to be silent on this issue the Commission will be forced to take note that the witness has avoided answering this vital question," he warned.

Angered, Jagan blurted out: "I believe the tenets of Communism to mean 'from each according to his ability and to each according to his need'. And I believe that represents the Communist belief and I accept it."

At last it was out. Anti-Jagan barristers and observers breathed a deep and satisfied sigh. His own legal advisers looked glum. Reporters scurried from the room to file stories which filled Georgetown's newspapers and made headline news around the free world.

Jagan went home to his one-storied wooden house on stilts to think about the next day's interrogation. In his simply furnished home with the pet monkey downstairs and the tightly packed bookshelves upstairs he must have done a lot of pondering.

For thousands of Guianese it was a day of triumph. Ever since the colony's constitution was suspended in 1953, people had been asking Jagan "Are you a Communist?" Always he had been vague and evasive. "I am a Marxist-Socialist," was the way he put it to me.

A remarkable pattern of events has led this slim, handsome, suave Indian dentist-turned-politician to the top of the political tree in British Guiana. A remarkable pattern—and a tragic one too. For this British Colony on the north coast of South America is a country divided within itself by racial conflict: not, as in parts of Africa, racial conflict in terms of white settler minority against African majority, but in terms of Negro (in British Guiana the word is never used, they say African) against Indian; urban dwellers against rural ones.

British Guiana, 83,000 square miles of densely wooded, mountainous, many-rivered fertility, is Britain's last possession on the mainland of South America. It is larger than England and Scotland together. Geographically, it is just out of the Caribbean area—for the Atlantic Ocean washes its thickly-populated north coast. Venezuela lies to the west, Surinam (Dutch Guiana) to the east and Brazil to the south. It is a land of sugar and bauxite, of sophisticated African city dwellers and poor, largely illiterate, Indian sugar cane workers. The Africans number some 190,000; the Indians, some 279,000 and their birth-rate is higher. Other races—English, Portuguese, Chinese, mixed descent and Amerindians—make up more than 104,000.

Cheddi Bharratt Jagan (pronounce the first a as in bag) has been the most important political factor in the country for a decade. He is a born actor. He has the looks for it—at 45 he looks 35 and is certainly the handsomest politician in his part of the world; he has the voice for it—sometimes loud and demanding, sometimes soft and cajoling; and he has the personality for it—gay, witty, charming, or forceful and emotion-packed.

He exerts an almost magical power over his devoted followers—the majority of them are Indians like himself. He is a man of the people. His family, like theirs, went to British Guiana from India—mostly from Bihar—to work on the sugar plantations and do the jobs that the freed African slaves would not do.

He was born on 22nd March, 1918, on a sugar plantation at Port Mourant in the flat, canal-drained Corentyne, east of Georgetown, the colony's beautiful capital. The locals like to say that the finest Guianese come from the area. His father was a "driver"—foreman—on the estate. His mother still lives there in one of the workers' houses without either a sink or running water. So does his brother Udit who is an estate worker. There were eleven children. Other brothers—Sirpaul, Vidia and Chunilal—have made their way in various fields in British Guiana. Chunilal—who changed his name to Derek—is a lawyer and a keen worker in Jagan's party. All but one of his sisters have taken English names.

Cheddi went to Queen's College, Georgetown, and, later, after a lucky $500 win, the elder Jagan was able to send him off to study dentistry in the United States. He attended the Negro Howard University in Washington and Roosevelt College, Chicago. The money did not last long and he worked his way through dental school for seven years.

Jagan made a very successful dentist with his charming chairside manner, his well-groomed appearance and comforting smile. But he was cut out for bigger things.

In Chicago, in January, 1943, while he was in his last year, Cheddi Jagan met the girl who was to become his wife, political helpmate, and herself a key figure in British Guiana.

Janet Rosenberg was two years his junior, a slim, fun-loving, brown-haired girl. She had attended the University of Detroit, Wayne University and Michigan State University where she had studied chemistry and excelled in swimming, fencing, ice-skating and archery. When they met she was taking a course at the Cook County School of Nursing preparatory to joining the services as her part of the war effort. Her father, a Jewish immigrant, was a plumber and heating engineer. She had an elder brother.

She also had well-defined Left-wing ideas.

By summer she and Cheddi were married. They could not afford the fare for both of them to travel to British Guiana. Cheddi could not afford to stay in the United States. So Janet took a job in Chicago while Cheddi, freshly qualified—B.Sc. (Sociology) and D.D.S.—from the North-western University, went home. Janet joined him in time for Christmas. They rented the second and third floors of a wood-frame building in Georgetown as a combination dental surgery and home. Cheddi hung out his shingle. Janet became his nurse.

Conditions in British Guiana were bad. The war, coupled with German U-boat activity off the coast making the shipment of sugar very precarious, had brought hard times to the colony which was already used to hard times. Political activity was virtually nil but trade unions were beginning to be formed. For constitutional reasons, and then the war, there had not been an election since 1935.

Jagan became easily the most popular dentist in Georgetown. He made the best dentures, did the finest work, and charged the lowest fees. Sometimes he did work free. Often he accepted credit. He prospered—his practice paid for all his brothers and sisters to be educated abroad—but he was dissatisfied. Dentistry did not offer the challenges of medicine.

In his search for the challenge that he loves, he turned his attention to unions and politics. Janet's Leftist principles had already made their mark. He read avidly, much of his reading matter being Marxist books and Communist pamphlets. The more he read and heard, the more convinced he became that only Communism could raise British Guiana from her impoverished condition to an acceptable standard in a reasonably short time. Other systems might do it in time, but time was not a commodity which the colony had in abundance.

In 1945 Jagan became connected with the Man-Power Citizens' Association, a fairly influential sugar estate workers' union. He left soon afterwards under strained and never properly explained circumstances.

But he had seen enough really to whet his appetite for politics.

Janet was active too. She had been a prime mover in founding the Women's Political and Economic Organization, a pressure group aimed primarily at getting women the vote, but also interested in bettering schools and social conditions.

Both Jagans wrote articles for *Indian Opinion*, the paper of the East Indian Association.

In 1946 Cheddi formed the Political Affairs Committee and began publishing the *People's Free Press*. The first elections in twelve years were held in 1947 and both Cheddi and Janet stood for election. She lost the election and also her U.S. citizenship for running in it. He was returned to the Legislative Council for East Demerara. The Political Affairs Committee as such ceased to exist soon afterwards but the Jagans and a group of friends carried on their political crusade.

They visited remote parts of the country often spending nights in tumble-down shacks, eating with the people, talking with them, identifying themselves in every way with the poor, the down-trodden, the hungry and the dissatisfied. Janet took to wearing a sari in an effort to identify herself further with the Indian population.

In 1948 they launched their own weekly newspaper as a "voice of the people" to counteract "distortions" in the Georgetown Press. They called it *Thunder*, taking the name from William Morris's: "Hark the rolling of the thunder/Lo the sun and lo thereunder/Riseth wrath and hope and wonder." Janet became editor and the paper carried articles sent out by Britain's Communist *Daily Worker*.

By 1950 the few loyal friends who had helped the Jagans in their early campaigning had grown into a substantial body of followers of all races. The virtually-defunct Political Affairs Committee was officially buried and from its ashes rose the People's Progressive Party which was to play such a large part in British Guiana's immediate future. Cheddi was President; Janet, Secretary-General. Good men joined them: men like African barrister Linden Forbes Sampson Burnham—"Odo" to his friends—a brilliant orator who had returned from law school in London the year before. A score of others whose names would be much in the public eye also rallied to the P P P.

The same year Cheddi and Janet had their first child, a son. They called him Cheddi—after his father—and nicknamed him Joe—after Joseph Stalin. Janet took him to America for medical treatment, and when she returned Cheddi's sister Edith moved in to look after him while his parents carried on with politics. In 1951 Janet won a seat on the city council.

H

A new constitution—and with it a general election—was in the offing. Cheddi put his plans into action. The Jagans toured the country. Cheddi set up clinics in remote places and did free dental work. Janet, in her sari, spent days away from home and family campaigning vigorously and getting to know British Guiana better than most of the locals. The P P P was multi-racial, although even then Cheddi realized that a great deal of the voting would be done on a racial, not a party, basis. He concentrated on areas where the Indian population was in the majority. Burnham campaigned in isolated African communities and focused his attention on predominantly-African Georgetown.

Other parties were in the field—most of them campaigning against the P P P. The election, the first under full adult suffrage, was to be held on 27th April, 1953. The new House of Assembly had twenty-four elected seats. Other parties, fearful that the P P P would gain a controlling number, frequently begged voters to vote for any party—other than the P P P. On the eve of the poll Georgetown's newspapers carried paid-for supplements drawing a fearful picture of Communist slave labour camps and "exposing" the wicked plans that the P P P was supposed to have for peasants' land. The voters, believing that the advertisements had been paid for by sugar kings and bauxite barons—which they were not—took the view that "if they are so much against the P P P it must be good for us".

Accordingly they went out to vote for the P P P. There were 130 candidates—seventy-nine of them independents—contesting the twenty-four seats. The P P P only contested twenty-two of them, but when the voting came in they had won eighteen seats in a landslide election. Cheddi became Minister for Agriculture, Lands and Mines. Janet did not take a cabinet job. Instead she became Deputy Speaker in the House of Assembly.

From the very beginning the P P P made it clear that they did not intend to work within the terms of the constitution which they declared was "too restrictive". The Guiana Industrial Workers' Union—virtually an arm of the P P P—called a general strike on the sugar estates. The party formed their own Council of Ministers and would present a united front at cabinet meetings with the intention of opposing Governor Sir Alfred Savage rather than doing anything constructive for the country. In the six months that they held office they did everything possible to bring about a crisis to embarrass Sir Alfred. Finally they undermined the police force, hoping that the Governor would intervene and give them the much-wanted constitutional issue.

Instead, on 9th October, 1953, the Governor, an experienced and unflappable colonial civil servant, suspended the constitution and 500 Royal Welch Fusiliers from Jamaica landed in Georgetown.

The White Paper on the suspension listed eleven items contrary to good government which had caused the British Government to take such drastic action. Among them were: fermenting strikes for political ends; removing the ban on the entry of West Indian Communists; attempting to repeal the Undesirable Publications Ordinance; spreading racial hatred; and threatening violence. Additionally, a plot to burn down the capital was revealed.

The Government of the colony passed into the hands of Sir Alfred. The P P P remained in displaced indignation for only a short time and then began to crack up. First it was the older and more conservative African element who left. "Cheddi is a Communist," they said. "We do not want a Communist Government in British Guiana." They tried hard to persuade Burnham to quit too but he remained with Jagan for the time being.

Cheddi dashed to London to lobby M.P.s to fight his case in the House of Commons. He made a goodwill tour of Britain speaking to working men's clubs up and down the country. Always he was expressive: "I just want the best that I can get for my country," he would say. "Is that wrong?" In November he went to India to ask Nehru to plead his case at United Nations. Nehru refused. He laid a wreath on the tomb of Mahatma Gandhi and was filmed doing so. The British Guiana Government banned the film when it reached the colony.

By February, 1954, he was back home. Under emergency regulations he was confined to Georgetown—where he had a lot of friends but little personal support for his party and was politically impotent. He filled in his time writing *Forbidden Freedom*, a book telling his side of the story. Later when he broke the confinement, he was jailed for three months.

At the penal settlement at Bartria a speeding car full of gunmen drove past and fired shots at him. They missed.

Janet held the fort while he was in jail and then she too was arrested—for being in possession of banned literature. She got three months. The day Cheddi came out of prison, Janet went in.

By early 1955 Burnham was having second thoughts about the Jagans. At a meeting of the party executive he managed to have them voted out of their top positions. They countered by calling another meeting and expelling him. A lot of his friends left too. Both groups continued to call themselves the P P P and both published the party paper. Burnham distinguished his by calling it the *PPP Thunder*. But by October he had ceased to try to run a rival P P P and had formed his own party, the People's National Congress. His paper became *New Nation*.

He broke with Jagan, he explained, because "I found he was more interested in peddling the latest Moscow line than in looking after the peculiar problems of British Guiana."

The same year Janet presented Cheddi with a daughter. They called her Nadira.

The emergency regulations were slowly relaxed. A new Governor, Sir Patrick Renison, arrived in 1955. By April, 1956, he had drawn up an interim constitution and was ready to announce new elections. The House of Assembly would have fourteen seats—as opposed to twenty-four under the 1953 constitution. The Executive Council would be entirely nominated.

Jagan knew that, publicly at least, he must soft-pedal his Communist views.

He called a secret party session—details of which leaked out— and told them: "It is clear from my analysis that in the period of our party's ascendency up to October, 1953, we definitely over-rated the revolutionary possibilities of our party. We allowed our zeal to run away with us; we became swollen-headed, pompous and bombastic. 'In order to smash powerful enemies,' said Stalin, 'it is necessary to have a flexible policy to take advantage of every crack in the enemy camp, and skill in finding allies.'

"Therefore a united front is absolutely necessary."

In 1953 the P P P had been multi-racial. By 1957 it had lost most of its top African members—Brindley Benn being a notable exception. Now it was an Indian party. Burnham's P N C was an African party. The ugly shadow of racial division hung over the colony. Jagan, while always making a great show of multi-racialism, was glad to have his supporters use the Hindu slogan "Apan Jhatt"—meaning "vote for your own"—in their campaigns. Burnham also recognized the value of racial voting but did little to encourage it. He knew that he could not expect to win with an African candidate in an Indian community. Therefore he concentrated his efforts in the towns and on isolated African communities, running a handful of Indians in their own areas.

Georgetown has a predominantly African population who saw their prosperity, even their very existence, being threatened by the rapidly growing Indian population. The same was true, to a lesser extent, of the European and Chinese populations. Indian businessmen feared Jagan's Communist policies.

The elections were held on 12th August, 1957. Jagan's P P P, much to his surprise, received 47 per cent of the votes giving him nine of the fourteen seats. Burnham got three seats. The United Democratic Party and the National Labour Front got one each. Cheddi gave up his dental practice to become Minister of Trade and Industry. Janet became Minister of Labour, Health and Housing.

Former party members continued to leave. And each one had something to say. Barrister Rudy Luck claimed he left the P P P because it had become "a vehicle for opportunists to ride on to eventual notoriety". Deposed Assemblyman Mohammed Khan declared that Jagan was "definitely working for Russia and did not propose to change".

Despite this, Jagan's new Government went from strength to strength. His development programme brought a large part of the country from dire poverty to comparative prosperity. He built new roads, hospitals and schools. He put up factories, encouraged investors when they could be found, and answered criticisms of his Government with the results of his efforts.

From his Georgian-style Government office Jagan issued directives to his civil service, briefed his Ministers, planned developments, and tried to strengthen his party.

A keen student of Professor Harold Laski, Jagan said once: "I have been greatly influenced by his writings. In this sense I have said on several occasions that I believe in Marxism. I am a Socialist in the sense that I believe that the means of production should be in the hands of the state. Public ownership of the means of production, exchange and distribution will result in greater distribution of wealth in favour of the poor and also mean the participation of the people themselves in the whole process of Government—in the administration, in factories, in other levels of Government."

On another occasion he said: "Because our economic set-up is hopelessly out of date and inefficient, I am a Socialist. If we try rebuilding it on conservative lines we should need a hundred years—and even then we'd fail. Socialism is our only way forward."

He has frequently said that he will go to either West or East for financial aid for his country. And he admits that the planned economy of the Soviet Union appeals to him.

"I am interested in what is happening there as I am interested in what is happening everywhere," he says. "I cannot say fully that there is freedom in the U.S.S.R. in the way we understand it in the West, but my feeling is that we have to learn from what is taking place in every part of the world, take the best of what is going and adapt it to suit our peculiarities and particular circumstances."

He sums up his political thinking this way:

"I am a passionate anti-Colonialist. I believe so strongly that colonialism is utterly wrong that I would gladly accept any help from whatever quarter to help me in my fight against it. I mean to pursue a policy of active neutralism. I have made no secret of the fact that I will not accept aid upon conditions which limit the sovereignty of my people. We do not intend to be a bridgehead or a base for anyone. I am not interested in the Cold War, in which in any case my small country can play no effective role."

Meanwhile Janet was busy with her portfolio and the party. From Freedom House, the run-down Georgetown headquarters of the P P P, she edited *Thunder*, kept tabs on the party's top men, and issued a continuous stream of propaganda. A miniature Cuban flag stands on her desk-top; a souvenir from her favourite country, as Fidel Castro is her favourite politician—next to Cheddi. Freedom House is also the home of the Guardian Library, the party's comprehensive collection of Communist literature which may be borrowed by members.

Janet has grown old faster than Cheddi. He is still handsome, the few grey hairs on his head making him look more distinguished. He is as immaculate and well-groomed as she is dowdy. In a rumpled dress she worked long hours both in her Government office and in Freedom House. Also she travelled. Her dumpy figure, thick horn-rimmed glasses, and bouncy personality became familiar at conferences in New York, London, Curaçao, Trinidad, Denmark and Cuba. It is also rumoured that she travelled as far afield as Hungary, Czechoslovakia and other Eastern *bloc* countries. Her frequent smiles, and the incessant, embarrassed and ingratiating little giggle that punctuates her speech, were seen and heard in high places far from British Guiana.

Cheddi travelled too: London, New York, Washington. He went to Chile to get British Guiana accepted as an Associate Member of the Economic Commission for Latin America. He lobbied delegates in New York to plead his country's case at the United Nations.

The Communist tag was hard to shake off despite Jagan's protestations that he was a Marxist and believed in Socialist principles. His carefully couched statements and well-thought-out replies to questions lost a lot of punch when various party members were less discreet.

Jocelyn Hubbard, now Minister of Trade and Industry, said in the budget debate in 1960: "To call a man a Communist is to write for him a certificate of the highest integrity; and, similarly, to call him an anti-Communist is to imply the opposite."

Jagan's staunchest African supporter Brindley Benn, P P P Chairman and Minister of National Resources, said: "This Government is not worried about the accusations of Communism. You cannot stop Communism. It is easier to stop tomorrow than to stop Communism." One of Benn's favourite phrases is: "Heads will roll."

Even Janet made provocative statements. On one occasion she said: "Cheddi will never be satisfied until the British are driven out of the colony. He has no use for half-measures. He wants British Guiana to be free." Later she said: "Cuba is an example of what can be done when an honest government with real power in its hands has the full support of all the people."

In November, 1960, a new political party appeared on the scene preparatory to the elections which would precede the granting of full internal self-government—the last stage before full independence. It was headed by Peter D'Aguiar, a prominent Georgetown businessman of Portuguese extraction. He called it the United Force and soon attracted many supporters from business, the civil service, racial minority groups and religious leaders, including the President of the powerful Muslim Anjuman. It is the only really multi-racial party in the country. Jagan immediately branded it "Fascist" and "ultra-Conservative".

Elections were announced for 21st August, 1961, and the three parties got busy. There were thirty-five seats to be contested under the new constitution. Race became an even bigger issue than it had been in the 1957 election, with the PPP and PNC campaigning strongly on it. The Africans realized that this would probably be the last time that they could hope to beat Jagan on a racial basis because of the numerically larger Indian population and their higher birth-rate.

But Jagan romped home again with 42.63 per cent of the votes giving him twenty seats; Burnham got 40.99 per cent and eleven seats; D'Aguiar, 16.38 per cent and four seats. Cheddi became Minister of Economic Development and Production. Janet had not run in the elections.

Soon after the election which made him Premier of British Guiana again, Jagan sent for an old and trusted friend to be his Public Relations Adviser. He was Jack Kelshall, a wealthy man regarded in his native Trinidad as a top Communist and very dangerous. Jagan had always attacked the appointment of ex-patriates to Government posts, but defended his action in sending for Kelshall.

"It is important to me to have someone close to me who shares my philosophies," he said.

Kelshall took an immediate line with people who opposed the PPP, promising that after independence "we will ship people out".

Shortly afterwards Cheddi flew to Washington to try to negotiate financial aid with President Kennedy. Janet flew to Cuba at the invitation of Fidel Castro. A number of Guianese were already in Cuba on agricultural scholarships and a deal had been made with Cuba to buy Guianese rice.

Jagan had already demanded independence by 31st May, 1962 —the date set for the ill-fated West Indies Federation. But in February, 1962, his austerity budget—drawn up by Cambridge economist Nicholas Kaldor—led to riots and arson in Georgetown. Jagan had to call for British troops to hold on to his Government. Janet dashed home from Cuba in time to see enraged mobs roaming the streets of the capital.

The soldiers restored order and a constitutional conference, arranged for May, 1962, was put off until July, only to be again postponed pending the report of the three-man Commission of Inquiry who were sent to investigate the rioting. Jagan made an impassioned plea to the United Nations, begging support for British Guiana in the face of Britain's "stalling". But it was to no avail. When the conference was finally held in October, 1962, it broke up in disorder and without fixing a date for independence.

In June, 1962, he expelled Minister of Home Affairs, Balram Singh Rai from both his office and his party, thus ending a sixteen-year association. Rai, a barrister, had openly accused Jagan of "coercion and fraud" at the party's elections in April. An anti-Communist, Rai had frequently disagreed with Jagan over policies but had always given way to majority decisions. There were signs that Jagan was reluctant to expel Rai—who is President of the powerful Hindu Maha Sabha, a religious organization—but Rai refused to withdraw his allegations.

Jagan, a firm believer in nationalization, has given an under-taking that he will not take over the foreign-owned sugar and bauxite industries, the country's largest exporters. And when he did take over the privately-owned electricity company he paid fair compensation for it.

He has also said that he believes in democracy, human rights and wants British Guiana to remain within the Commonwealth. Few of the people who were close to him in 1953 are still in the party.

The public face he presents gives little cause for alarm.

"What I am interested in is to set up a democratic régime in British Guiana," he says. "My party has taken the lead in seeing to it that democratic rights—the bill of rights—are written into our constitution. To put my position very clearly, I would say that I believe in the parliamentary system of democracy. I am wedded, dedicated, to parliamentary democracy. But I do not believe in capitalism. I do not believe that free enterprise will, in present day circumstances, develop my country.

"So far as I am concerned the personal liberties of the Guianese people and democratic processes will not be sacrificed. I am a Socialist. I believe in planned economy, but I can assure the world that this will not take precedence over the liberties of my people.

"Even if we become a republic, as India is, we will still be a member of the Commonwealth of Nations."

It is his private face, as indicated by a leak which came out of the P P P's 1962 annual Congress, that is dangerous.

For he told his followers: "We must not be divided on the issue of Communism. Communism is winning throughout the

world—it will win everywhere . . . every man must have a gun
in his house to defend the elections."

Both faces say: "Nobody will run my own show but me."

Cheddi Jagan is all things to all men. For some—his own people
—he is a racial leader. For others—the more extreme Indians—he
is failing to be a racial leader, five of his nine Ministers are African.
For some he is to be distrusted because he is a Communist. For
others he is to be distrusted because he has ceased to be Communist
enough and is now just another Colonial politician caught up in the
race for power.

All things to all men: but still the Premier of British Guiana.

EVALUATED BIBLIOGRAPHY

It would clearly be impossible to attempt to list even a tenth of the books which have been published on Caribbean America. Below I offer a selected list of some of the better and more recent books with a few comments on them. The vast majority of them are in English, but I have included where pertinent the writings in Spanish—and in one case French—of men who are now the political leaders of their countries. Most of the books—both American and British editions listed here—are in print. Those which are not are easily available from the better libraries.

ALEXIS, Stéphan, *Black Liberator: The Life of Toussaint L'Ouverture*, (Macmillan, New York, 1949). An English condensation of the French original by a Haitian author.

ARCINIEGAS, Germán, *The State of Latin America*, (Cassell, London, 1953). Conditions have changed considerably since the distinguished Colombian author wrote this book. But it is still pertinent in many respects and is certainly necessary reading for an understanding of the area. Obviously larger in scope than Caribbean America, but full of interesting material about the region.

AYEARST, Morley, *The British West Indies: The Search For Self-Government*, (Allen and Unwin, London, 1960). Indispensable guide to the politics of Britain's Caribbean territories by an American professor who spent time collecting his facts in every territory. Occasional factual errors but for the most part correct down to the last detail.

BATISTA, Fulgencio, *Cuba Betrayed*, (Vantage Press, New York, 1962). Overthrown dictator Batista tells his side of the story. Full of indignation and self-justification, but nevertheless an interesting book showing how a dictator's mind works when he is no longer in power.

BENTON, William, *The Voice of Latin America*, (Weidenfeld and Nicolson, London, 1962). Good book, by an American Senator. Detailed, concise and containing tables of figures not easily accessible elsewhere.

BETANCOURT, Rómulo, *Rómulo Betancourt: Pensamiento y Acción*, (Mexico, 1951). The present President of Venezuela writing on his thoughts and deeds while in exile. In Spanish.

——, *Venezuela: Politica y Petróleo*, (Fordo de Culture Económica, Mexico, 1956). Venezuelan President writes of politics and oil. In Spanish.

BIANCHI, William J., *Belize*, (Las Americas Publishing Co., New York, 1959). A full-scale legal discourse on Guatemala's claim to British Honduras by a top New York lawyer.

BLOOMFIELD, L. M., *The British Honduras-Guatemala Dispute*, (Carswell, Toronto, 1953). A useful and competent historical and legal analysis.

BURDON, Sir John, *Archives of British Honduras*, (3 volumes, Sifton Praed, London, 1931-35). Volume one deals with the 17th and 18th centuries and contains most of the important documents of the period. Volumes two and three, covering the period 1800-84, are confined to documents preserved in the colony itself. The best printed collection of prime source material.

BURNS, Sir Alan, *History of the British West Indies*, (Allen and Unwin, London, 1954). Mammoth 700-page tome giving the history of all the British territories and most of the non-British ones too. Minutely researched and documented. Several tables of statistics not available elsewhere.

CAIGER, Stephen, *British Honduras Past and Present*, (Allen and Unwin, London, 1951). Brightly written, but not always accurate, history of British Honduras.

CAIN, Ernest E., *Cyclone Hattie*, (Arthur H. Stockwell, Ilfracombe, 1963). Privately printed account of the hurricane which devastated British Honduras on 30th October, 1961, by a man who was there. Much interesting information on a major disaster.

CARMICHAEL, Gertrude, *History of the West Indian Islands of Trinidad and Tobago*, (Alvin Redman, London, 1961). Painstakingly researched history from earliest times to the end of the nineteenth century.

CARR, David, and THORPE, John, *From The Cam To The Cays*, (Putnam, London, 1962). A good general account of the many aspects of British Honduras by members of a Cambridge University expedition to the country 1959-60.

CASSIDY, Frederic G., *Jamaica Talk: Three Hundred Years of the English Language in Jamaica*, (Macmillan, London, 1961). Just what the title says it is. Fascinating study of Jamaican Creole with copious lists of common phrases and their derivations.

CASTRO, Fidel, *History Will Absolve Me*, (Liberal Press, New York, 1959). This is the text of Castro's speech at his trial for the attack on the Moncada Barracks in 1953. It was delivered on 16th October, 1953, and published, in a slightly enlarged and altered form, after he came to power. Many believe that here is heard the authentic voice of Castro the revolutionary and liberator, unbesmirched by Communism.

——, "Why We Fight", published in *Coronet* magazine, (New York, February, 1958), as an exclusive interview during the campaigning in the Sierra Maestra range.

CAVE, Hugh B., *Haiti: Highroad to Adventure*, (Henry Holt, New York, 1952). Readable, informative and at times humorous account by first-rate English writer who spent several years living in Haiti. Well illustrated.

——, *Four Paths to Paradise*, (Alvin Redman, London, 1962). One of the best modern books about Jamaica by a fine reporter with an inquiring mind and a knack of combining historical snippets with his own on-the-spot reporting. Illustrated.

CHANDOS, Dane, *The Trade Wind Islands*, (Doubleday, New York, 1955). Sprightly account of what the American author calls "an informal journey through the West Indies". Careful reporting and a nice eye for detail. Chapters on Cuba, Jamaica, Haiti, Dominican Republic, Puerto Rico, Barbados and Trinidad with short stops in some of the smaller British West Indian islands in the Lesser Antilles. Pleasant reading.

CLEMENTI, Sir Cecil, *A Constitutional History of British Guiana*, (Macmillan, London, 1937). Detailed book tracing colony's political life from the days when it was Dutch.

CRAIG, Hewan, *The Legislative Council of Trinidad and Tobago*, (Faber and Faber, London, 1952). Detailed study of the islands' legislature. Part of the series Studies in Colonial Legislatures issued under the auspices of Nuffield College.

CRAIGE, John H., *Black Baghdad*, (Minton, Balch, New York, 1933). Tough account of Haiti under the occupation of the American Marines by one of them.

DE LEEUW, Hendrik, *Crossroads of the Buccaneers*, (Arco, London, 1957). Travel book of the Lesser Antilles with chapters on all the islands, British, Dutch and French. Sloppily written, but giving a good general idea of each island historically and up to 1940.

DE MADARIAGA, Salvador, *Latin America Between the Eagle and the Bear*, (Hollis and Carter, London, 1962). Noted Spanish writer at grips with a subject he is not at home on: the Russian and Chinese political infiltration of Latin America. Mostly concerned with South America but some material on Central American republics as well as Haiti, Cuba and the Dominican Republic. Some good arguments but much unimportant data.

DENIS, Lorimer, and DUVALIER, Dr. François, "La Civilization Haïtienne: notre mentalité, est-elle africaine ou gallo-latine?", *Révue de la Societé d'Histoire et de Géographie d'Haiti*, (Volume VII, No 23, pages 1-31, May, 1936). Magazine article by the now President of Haiti and a collaborator on why the *élite* in the country should not foreswear their African heritage. A number of other articles by Denis and Duvalier appeared in the Haitian publications *Les Griots* and the *Bulletin du Bureau d'Ethnologie* between 1938 and 1955.

DEREN, Maya, *Divine Horsemen: The Living Gods of Haiti*, (Thames and Hudson, London, 1953). The best account of voodoo by a talented American writer-photographer who took part in ceremonies. Detailed, documented and illustrated.

FLUHARTY, Vernon L., *Dance of the Millions: Military Rule and Social Democracy in Colombia 1930-1956*, (University of Pittsburgh Press, 1957). Good survey of the period of Colombia's political history, but dictator-president Gustavo Rojas Pinilla comes off rather better than he deserves.

FREETH, Zahra, *Run Softly Demerara*, (Allen and Unwin, London, 1960). Interesting account of life at Mackenzie, the bauxite mining town in British Guiana, by an English woman who lived there. Well illustrated.

GREATOREX, Wilfred, *Diamond Fever*, (Cassell, London, 1957). First-rate adventure story of an Englishman who mined diamonds and gold in the unexplored interior of British Guiana. Illustrated.

GUÉRIN, Daniel, *The West Indies and Their Future*, (Dennis Dobson, London, 1961). Painstakingly and copiously documented book dealing with all the Caribbean islands. Marxist in outlook, but not to be dismissed lightly.

GUNTHER, John, *Inside Latin America*, (Hamish Hamilton, London, 1942). Largely out of date by now, but still interesting book by the well-known American reporter. Very political and very taken up with the Axis activities in the area. Published before America came into the Second World War.

HICKS, Albert C., *Blood in the Streets*, (Creative Age, New York, 1946). A detailed exposé of Trujillo's régime in the Dominican Republic.

HOYOS, F. A., *Barbados, Our Island Home*, (Macmillan, London, 1960). Limp covered book giving a general look at the island. Aimed primarily at schools but still a useful handbook. Illustrated.

HUGHES, Marjorie, *The Fairest Isle*, (Victor Gollancz, London, 1962). Interesting book of impressions of Jamaica and the Jamaicans by an English woman who spent several years living in the island.

HUMPHREYS, Professor R. A., *A Diplomatic History of British Honduras, 1638-1901*, (Oxford University Press, London, 1961). The best-documented and most scholarly study of British Honduras. Material taken from primary research sources and neatly presented. Pocket of valuable maps at back showing colony's geographical limits at various periods in its history. Issued under the auspices of the Royal Institute of International Affairs.

INTERNATIONAL COMMISSION OF JURISTS, *Cuba and the Rule of Law*, (Geneva, 1962). A report on the Rule of Law in Cuba, containing passages from some of Castro's speeches, the constitutional and criminal legislation of present-day Cuba and the accounts of released political prisoners. The last-mentioned are particularly hair-raising.

JAGAN, Dr. Cheddi, *Forbidden Freedom*, (Lawrence and Wishart, London, 1954). Premier of British Guiana writes his side of the story about the suspension of the country's constitution in 1953. Marxist approach to colonial problems.

JAMES, C. L. R., *The Black Jacobins*, (Dial Press, New York, no date). The Haitian revolutionary period told by a Trinidadian writer.

JENSEN, Amy Elizabeth, *Guatemala: Historical Survey*, (Exposition University Press, New York, 1955). Fact-packed book on Guatemala with particular accent on the politics right up to 1954. Slightly hysterical in its approach to every President after Jorge Ubico, but containing a wealth of detail. Badly presented and therefore something of a drudge to read.

KARNES, Thomas L., *The Failure of Union: Central America, 1824-1960*, (University of North Carolina Press, 1961). Sound and careful survey of the area and its problems.

KREHM, William, *Tiranías y Democracies en El Caribe*, (Unión Democrática Centra America, Mexico City, 1949). Competent study of political situation in Caribbean America by a leading *Time* magazine correspondent. In Spanish.

LAVIN, John, *A Halo for Gómez*, (Pageant, New York, 1954). Life and times of General Vincente Gómez, dictator-president of Venezuela from 1908 to 1935.

LEIGH FERMOR, Patrick, *The Traveller's Tree: A Journey Through the Caribbean Islands*, (John Murray, London, 1950). One of the great travel books. Discerning writer on trip up the islands from Trinidad to Cuba. Only St. Vincent and Montserrat missed out. Delightfully written and superbly illustrated.

LEYBURN, James, *The Haitian People*, (Yale University Press, 1941). Now slightly dated but still a valuable book on the island and its inhabitants.

LIEUWEN, Edwin, *Venezuela*, (Oxford University Press, London, 1961). The best easily accessible account of the country from all points of view: historical, economic and political. Issued under the auspices of the Royal Institute of International Affairs.

LOWENTHAL, David, (Ed.), *The West Indies Federation: Perspectives of a New Nation*, (Columbia University Press, New York, and Oxford University Press, London, 1961). Four papers dealing with aspects of the Federation of the West Indies which lasted from 1958 until 1962. Useful tables and charts not available elsewhere.

MACMILLAN, W. M., *Warning From The West Indies*, (Faber and Faber, London, 1938). Timely (in 1938) and succinct appraisal of the situation in the British Caribbean. Much of the material is still relevant today.

MARTZ, John D., *Central America: The Crisis and The Challenge*, (University of North Carolina Press, 1959). Descriptive survey of the Central Americas.

METRAUX, Alfred, *Voodoo in Haiti*, (Andre Deutsch, London, 1959). Copiously documented and illustrated account of Voodoo by a French sociologist and anthropologist who spent some years in the island. Definitive.

MILLER, Warren, *The Lost Plantation*, (Secker and Warburg, London, 1961). First-hand reporting by an American writer who knew Cuba under the old régime and went back after the Castro Government came to power. Detailed, balanced and interesting.

MITTELHOLZER, Edgar, *With A Carib Eye*, (Secker and Warburg, London, 1958). Out-of-the-rut travel book by the doyen of West Indian writers. Mittelholzer comes from British Guiana and writes engagingly of his own country as well as Trinidad, Grenada, Barbados, Jamaica, St. Lucia. Illustrated.

MONTGOMERY, Field-Marshal the Viscount Montgomery of Alamein, *Three Continents*, (Collins, London, 1962). The travels of the author in the Americas, Asia and Africa. Interesting reporting of his meetings with the Presidents of Guatemala, Nicaragua and Honduras.

NAIPAUL, V. S., *The Middle Passage: The Caribbean Revisited*, (Andre Deutsch, London, 1962). Brilliant Trinidadian novelist turns to factual reporting. Sparkling wit and perceptive details about British Guiana, Trinidad, Antigua and Jamaica. Martinique and Surinam (Dutch Guiana) thrown in for good measure.

NORRIS, Katrin, *Jamaica: The Search for an Identity*, (Oxford University Press, London, 1962). Limp covered booklet on contemporary Jamaica. Coming immediately after independence it discusses some of the many things which make Jamaica as fascinating and unsure of itself as it is. Issued under the auspices of the Institute of Race Relations.

PARRY, J. H. and SHERLOCK, Philip M., *A Short History of The West Indies*, (Macmillan, London, 1954—revised 1960). Brief history of all the islands in the Caribbean up to the present day. Workmanlike book. Illustrated.

PHILIPS, R. Hart, *Cuba: Island of Paradox*, (McDowell, Obolensky, New York, 1959). Interesting and objective study of Cuba since the Castro revolution.

PORTER, Charles O., and ALEXANDER, Robert J., *The Struggle for Democracy in Latin America*, (Macmillan, New York, 1961). Up to the minute account by two American senators of conditions south of the United States. Not all Caribbean American countries discussed but material on Colombia, Honduras, Venezuela, Cuba, Dominican Republic, Haiti and Nicaragua. Invaluable.

PROUDFOOT, Mary, *The U.S.A. and Britain in the Caribbean Islands*, (Faber and Faber, London, 1954). Definitive study of British and American islands in the Caribbean. Political, geographical and economic facts and figures. Now slightly dated. Part of the series in Colonial and Comparative Studies issued under the auspices of Nuffield College.

ROBERTS, W. Adolphe, *The French in the West Indies*, (Bobbs-Merrill, New York, 1942). Excellent historical account by eminent Jamaican historian of the French West Indian territories from discovery up to 1942. Chapters on Haiti. Gets away from the Caribbean and writes of Mexico and Louisiana too. Illustrated.

RODMAN, Selden, *Haiti: The Black Republic*, (Devin-Adair, New York, 1954). Superbly illustrated, carefully detailed and thoroughly workmanlike book on Haiti. Every aspect of the island's life is dealt with. Information for tourists included. A visit to the country without this book is unthinkable.

ROURKE, Thomas, *Gómez: Tyrant of the Andes*, (Morrow, New York, 1941). One of several books on General Vincente Gómez, dictator-president of Venezuela from 1908 to 1935.

SCHMID, Peter, *Beggars on Golden Stools*, (Weidenfeld and Nicolson, London, 1956). One of the better travel books on Latin America. A Swiss journalist travels all over Central America. Only Caribbean American mainland countries not written of are British Honduras, Venezuela and British Guiana.

SHERLOCK, Philip M., *Jamaica Way*, (Longmans, Green, London, 1962). Limp covered booklet on the island. Everything the tourist might want to know and a great deal more. Well illustrated.

SMITH, Raymond T., *British Guiana*, (Oxford University Press, London, 1962). Probably the best single volume on the country. Carefully researched and documented with all aspects covered from early history to present day politics by an English professor who spent a great deal of time in British Guiana. Fold-out map at back. Issued under the auspices of the Royal Institute of International Affairs.

UNITED NATIONS MISSION OF TECHNICAL ASSISTANCE TO HAITI, *Mission to Haiti*, (Lake Success, New York, 1949). Advice, and a great wealth of facts and figures not available in other places.

VANDERCOOK, John W., *Black Majesty*, (Literary Guild, New York, 1928). Fictionalized life of Henri Christophe, but basically accurate and documented. Highly readable.

WADDELL, D. A. G., *British Honduras: A Historical and Contemporary Survey*, (Oxford University Press, London, 1961). Short but data-packed book covering most aspects of the colony in accurate detail. Historical, economic and political material. Issued under the auspices of the Royal Institute of International Affairs.

WALLSTROM, Tord, *A Wayfarer in Central America*, (Arthur Barker, London, 1955). The travels and adventures of a Swedish journalist. Chapters on Guatemala, Honduras, Nicaragua, Costa Rica and Panama. Brightly written and enjoyable. Some political writing in Nicaragua and Costa Rica chapters. Illustrated.

WELLES, Sumner, *Naboth's Vineyard*, (Harcourt, New York, 1928). Well-written book on the U.S. occupation of the Dominican Republic, with some hard things to say about Marine treatment of the population.

WILLIAMS, Eric E., *The Negro in the Caribbean*, (New York, 1942, London, 1945). Scholarly discourse on the subject by present Prime Minister of Trinidad and Tobago.

——, *Capitalism and Slavery*, (Chapel Hill, 1944). As above.

——, *Education in the British West Indies*, (Port of Spain, 1950). As above.

——, *Documents on British West Indian History, 1807-1833*, (Port of Spain, 1952). As above.

WILSON, Charles Morrow, *Central America*, (Allen and Unwin, London, 1942). Somewhat dated but still interesting book on the opportunities in Central America. Largely on agricultural topics but well written and pleasingly descriptive. Illustrated.

WIRKS, Faustin and DUDLEY, Taney, *The White King of La Gonave*, (Doubleday, New York, 1931). A Marine sergeant's experiences on La Gonave during the Haitian occupation.

WOLLASTON, Nicholas, *Red Rumba: A Journey Through the Caribbean and Central America*, (Hodder and Stoughton, London, 1962). One of the great travel books of the decade. A sensitive writer with a good eye for detail on a tour through Cuba, Guatemala, Honduras, Nicaragua, Costa Rica, Panama, Puerto Rico, Haiti and the Dominican Republic. El Salvador is thrown in for good measure.

WORKS PROJECT ADMINISTRATION, *Puerto Rico: A Guide to the Island of Borguén*, (University Society, Inc., New York, 1940). Good general guide of the island with a great deal of assorted information, some of it now slightly dated. Well illustrated.

ADDENDA

Since this evaluated bibliography was compiled several books have been published which I would have included in it.

ESKELUND, Karl, *Revolt in the Tropics*, (Alvin Redman, London, 1963). Well-known Danish travel writer and his Chinese wife on a trip which took them from Cuba to British Guiana, touching at Jamaica, Haiti, Puerto Rico, Antigua, Dominica, Barbados, St. Lucia and Trinidad. An interesting journey, generally well told, some errors of fact, but entertaining reading. Illustrated.

MANNING CARLEY, Mary, *Jamaica: The Old and The New*, (Allen and Unwin, London, 1963). An English woman writes interestingly on Jamaica, her home for a number of years. Illustrated.

MARTZ, John D., *Colombia: A Contemporary Political Survey*, (North Carolina University Press, 1962). The best book on the political situation in Colombia. Sourced and documented right up to the hilt. Ends in 1960 with Lleras Camargo in office.

MIELCHE, Hakon, *Calypso Islands*, (Herbert Jenkins, London, 1962). Danish writer on leisurely journey through Caribbean. A tendency to stress the exotic, but generally pleasing. Material on Trinidad, St. Lucia, Barbados, Martinique, Antigua, U.S. Virgin Islands, Puerto Rico, Dominican Republic, Haiti, Jamaica and Cuba. Illustrated.

STOPPELMAN, Francis, *Jamaica*, (Ernest Benn, London, 1963). Superb collection of some two hundred and fifty photographs by this noted Dutch photographer. Gives a better picture of what Jamaica is really like than a dozen travel books.

INDEX

241

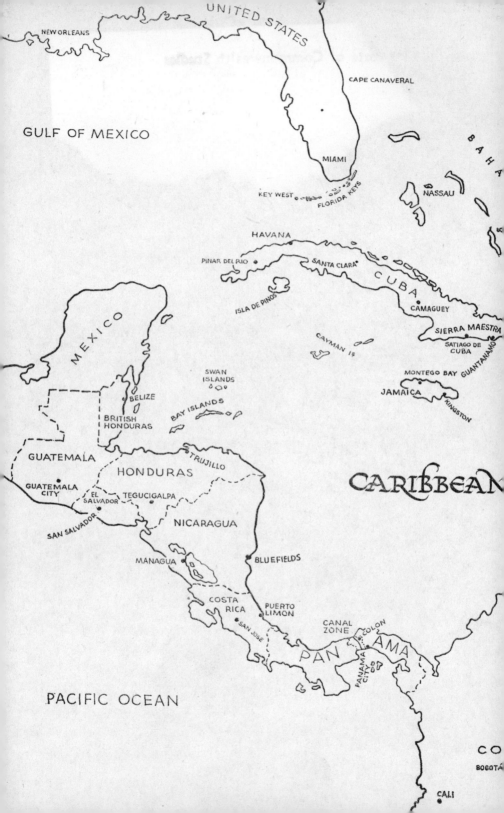